PRAISE FOR *BLACK SUFFERING*

"Writing from within a matrix of hope and despair, the author of this book, an African American scholar and preacher, reflects on his life's experience and work among people who are both resistant and resilient. Drawing upon the resources of ethnography, storytelling, history, literature, philosophy, and theology, he analyzes and describes the pathos of Black suffering from the time of slavery up to the present day. This perceptive meditation on the experience of suffering and hope will inspire all readers to think and work more diligently for a better world."

—**Peter J. Paris**, Elmer G. Homrighausen Professor
Emeritus, Christian Social Ethics, Princeton Theological
Seminary

"*Black Suffering: Silent Pain, Hidden Hope* provides readers an opportunity to think deeply about a collective response to the universality of Black suffering. In an era where increasingly #BlackLivesDontMatter, this text is a timely reminder of the poignant strands of hope that call us individually and collectively to the work of justice."

—**Angela D. Sims**, president, Colgate Rochester Crozer
Divinity School

"James Henry Harris has crafted a creative book on the perennial problem of Black suffering, a text that is more relevant now than ever because, in Harris's words, Black suffering is becoming difficult to recognize, since it is concealed in the normalization of Black death and the shifting ways that make it difficult to recognize, for example, in the COVID-19 pandemic that is directly tied to racism, poor health care, unemployment, and the stressors that are intricately tied to being Black in America. While Black suffering is global in scope, Harris hones in carefully on the particular situation of African American suffering in the United States, and the hip-hop "mixtape" serves as a metaphor for his method that draws upon a myriad of Black intellectual and cultural sources to investigate, make sense of, and call prophetically for an end to the disproportionate suffering that attends Black existence.

Harris utilizes a kind of living ethnography from his present and long-term relationship in the Randolph community of Richmond, Virginia, where he is pastor of the Second Baptist Church; African American literature; Black intellectual history; the history of Black resistance; philosophy; and Black theology to give readers a full and powerful picture of the suffering that white supremacy creates and the joys and hope of Black living that yet endures. Scholars in many disciplines—from religious studies, anthropology, theology, history, and beyond—would benefit from this updated treatment of Black suffering. Every American who cares about America and understanding where it now stands and how much work is left to be done should read this book."

—**Stephen C. Finley**, associate professor, Louisiana State University

"At once, with storytelling rich in experience; prose that is sermonic in tone; and arguments steeped in biblical analysis and philosophical and theological depth, James Henry Harris offers us a view of Black suffering that is more than data and cognitive mapping. He uncovers the evil of the experience of Black suffering amidst the silences that point to *something else*: a way to a hidden hope imprisoned by a subjugated consciousness that we must liberate from the white imaginary that holds the key to the prison door."

—**Walter Fluker**, professor emeritus of ethical leadership at Boston University and Dean's Professor of Spirituality, Ethics, and Leadership at Candler School of Theology

"In this timely and necessary work, James Henry Harris gives voice and insight into the present reality and historical complexity of Black suffering and silent pain. It is a powerful and poignant wake-up call to those who have become numb to their own pain and that of others. This is a textbook for any preacher, pastor, and practitioner of the gospel hoping to engage in relevant healing and liberative ministry."

—**Jacqueline A. Thompson**, senior pastor, Allen Temple Baptist Church, Oakland, California

Black Suffering

Black Suffering

Silent Pain, Hidden Hope

James Henry Harris

Fortress Press
Minneapolis

Print ISBN: 978-1-5064-6438-1
eBook ISBN: 978-1-5064-6439-8

Cover design: Laurie Ingram
Interior design and typesetting: PerfecType, Nashville, TN

Dedication

*This book is dedicated to members of the
Black community everywhere who continue to
carry the banner of freedom and justice.*

*I also dedicate this work to my dear mother,
Carrie Anna Jones Harris (deceased),
and my father, Richard Harris (deceased).*

*To my wife, Dr. Demetrius Bright Harris,
and my sons, Attorney James Corey Alexander and
Cameron Christopher David Harris, a filmmaker.*

CONTENTS

PREFACE

For the past ten years or more, I have been toiling away at this very vexing subject of Black suffering. The illusiveness of the topic lies in its pandemic presence and its ability to be embedded into the fabric of everyday existence. This makes it difficult to tackle. This is the irony.

My first few attempts at this project took the exclusive form of short stories, which I used as a way of expressing the topic of Black suffering through characters and plot. This, too, was hard. I later focused on narrative history, using the first-person singular as a tool for telling the story of Black suffering. It is a difficult and painful subject for me because it is my life's story as well.

I want to thank the following persons who read and commented on this book: Larry Bouchard, Peter Paris, Charlie Gillespie, Tony Baugh, Lisa Wilson, James Corey Harris, Charlotte McSwine-Harris, Jennifer Geddes, Tanya Boucicaut, Paul D. Jones, Hal White, Tim Lee, Venessa Bond, Corey D. B. Walker, Angela Simms, and Charles F. Abel. Dr. James E. Jones, Dr. Alton Hart, and Dr. Robert Wafawanaka—a surgeon, internist, and Hebrew Bible scholar respectively—read every page of the manuscript and offered very helpful comments related to the subject of Black pain and suffering. I am thankful to the members of Second

Baptist Church (West End), Richmond, Virginia, who attended my Tuesday "Lunch and Learn" seminars and readings, where much of this work was first shared. Sometimes, we had over fifty people in attendance. Moreover, the Dialectical and Literary Society at the Graduate School of Theology at Virginia Union University allowed me to lecture on this topic. All of my undergraduate and graduate students who have given listening ears to portions of this book are not only appreciated but cherished. I want to thank Rev. Yohance D. Whitaker for his teaching assistance, untiring support, and help in editing the final draft of this book. Additionally, Andrew Blossoms was instrumental in reading and reviewing every page of the book in its early development.

I want to thank Debra Haggins, Dwight Riddick Sr., and William Harvey for their invitations to deliver the Hampton University Ministers' Conference Lectures in 2016 and 2018. Some of this material was first developed for and delivered to the thousands of ministers and laity in attendance. Also, thanks to the participants in the Black Theology Conference in Johannesburg, South Africa, held at the University of South Africa in the summer of 2016, where I first lectured to an international audience on the topic of Black suffering.

I want to thank my editors at Fortress Press, Scott Tunseth and Rachel Reyes, for their expertise and untiring efforts to bring this book to publication. Thanks to Mary Edosomwan and her husband, Johnson A. Edosomwan, who made it possible for me to study and write at their retreat center near Emporia, Virginia.

As always, thanks to my lovely wife, Demetrius, and sons, Corey and Cameron, who always support my writing efforts and my efforts to help ameliorate Black suffering in our community and world.

Again, thanks to everyone named and unnamed who has read or listened to me as I have struggled to find a way to approach this complex and slippery topic. Any weaknesses or shortcomings in this book are mine and mine alone.

Introduction

I can't breathe. —George Floyd's last cry for help, May 25, 2020

Go back to America, where they hated Negroes! To America, where Negroes were not people. To America, where Negroes were allowed to be beggars only, of life, of happiness, of security. To America, where everything had been taken from those dark ones, liberty, respect, even the labor of their hands. . . . Helga couldn't, however, help it. Never could she recall the shames and often the absolute horrors of the Black man's existence in America without the quickening of her heart's beating and a sensation of disturbing nausea. It was too awful. The sense of dread. —Nella Larsen, *Quicksand*

I have talked to hundreds of people from various neighborhoods and backgrounds: pastors, community leaders, and church folk of all ages and educational achievements in search of understanding the issues of Black suffering. I have also observed film, television, and museum exhibits at the Center for Civil and Human Rights in Atlanta, Georgia; the King Center for Civil and Human

Rights in Atlanta; the Civil Rights Museum in Memphis, Tennessee; the National Museum of African American History and Culture in Washington, DC; and the archives at the Wilder Library at Virginia Union University. I have interviewed hundreds of youth and adults in depressed urban communities throughout the United States. Additionally, I have spent my life working with Black people in the struggle for justice and fairness, especially in our core cities. My laboratory is the Randolph community and Second Baptist Church in Richmond, Virginia, where I have lived and worked among my own Black people for the past twenty-eight years.

In the summer of 2016, I spent a couple of weeks talking to people on the South African streets of Johannesburg, Pretoria, and Soweto, trying to observe firsthand the struggles and sufferings of Black people in that part of the world. I also observed and talked to people in Freedom Park in Pretoria, the Hector Pieterson Memorial and Museum in Johannesburg, and the Nelson Mandela National Museum in Johannesburg. That same summer, I introduced the subject of Black suffering in a short lecture during a Black theology conference at the University of South Africa in Pretoria.

On a Sunday evening, sunny and bright, one day after I arrived in South Africa, I visited the little house where Mr. Nelson Mandela lived while practicing law in Soweto as a young man. As I was standing in the street, a young child, around the age of nine or ten, asked me if he could dance and sing for me. I agreed and gave him a few American dollars. He joyfully took it, but as he was beginning to leave my presence, he said, "Don't be afraid. You are safe with us here. We will not hurt you." Wow! Those few words were precipitated by something this young Black child could sense in my demeanor. They brought tears to my eyes. Even now, when I continue to hear this child in my memory, speaking comfort and assurance to me, I begin to cry. His bare feet, small and skinny frame, and tattered clothes betrayed the rugged resolve and strength of his comforting words. This nameless

Black African child spoke wisdom to my soul and bolstered my understanding of Black suffering, which seems universal to me. I have determined my subject is a painful one for everyone in the Black and brown world community. Yet it is so normalized. And herein lies a major part of the problem. I have been told and I have witnessed time and time again that Black people do not want to hear of their suffering. White people do not want to acknowledge their role in the phenomenon, nor even characterize the negativity surrounding the Black experience as suffering. This means my efforts as an ethnographic researcher and cultural critic are complicated and confounded by denials and deceptions. Nevertheless, as a social scientist, theologian, and preacher, I have sought to synthesize theory and practice in a qualitative analysis that includes stories, anecdotes, vignettes, history, and sermonic discourse—all in service to understanding and explaining the "mixtape" experience of Black suffering.

Every day at the church where I serve, I encounter poor Black children, youth, and young adults seeking food, shelter, water, and money. Their lack of economic resources has resulted in poverty and suffering. Every week, we provide for hundreds of homeless and poor people that bombard the church in search of a hot meal and other food items. And when possible, I often put folk in my car and buy them a hot meal, clothes, toiletries, and the like, hoping it will make a small difference in their difficult and troubled lives. I recognize Black suffering is all around me, all the time. Only a nationwide quantitative study will help prove definitively and statistically what I experience, know, and understand in my body, mind, and heart: Black suffering is a monstrous reality in my community, state, nation, as well as around the world, and it is becoming ever more insidious and less recognizable.

The fact of Black pain and suffering is not only an abject reality but also a tragic one. The cruelty of subjecting Black folk to the evils of dehumanizing violence and hatred goes almost without saying. The unspeakable reality of this cruelty mutes any response, except for an internalized pain, which has turned into suffering over the years of its effects. Yes, I struggle with this topic. It is difficult and painful about which to write and read. It is such a hard topic to put into words, so time-consuming, so draining on the Black woman and man, because it affects the body and mind in ways as yet unimagined. Some days, I do not want to read another statistical report or newspaper story, hear another television news piece, or see another Black man, woman, or child shot by a white racist police officer in the back, or in the head, or in his bed. Suffering is a dread that stifles the Black body in ways that make one almost sick to death. And yet we must live in an environment that keeps us itching and scratching, searching for ways to keep ourselves sane and focused. We must not let bitterness and the evils of others consume or destroy us. This is a mental struggle, a psychological nightmare, and a physical weight almost too heavy to bear.

The pandemic spread of the coronavirus is shining the light on blatant and insidious health and economic disparities between whites and African Americans in every state, city, county, and locality in America. For example, in Louisiana 70 percent of the folk with COVID-19 are Black, and Blacks make up only 34 percent of the population.[1] The state of Louisiana has become a metaphor for Blacks suffering from COVID-19. On the same broadcast, Magic Johnson, a former basketball great, said that too much misinformation was being disseminated in the Black community such that rumors and myths were more widespread than truth and facts. The narrative that "Blacks couldn't get the disease" and other falsehoods have also contributed to the disproportionate number of Blacks who have contracted the disease and those who have died. Black men seem to be at the top of the list in both categories.[2] Moreover, this is highly correlated with the long-standing social, health, and educational inequalities in the Black community that manifest themselves in a higher incidence of diseases such as asthma, obesity, diabetes, high blood pressure, and heart and lung disease. There is a clear and undisputed relationship between income inequality, joblessness, gun violence, lack of health insurance, and being Black. The structural inequalities in society due to injustices and racial discrimination toward Blacks and minorities are seen in the disproportionate numbers of Black folk dying from chronic diseases, including coronavirus, in cities like New York, Chicago, Detroit, and New Orleans. The problem is that the fact of this reality doesn't seem to ever change regardless of who is in the White House, Congress, or the Governors' mansion. It appears that governments and businesses tend to be unconcerned about the blatant presence of racism in every corner of the world. Again, Black suffering is seen every day and in every place where the sun seems to shine, where the rain falls, and wherever the wind blows. And, yet we act as if it does not exist.

In the news segment "High rate of infections among Black Americans is alarming," Dr Valerie Montgomery Rice, President and Dean of Morehouse School of Medicine, said that the problem is one of systemic disparities among African Americans. Systemic racism results in three times the rate of death and six times the rate of the novel coronavirus infections that saddle the Black community, which is laden with other pandemic issues such as poverty, poor housing, lack of health insurance, homelessness, food deserts, and a panoply of other negative economic and social ills. Too often the issues in Black communities in the United States mirror those seen and felt in third world countries.[3]

Black suffering in America undoubtedly persists. Painful incidents repeatedly echo the past, whereby heinous crimes are unjustly committed against Black bodies. In May of 2020 George Floyd, a forty-six-year-old Black man described by family and friends as a "gentle giant," was murdered outside a Minneapolis restaurant by four police officers for being Black. For nine minutes the white police officer Derek Chauvin kept his knee and his full weight on Mr. Floyd's neck as he struggled and pleaded that he could not breathe. He died at the scene as three other officers, Tou Thao, J. Alexander Kueng, and Thomas Lane, looked on in complicity. The police are indeed a threat to Black life and this sad reality becomes more and more apparent, as cell phone cameras and other videos demonstrate. The "resisting arrest" narrative continues to be advanced as an excuse to murder Black men and women. Resisting arrest is a trope that accompanies almost all murders of Blacks at the hands of police officers. A few months earlier Ahmaud Arbery of Brunswick, Georgia, was chased down and murdered by three white men simply for being Black. This time the Black man was purportedly trespassing on an unoccupied property that was under construction. The Black man was chased, wrestled down, and shot dead based on a perception that because he was Black, he must have committed a crime, and these three vigilantes had the right to murder him for the greater good of society. Every day in America, these realities seem to grow bolder and more egregious, thus becoming more normalized. The tragedy is that the murders of Blacks seem to increase rather than diminish. And, the cycle continues: a Black man is murdered for no reason except being Black, a multitude of people march and protest in the streets for a while, then there is calmness, and suddenly there is another murder and the cycle starts over again. Nothing changes except the names of the cities, the names of the murdered, and the names of the murderers. These incidents magnify the dereliction of justice and deepen the wound of apathetic disregard towards Black pain. The race of the victims remains Black and the police continue to do what they have always done to Blacks: harass, violently beat, arrest, and murder under one or many of these fictive, scapegoated tropes: "resisting arrest," "a taillight is out," "he's reaching for a gun," or "I felt that my life was being threatened." It seems that members of law enforcement have cornered the market on justifying racism and murder by shrouding their unlawful, evil acts under the guise of protecting and serving. To the majority of Blacks in America, the shield and the "boys in blue" are symbols of anti-protection and oppression. This is how racism and law enforcement work in harmony to diminish the value of Black life and to guarantee that Black suffering remains a global pandemic—a health crisis of epic proportions.

The persistent police violence is like a cancerous disease that not only affects Black men but unfortunately Black women, who are equally as dehumanized, oppressed, and victimized. For example, Louisville police officers shot and killed Breonna Taylor in her own home at least eight times during a "no knock" drug search warrant in March 2020. There were no drugs found. Miss Taylor was a young Black twenty-six-year-old EMT who aspired to become a registered nurse. This horrific murder by the police is made worse by the fact that it took two months for the media and the world to notice that yet another innocent Black woman was murdered by the police—an arm of the State. This is another vivid and vicious example of Black suffering and pain that causes me to struggle to hold back tears even as I write these words. I confess that this writing is exhausting and painful because there seems to be no end to the violence and hatred perpetrated against Black bodies. The mentality and practices of the slavocracy live on and the cries of Black folk continue to be unheard and unheeded.

A Call to Consciousness

This book is a call to consciousness, a call to wake up from our slumber and challenge the world to take its feet off of the necks, backs, and rib cages of Black folk. This book is indeed a "mixtape," a type of "remix" of the suffering seen and felt in the everyday lives of Black people—a suffering so persistent it has become normalized. For example, from the time my sons were able to speak and listen, I have sought to explain the hatred and indifference society has for Black males in particular. I have encouraged them to be respectful and polite to the often biased and hateful police officer when stopped for a broken taillight or speeding. In the United States of America, police are not friendly to Black people, and Black people are always threatened by the police to the point of feeling unsafe in their presence. Too many Black people have lost their lives at the hands of a racist, trigger-happy police officer under the auspices of "reaching for a gun" or "resisting arrest." Rectifying these lies must be a part of police training.

I worked with a family whose son and brother, Marcus-David Peters, was shot and killed by a Black Richmond police officer from Ghana. This young Black man, college educated, was a high school science teacher who aspired to become a doctor someday. One afternoon, after teaching school all day, he experienced an unexpected mental crisis. He was driving his car while naked, completely in distress, and unarmed, when he was shot and killed by another Black man—a police officer. This senseless killing caused a lot of pain and suffering for the young man's family and throughout Richmond's Black community. It still reverberates in my consciousness. I wonder if I am next—or if not me, who else may be the next Black victim of these acts of evil and injustice, so often sanctioned by the government and its operatives? This senseless killing was ruled a "justifiable homicide" by a Black Commonwealth's attorney. A Black person cannot get a break from anybody wearing a badge and a gun, and swearing an oath to uphold the United States Constitution. It seems suffering and death are the only options that ultimately characterize much of the Black experience.

In contrast to the police killing of Marcus-David Peters, in Pittsylvania County, Virginia, a couple of hours southwest of Richmond, a white man—who was a suspect in a triple homicide—considered so "armed and dangerous" that schools were placed on lockdown—charged a retreating state police officer, jogged through pepper spray, and briefly choked a bystander before being chased away by a baton-wielding officer." This white man, Matthew Bernard, was naked and more threatening than Marcus-David Peters. Yet, he was allowed to walk away and eventually stand trial. The major difference here is that one naked man was Black and the other was white.[4]

A Work of Uncovering

In this book, my work of uncovering something is twofold: First, I look at the phenomenology that seems to preclude Black people from being aware of their suffering. Second, I explore reasons why it is of paramount significance that Black folk quickly become cognizant of that same, very extant suffering. This text is an attempt at a novel mode of liberation, one that cajoles the Black person in America out of the pangs of her comfortability and complacency, away from the concrescence of material culture, and toward a consciousness of concern relative to her woefully enduring suffering.

I do this by responding thoughtfully to the suffering that seems to be everywhere, and I use different genres to try to capture this suffering. You will find narrative essays interspersed with short-story interludes; and because my life as a Black preacher cannot be segregated from this subject, you will also find some of my homiletical reflections. I am convinced the work of the Black preacher today is as important as ever before.

Using these various genres helps my critique to be mindfully impartial, ultimately a monumental and lateral position, that of an agapeic lover of Black people. This is *Black Suffering*.

The Matrix of Despair and Hope

Because of white supremacist mentality concomitant with market morality, outsourcing of jobs, and technological advancements open only to highly educated persons, Black men were deindustrialized from 1970 to 1987, from 70 percent employment to 28 percent, leading to radical poverty in urban communities. This led to the illegal pursuit of monies through the sale of crack cocaine and marijuana among Black men. White men are seven times more likely than Black men to possess crack; seven times more likely to use crack, powder cocaine, and heroin; and equally likely to use and possess marijuana—but Black people are five times more likely to be imprisoned for drug possession and use. Half of the people incarcerated in our nation are there for drug offenses. Eighty to 90 percent of all drug offenders sent to prison are Black. By the year 2006, one out of every fourteen Black men in the United States was behind bars.

All the while, by 1987, during the vestiges of the Reagan administration, the funding for drug abuse centers nationwide dropped from $274 million to $57 million. Funding for drug education dropped from $19 million to $3 million. In 1994, under Bill Clinton, Black people's second favorite president, $17 billion were removed from public housing initiatives, a drop of 61 percent, while $19 billion went toward the construction of new prisons, a boost of 171 percent. This shift in funding hastened an increase in the number of people caught in Michel Foucault's "carceral circle" and created what Michelle Alexander calls a racial "under-caste."[5] It is not unusual for me to talk to people on the street and in the churches who have fathers, mothers, cousins, and other relatives who are incarcerated. The experience of incarceration is a Black experience. This, too, is a ubiquitous example of Black suffering.

These are but some of the ways Black people suffer today, anesthetized by the prospects and promises of a post-Obama colorblindness, yet somehow subject to a monarchical legal tyranny that consumes Black life economically, educationally, socially, infrastructurally, and psychologically. I intend to disclose all of these realities within the framework of a phenomenology that can no longer be denied, resultant of a trauma that is not fully known, stemming from a brutal past and a recidivist present.

In his book, *Appeal, in Four Articles: Together with a Preamble, to the Coloured Citizens of the World, but in Particular, and Very Expressly, to Those of the United States of America*, David Walker attempted to galvanize a people who were yet in the throes of bondage and subjugation during the years of American chattel slavery. Writing in Boston in 1829, Walker, on one hand, wished to adumbrate the moral vacuity of a nation that held people captive, highlighting the suffering of Black folk in slavery; on the other hand, he hoped to encourage his kinsmen who were yet enslaved. Similarly, my book *Black Suffering* seeks to expose the ways that even to this day, 190 years removed from Walker's treatise, Black people still suffer in the United States and throughout the world.

This book is my meager submission and request to the world to listen to the cries of Black folk, cries that stretch from slavery to the present moment. I have only a few concrete answers to the historically troubling and painful reality that Black people face daily. And yes, in full disclosure, I am paranoid and afraid. This is because I see and feel suffering. I am grateful I have not lost my mind to the searing effects of hatred and evil, as so many others have. So I get up every day, caught in a matrix of despair and hope, trying to negotiate the dialectic of understanding and explaining the savage reality of Black suffering—explaining it to myself, to my sons, to my church, my students, my community, and the larger world.

Prelude:
"The Color of Suffering"

"Now I know why Baby Suggs pondered color her last years. . . . Took her a long time to finish with Blue, then yellow, then green. She was well into pink when she died. I don't believe she wanted to get to red and I understand why." —Toni Morrison, *Beloved*

The work of creative nonfiction below reflects my experience with my maternal grandmother and Deacon Stanley A. Lucas. They are the inspiration for the piece, which is a combination of memoir and narrative history. Memories of my grandmother's soft, buttery biscuits will never be erased from my consciousness. They would melt in my mouth, and I used to watch her make them from scratch. In the account below, she is Susie, the judge's housekeeper.

Stanley Lucas is the inspiration for the piece's main character and protagonist, John Comer. Historically, Stanley Lucas was among the first five African Americans hired to drive the public buses for the Richmond Transit Authority. He helped to integrate the public transportation system in the late 1950s.

I have used my experience with these two important people in my life to construct this piece of creative nonfiction, "The Color of Suffering." Both individuals suffered in silence and did so without eliciting any semblance of pity or displaying any form of hatred toward white people and others who treated them with disdain and disrespect.

This piece is used as an introduction to *Black Suffering* because it sets the stage for the essays and narrative analyses that follow. The characters' experience of suffering is my experience, and, by proxy, my experience is their experience.

"The Color of Suffering"

Chattel slavery. Nigger. Harriett Tubman. Sojourner Truth. Nat Turner. Denmark Vesey. Gabriel Prosser. Auschwitz. Buchenwald. Darfur. Liberia. Chicago. Charleston. Sanford, Florida. Greenwood, Mississippi. South Los Angeles. Brooklyn. New Orleans. Richmond. Petersburg. These symbols, people, and places reflect the ravages of oppression and the pain of poverty. Race hatred. The color of suffering. From the Civil War to weapons of mass destruction. To the destructive and demonic power of Hurricane Katrina. To images of emaciated bodies and Black faces of the old, infirm, and poor. All too often, the color of suffering is Black.

John Comer, a draftee of World War II, faced death on foreign soil as President Franklin D. Roosevelt's speech, "The Four Freedoms," rang in the background:

> In the future days, which we seek to make secure, we look forward to a world founded upon four essential freedoms.

The first is freedom of speech and expression—
everywhere in the world. . . .

The fourth is freedom from want—which translated
into world terms, means a worldwide reduction of arma-
ments to such a point and in such a thorough fashion
that no nation will be in a position to commit an act of
physical aggression against any neighbor—anywhere in
the world.[1]

Roosevelt's speech was a constant reminder to John that
the powers that be could proclaim words of freedom and never
understand the true meaning of freedom for *all* people, especially
Black people, whose struggle still existed on American soil. John
faced Jim Crow laws at home while being forced to fight against
the ungodly, unholy regime of Hitler. Langston Hughes captured
John's thoughts in his poem "Beaumont to Detroit": "How long I
got to fight both Hitler and Jim Crow?"[2]

As the years slowly passed, John remembered Adolph Hitler
and the Ku Klux Klan as symbols of evil reflecting the nature of
man's inhumanity toward others, particularly Black males, and
the police torture that is not random but systematic. Something
of an unlettered philosopher, Comer was a self-made historian.
John Comer—a jackleg preacher, a lover of wisdom he was.
Before getting the job as a bus driver with the Richmond Transit
Authority, he was a cab driver in Jacksonville, Florida, during
the early 1950s. Before that, he had studied history at Virginia
State College with Professor Harold Tolliver, an expert on slavery
and Black history in Virginia. John never graduated from college,
although he scored an impressive, almost perfect score of 1570
on his SATs back in the mid-1950s. He was a genius of sorts, like
Nat Turner and W. E. B. Du Bois before him, but he was denied
admission to the University of Virginia because he was the wrong
color during the days of massive resistance in the Commonwealth

of Virginia. The Byrd Machine certainly was at work. Some called him a nigger. "An uppity nigger," the white folks would say. The governor and the legislature of Virginia, driven by racism, closed the schools rather than integrate. When desegregation did come down to the Southern states after *Brown v. Board of Education of Topeka, Kansas*, white folks just decided to extricate themselves from the ghastly situation by getting their churches and synagogues to build private schools that did not have to deal with suffering Black or poor people. This was the beginning of the exodus from public schools and public transportation by white people, who had coined the word "nigger" as a racial epithet during slavery and the Reconstruction Era.

John Comer had just moved to Richmond from Chicago when the city integrated its public transportation in the wake of Rosa Park's bold stance in Montgomery in 1955 and Martin Luther King Jr.'s many speeches and marches. In this same year, 1955, John mourned at seeing the picture of Emmett Till's mangled body on the front page of the *Chicago Defender* and on the cover of *Jet Magazine*. His first day on the job came after he studied for his commercial driver's license and passed the test on the first try. It was a cold blustery day in December 1959, four years after the Emmett Till murder had shocked the nation and confirmed the evils of the South's Confederate hate and the white practice of hanging and murdering Black people for sport.

The Christmas spirit was all in the air. Bells jingled on horse-drawn carriages; candles and lights were displayed in every shop. Downtown Richmond was bustling with shoppers. John pulled his bus up to the curb at Broad and 5th Streets. As the door opened, he saw three brightly dressed white ladies with their packages, ready and eager to climb aboard. They looked with amazement into John's dark, dusty, smiling face. They made one step toward the door and two steps back into the street and exclaimed almost in unison, "Oh my God. He is a Negro bus driver! We can't ride with a *nigger* driver. The nation is going to Hell in a hurry. Who is responsible for them driving our buses? What will they do next?" The women then continued to mumble at one another in complete disgust.

John replied with polite aplomb, "Ladies, if you are riding the bus, you need to get on now. I am holding up traffic."

"No!" one of them snapped, "We will wait for the next bus."

"The next bus has a Black driver, ma'am. All the drivers on this route out to River Road are Black. Suit yourself."

He closed the door and went to the next stop. As the bus made its return route, John Comer noticed cars had crowded out all the city bus stops. Cadillacs. Buicks. Oldsmobiles. Some Audi and Mercedes wagons. They were picking up the white men and women who worked and shopped downtown. But the drivers were still Black, dressed in their butler uniforms, opening doors and tipping their hats, smiling like Stepin Fetchit and Uncle Remus.

Two months later, pulling the big diesel engine bus to the curb on his way into the 7-Eleven to get a cup of Maxwell House coffee, John could not help but notice the smooth brown-skinned face of a petite Black woman in her mid-forties, waiting to board. He had seen her almost every week during the months he had driven the crosstown route from 23rd Street in Church Hill to the base of the Huguenot Bridge, making a "U" turn at River Road. In a matter of forty-seven minutes, he traveled from poverty to privilege. The East End of the city was a metaphor for squalor—rat-infested public housing projects and a litany of other problems known and unknown. The West End was where power resided. Lily white. Protestant too. A very few Jews. No Black people. It was written in the neighborhood covenants that Black people were not allowed on either side of Cary Street Road from the country club to Exeter Street past Mary Mumford School to the foot of the Huguenot Bridge.

In most places, income and land elevation are one and the same—the higher the income, the higher the elevation. A hilltop mansion. A villa overlooking the Pacific Ocean in places like San Diego. A mountaintop cabin in Vail, Colorado—or even in Wintergreen, Virginia. New Orleans is also like that, where the well-to-do live above sea level in old antebellum Southern mansions, not too far from the low-lying areas. But Richmond's impoverished Church Hill is different because it is way up high, towering above City Hall and the Federal Reserve Bank Building. High above the Governor's Mansion and the Jefferson Hotel. It "don't need no levee" to protect it from the floodwaters because water "don't" flow uphill. But downhill, you will drown without a levee or a car filled with gasoline. Around 1941, Langston Hughes wrote his classic poem "Mississippi Levee":

> Don't know why I build this levee
> And de levee don't do no good
> Don't know why I build this levee
> When the levee don't do no good.
> I pack a million bags o' sand
> But de water still makes a flood.
> Levee, levee,
> How high have you got to be?
> Levee, levee,
> How high have you got to be
> To keep them cold muddy waters
> From washin' over me?[3]

"Ma'am, good morning. How are you percolating today?" John asked the charming, classy-looking Black woman.

"Every day that the good Lord gives me and allows me to keep on keeping on is a mighty good day," she said. "I'm doing fine. I got my health and strength, and I'm able to go to work in Judge Powell's house two days a week and the other three days,

I work for the Levinsons in their clothing store on West Grace Street. Seamstress work. Tailoring. My name is Susie Jones, and I see your nametag. So, you must be John Comer?"

The two of them struck up a conversation that day, and a friendship too. They both loved to talk Black history, politics, current events, race relations, education, violence, poverty, suffering, and pain. Twice a week, Susie rode John's bus from the Hill district in the East End of the city to the outer edge of the West End, near the James River, where there were no sidewalks and no small clapboard houses. All of the houses were like castles, with gates and tall brick walls of protection. Williamsburg brick Colonials and two- and three-story brick Georgian mansions with parapet walls around slate roofs imported from Mexico and Spain. The tall fescue grass was always green, even in July and January. These houses reeked of white privilege, money, and power.

Judge Powell's house was a large, six thousand-square-foot English Tudor with six bedrooms, a complete law library, and a separate study. The house had forty-three double-paned windows and eight stained glass windows in its front parlor that made it resemble a monastery. It was hard to clean, but an easy place to learn if one could read and study in secret. Susie was especially fond of Judge Powell's cherry wood library. It had stacks of law books on torts, constitutional law, criminal law, and legal history and theory. Susie read from them all when no one was in the house but her. She also read some of his classic books by Cicero, Homer, and Plato; Aristotle's *Rhetoric*; and all the Supreme Court proceedings on the *Dred Scott* decision of 1857, a decision that established Black folk had no rights white people had to respect. And she even read the amicus legal briefs surrounding the *Brown v. Board of Education of Topeka, Kansas* decision.

Susie's secret ten-year goal was to read every book in the judge's library. But there were roadblocks along the way. She was already past a hundred titles because she would sneak a different book with her home every night she worked in the judge's house. She would make sure the books were all neat and evenly spaced so the judge would not suspect anything was missing. Even so, the judge could not dream that Susie was such an avid reader. Even when he could not find a book, he blamed it on his stress and hard work, never suspecting his maid and housekeeper was the culprit.

In the presence of the judge, Susie played the ignorant "Aunt Jemima" role. Black people had learned well how to stay in their place around white people by being agreeable and concealing their knowledge. Jim Crow was still alive and well in Virginia. Susie knew the enslaved had once been beaten and murdered throughout Virginia and the South for knowing how to read. It was a crime against the law. Judge Powell's law.

On the days Susie worked for Judge Powell, she cooked, cleaned, and served meals whenever there was a party or big gathering of the judge's friends. One cold day in January, Susie overheard Judge Powell talking to just such a friend, the Governor of Mississippi, about Martin Luther King Jr. and "the Negro problem." She was preparing to pour the judge's tea in the small room off from the library when she overheard him say, "The world would be much better off without niggers like King. He's a Communist, you know?" The judge was emotional and almost yelling into the black rotary telephone. Susie dropped the entire pitcher of tea and the crystal glasses, which had been imported from China. Everything fell to the floor and splattered into a hundred little pieces of broken glass.

"Susie," Judge Powell yelled, "what in the holy hell is going on in there?"

"Nothing, sir. I's so jittery and nervous today. I forgot to take my medicine. The doctor prescribed Valium for my nervous tension. I'll be all right by tomorrow."

"Yes, you need to get yourself together. Get ready to go before you miss your bus. The last run is in a half-hour, you know," said

Judge Powell. "You may need to take a few days off to calm your nerves. This is the third time in the past few months you have dropped and broken something valuable. Last month, you broke our marble carving of the Pieta, and before that, you dropped my glass-framed diploma from Brown. Do you remember?"

"I do, your honor," she replied with furtive alacrity. "I promise you it won't happen again."

"It had better not. You'll have to be punished by making restitution if it does."

Susie was still trembling when the bus pulled up just a few blocks from the large stately mansion. As she boarded the bus and took her seat across from the driver, John noticed she seemed unusually troubled. He tried to ignore her nervousness, but decided to ask, "What's the matter? Is everything okay with you today? You seem a bit fidgety."

"Yes, I am. I am very shaken by something that happened an hour or so ago. You won't believe what I heard come from the mouth of the judge today."

"It must'a been bad," John said.

"He was on the telephone with a governor from the Deep South. Mississippi, I believe. Now I know they say the law is supposed to be impartial and colorblind. Ain't that right, John?"

"Yes, ma'am, so they say."

"But you and I, we both know the law, the Constitution, ain't much help to us Colored folk. For white folks, it is sacrosanct, holier than the Bible. But for Black folk, the law and the Constitution don't mean nothing but suffering and pain. It's always been against us, you know?"

"I know that's right, all the troubles I have had," John commented, shaking his head.

"Judge Powell, who I been cooking and cleaning for going on almost twenty years now, said some evil things this very day. I don't know why, but I was sickened by what I heard."

"You shouldn't be surprised, though."

"Well, I was caught off guard. That's all. To think that I nursed his son, Colin, from the time he was two months old. Did so from my own breasts with the milk of my body and my soul. I changed his diapers and read him his nursery rhymes, picture books, and taught him how to read and write 'cause the Judge was too busy deciding cases 'gainst Black folk and 'gainst women and civil rights, you know? And his wife was too sick to do anything useful. She was confined to the bed for eight months after the baby was born, and I waited on her night and day, hand and foot. Like a slave."

"You never told me that part," John chimed in.

"Yes, sir. Even when Colin followed his father's footsteps and went up there to Providence to attend that school built by slave trader money back in 1770."

"You mean Brown University?"

"Yes, sir. I washed and ironed his shirts every week. For four years, I received them dirty clothes from the mailman on Tuesday mornings, and guess what? I washed, starched, ironed, and packed those clothes to be sent back to Providence on Wednesday mornings. I never missed a week the whole time he was up there. Sometimes, I stayed up 'til two o'clock in the morning washing and ironing. Like a slave, I labored without saying a mumbling word. And today, I heard two words from the judge's mouth that almost made me lose my sanctified religion. I fell to my knees and cried into my calloused hands.

"'Niggers.' 'Black bastards.' He said that about Dr. King and millions of Negro marchers and protestors in America who put their lives on the line for our freedom and the freedom of white folks who hate him and the rest of us."

Ms. Susie Jones rambled nervously on and on. She was shocked by her own disillusionment. She was pained by the reality of racism that permeated the entire legal, political, and social justice system. She understood clearly that she worked in the house of a white racist. A judge. A Klansman. The new sovereign slave master. So American. So Jeffersonian. So duplicitous. So indispensable to American jurisprudence. So evangelical, so Christian.

John listened intently to every word flowing from Susie's mouth. But her language struck him as odd and peculiar.

John raised his voice and asked her, "What do you mean by saying, 'The freedom of white folks?'"

"Well, God made everybody," Susie observed.

John was tense. "The white man is in control of everything. Money, guns, drugs, politics, the law, government, God, and the church," he retorted. "He is already free. We are the ones suffering in bondage. You and me. Black folk are still suffering and in perpetual pain in this country. The nerve of him calling Martin Luther King Jr. a 'nigger.' He probably thinks even worse of you, Susie."

"That may be true. No. That is the truth. But white folks still aren't free until Black folk and other folk are free. As long as there are oppressed people, they are not free."

"That's crazy. You sound like you been doing more than reading. You sure you ain't been sampling the judge's Jack Daniels?" John quipped.

"Whenever the privileged oppress the poor, Blacks, and even white womenfolk, the oppressors are not free," Susie responded. "White women, you know, have been victimized by white men, although not as much as Blacks. Don't you think the little white plantation mistresses during slavery knew their husbands' rape of the enslaved? Some say that white women were complicit in this oppressive behavior. At least that's what I think. Don't you think Jefferson's wife knew about her husband's assault continuously made on Sally Hemings, the young fourteen-year-old slave girl? Some say she was the mother of six of his children. I've even heard that his wife too was no saint when it came to that. She had a Black lover. This author of a book in the judge's library, I can't think of his name, said a lot of white folks were enamored with the Black body. It was a power thing. A fetish. Just like Huckleberry Finn was obsessed with Miss Watson's slave, Jim. You ever heard that?"

"Well, it was also economic and hedonistic, too, since the slavers paid money on the auction block for Blacks and since the same folk wrote the laws and the Constitution denying Blacks their status as humans," John said. "Blacks became chattel slaves, like a pair of shoes or a hog, for example. And property rights is a big thing in the law—especially since the same folks took the property from the Native Americans through murderous pillaging called 'discovering America' and 'manifest destiny.' I know you read about torts and all sorts of stuff like that in the judge's books. You know he's an expert on torts as it relates to others. White folks have never done any wrong, as far as the law is concerned. At least, they make no such confessions. Saint Augustine and Saint Thomas Aquinas be damned. The Framers were the architects of injustice and man's inhumanity toward other men. Black folk, especially." He went on and on. "When I ride around this state, Virginia, everywhere I look, I see a plantation mentality in the words and deeds of white folks. Chesterfield. Charles City. Hanover. King William. Southampton. Chesapeake. Orange. Halifax. Giles County. Richmond. Henrico. Louisa. Goochland. Fairfax. Loudon. The Mattaponi Indians and all their ancestors have been cleansed from the public square and placed on reservations. This is the land of the free, where ethnic cleansing was initially written into the Constitution."

Susie stared into his rearview mirror, watching his eyes glued to the road. He glanced back into the mirror at her as he anticipated her response. "John," she said, "some of the stuff you say is above my head. Sounds a bit paranoid. You seem to be stuck in the past."

"Well," said John, "the past is still haunting us today. Although chattel slavery is gone and Jim Crow is on his way to the graveyard, the vestiges of slavery live on in the minds of folks like your judge. White folks who speak derisively and hatefully about Blacks are still calling us 'niggers.' Oh, I know we call ourselves different things, bad words, too, because we claim to love each other, but no white person has the right to say it, because they use it as a hateful racial epithet. As far as I'm concerned, they should never again be allowed to say the word 'nigger.' They can think it, but they can't be allowed to say it. I ain't down with that. Huck Finn and Mark Twain be damned. And yet, I also know Black folks hate each other and at the same time have an irrational love for whites. Black people love white people."

"God got tired of Black people being treated like animals— kept in bondage," Susie reflected. "And God put it in Abraham Lincoln's heart to help free the slaves. Jefferson Davis, Robert E. Lee, and Stonewall Jackson didn't like that too well. And neither did millions of poor white folks in the South. So many of them would rather die before seeing Black folk free. You know I learned some time ago that all of Judge Powell's ancestors were slave owners right here in Virginia. His great grandfather was a colonel in the Confederate army too." She recounted this sordid history with sorrow.

John gave his reply. "Slavery didn't end with the Civil War. Richmond and points south are still fighting the War. The war rages on in the hearts and minds of those who feel legacy and privilege supersede justice and fairness. And to think some of these folks still sit on the bench in the county courthouse. Every courthouse in America. Why do you think your judge was so callous and adamant about calling Dr. Martin Luther King Jr. a 'nigger?' It's because King is a threat to democracy as practiced by the architects of maintaining difference and otherness. Because King wants America to embrace and practice the ideals of the Constitution, your Judge Powell called him a 'nigger' and a Communist, a violation of democracy. You understand me?"

Susie, after hearing John's diatribe about the suffering of the innocent, the neglect of the poor, and all the troubles of Black Americans, ventured to respond, "Well white folks, they suffer too."

John, looking away from the sparsely traveled road, said, "Let's save that discussion for tomorrow, but today, as far as I can see, the color of suffering is Black. Also, violence and suffering are interrelated. And violence constitutes evil. Violence, you know, Susie, comes from the word violate. Violence violates some aspect of human dignity. Suffering is often an attack on the poor, the powerless—Black children, old men, and women. Hopeless young people with faces colored Black."

"That's true," Susie said, "but white folks, they suffer too. Take Judge Powell's wife. I have seen her crying and weeping early in the morning when I first come in the door. She sometime cries all day and night long—suffering the pain of neglect and abuse in that big house. Did I tell you she confided in me just the other day that Judge Powell hasn't touched her in over two years? She thinks that he has a mistress, you know. She is still in her forties, full of life, while her desire and passion go unrequited. That looks to me like a type of suffering too. What color is that, since you are so smart?"

"Tomorrow, Susie. Tomorrow. Since you think suffering has no color, while the pain in your back keeps you up at night, as does the pain in your knees from lifting furniture and scrubbing floors. I think you are living in an illusion about your own suffering. We will take that up tomorrow. But the unhappiness experienced by the judge's wife is not like being called a 'nigger,' and surely her lack of sexual pleasure and her unfulfilled desire are not the same kind of suffering I have been talking about. You do understand that, don't you, Miss Susie?"

"Not only do I understand it, I can explain it better than you can, because Black women know more about suffering than men do," Susie said.

"There you go again. It ain't about who knows more or who knows less. It's about experience. It's about life," he said as tears began to roll down his face.

"Why are you crying, John? Did I say something to hurt you?" Susie asked.

"No, no, no. I was just thinking. Remembering, that's all."

Evil and Black Suffering

And not only that, but we also boast in our sufferings, knowing that suffering produces endurance, and endurance produces character, and character produces hope. —Romans 5:3

Even when I cry out, "Violence!" I am not answered; I call aloud, but there is no justice. —Job 19:7

"Oh Lord," inquired Isabella, "what is this slavery, that it can do such dreadful things? What evil can it not do?" —Sojourner Truth, *The Narrative of Sojourner Truth*

Evil is more than a symbol. Evil is an external act that results in suffering for Black people. For sure, suffering is a human condition. All people have the experience of suffering in their consciousness and bodies; therefore, suffering is a biological and psychological trait of the human species, and of other animals as well. Suffering is endemic to being conscious. However, it is the lack of consciousness regarding the suffering of Black people in particular that concerns me. In other words, when individual suffering is so confined to the realm of particularity that it is unable to extend to the Other, this, in effect, constitutes a state of deliberate unconsciousness. When Black suffering is outside of the milieu of experience for a specific race of people, this lack of consciousness redounds regarding the nothingness of Black suffering in the eyes of the majority culture. Yes, white people, Black people, and all others suffer on one level or another. Individual suffering is incontestable. However, it is the lack of consciousness or concern for Black suffering that is of paramount interest here. Suffering is not only the "agony of the despair over the inability to die," but it is also the struggle to live in freedom against the will of the oppressor.[1]

All Black suffering relates back to evil—an evil grounded in American chattel slavery, Jim Crow laws and practices, and the residuals of perpetual hate. Sojourner Truth is right in saying the evil of slavery is everlasting and ubiquitous in Black life. The banality of suffering and evil are one and the same for Black people, who are born into the world encumbered by both phenomena due to racial hatred. Suffering and evil are experiences of the material world, something more than a "datum." Philosopher Emmanuel Levinas's essay "Useless Suffering," one of the most challenging and dense post-Holocaust writings, prompts me to postulate that suffering is a thoroughgoing cognitive and visceral response to what I perceive as logical gaps in his text—maybe gaping holes—so characteristic of almost all European theologians and philosophers, from Immanuel Kant and Georg Wilhelm Friedrich Hegel to Reinhold Niebuhr and Paul Tillich. Don't misunderstand me here; the analyses of these giants in philosophy and theology are contested by me because of their systematic exclusion of Black suffering from their lexicon, their language. This allows me to conclude their racism and white supremacy flatten or stamp out any claim to cognitive strength, indifference, and disinterest (i.e., objective truths).

Levinas joins this insouciant caravan of those who treat Black people not only as the Other, but to a large extent as nonexistent—not worthy of being mentioned even as a footnote in their theoretical discourse. In a very real sense, Black suffering is erased or excluded from the consciousness of white people, starting with the intellectuals and trickling down to the factory workers and churchgoing evangelicals. This intentionality itself constitutes a negative phenomenology of suffering. And this is nothing about which to boast. The memory or inability to remember suffering creates a silence, a moan, a woe that is too deep for words. A century and a half after slavery, the memory and vestiges of it still haunt my social imagination. This suffering produces systemic anger and distress. But more than that, it produces pain that lingers for generations, pain that is at least as ritualistic as it is hopeful. Suffering produces a painful enduring sickness in the body and mind—an inability to recognize and acknowledge suffering as suffering. That, to me, is the Black problem—and the problem of the white architects of Black suffering.

Levinas says consciousness is not fixed. Evil is parasitical. It feeds off of being. Therefore, suffering deals with the issue and question of materiality. Consciousness is impacted by the materiality of data; and if consciousness is influenced by materiality, then consciousness of the Holocaust has made us act as human beings regardless of race and ethnicity.[2]

Black suffering is grounded in the experience of being the hated Other, the victim of American materialism, exceptionalism, and the grand narrative of an American identity shaped and shorn by a Jeffersonian "Anglo-Saxon myth." The Very Rev. Dr. Kelly Brown Douglas explains this mindset in detail and asserts its meaning using the following language:

American exceptional identity was grounded in the Anglo-Saxon myth. To reiterate, this myth stressed that it was Anglo-Saxon institutions that best respected individual rights and liberty. Inasmuch as America stayed true to its Anglo-Saxon character when forming its governing institutions, then it would maintain its exceptional identity. . . . [Its] Anglo-Saxon character and its "chosen" nature.[3]

Professor Brown Douglas goes on to explain the synchronicity between these two elements of mythmaking and illustrates how this constructed exceptional identity morphed into abject racism. To be American means to be white—just as Charles Long, the historian of religion, asserts that once persons from other countries land at John F. Kennedy Airport in New York, they take on an American identity almost immediately. They understand that to survive, to excel, and to avoid being shot and killed by the police, "whiteness" is a necessary racial identifier. They are no longer German, Irish, Turkish, or even Asian. They immediately become white,[4] says Long.

Consciousness combats the deep layers of suffering we would rather not face or experience, especially if we are the purveyors of the suffering imposed on the Other, and even if we are not. This understanding is extended to and is apparently the case for Levinas, whose discourse on the phenomenology of suffering never once hints at American chattel slavery and the suffering it caused millions of enslaved people for 250 years—a fact that constitutes the essence of the experience of suffering as a human atrocity and as an illogical or irrational social and psychological construct. Levinas outlines and explains the exceptional nature of the Holocaust and wonders what kind of God would allow such evil to happen to adults and children, and further suggests, like other Jewish scholars,[5] the evils of Auschwitz make Friedrich Nietzsche's claim that "God is Dead" not only a real possibility, but also a viable and substantiated probability. The sheer evil of murdering children and adults continues to reverberate in society even today; the ninety-four-year-old "accountant of Auschwitz," Oskar Gröning, was sentenced in 2015, to four years in a German prison for his role in the deaths of 300,000 Hungarian Jews. One of the unnamed Holocaust survivors of Auschwitz hugged and embraced the convicted accountant; when a reporter in awe asked her how she could do that, she replied, "Forgiveness is the best revenge."[6]

Wow! My mind vectored immediately to the Emmanuel African Methodist Episcopal Church in Charleston, South Carolina, and to the family members of the nine Black Bible study and prayer meeting participants massacred there. They, too, were forgiving of the killer during the arraignment hearing, just a day or so after the murders. With a rare and surprising univocity, they each said, "I forgive him." Black people are extraordinarily forgiving of the evils perpetrated against them by white people. How else can they keep their sanity in the midst of being dehumanized on every hand?

It seems to me that Black suffering is outside the realm of consciousness for most white scholars and philosophers. It is beyond the traditional understanding of the phenomenology of suffering. Black suffering does not even seem to qualify as "a datum in consciousness," as Levinas rather scientifically describes suffering, meaning it does not constitute a given or an "of course" to scholars that this, too, is suffering. It appears Black suffering is psychologically and intentionally outside the realm of consciousness of white people, such that the sensation of pain and the experience of color tend to escape the awareness of these philosophers and scholars. Since being white is the experience of privilege, the experience of color is one that represents the negation of being, i.e. Blackness, especially to white folk. To be Black is to experience acts of evil and suffering daily. It is to be in a constant fight and struggle to be seen and heard. It is to be enraged and hopeful at the same time. Could this be an unconsciousness so ubiquitous that it could be said to be ontological or endemic to being non-black? While this idea, to me, is an epic absurdity and evil, it may purport to explain why the lynching of the Black body, the castration of Black males, and the burning and torture of Black men and women throughout American Southern history are not thought to be suffering, but something else, akin to a type of carnivalistic pleasure. A warped and sadistic entertainment, as seen, for example, in the 2012 movie *Django Unchained*—the taking of pleasure in the pain and death by torture of the Black body.[7]

Black suffering is not considered suffering in the white American consciousness. This is what I call "the Black Suffering Principle." Its extreme Otherness constitutes an ontological negation of being within the mind of the dominant culture. Historically, this suffering is seen as a type of spectacle, a dissociation from the Other. It is what I, mimicking the provocative and often controversial Black recording artist and rapper Kanye West, call an "other-other," which is an explainable suffering that apparently does not signify negativity. Rather, it signifies the antithesis to negativity and evil. And yet Levinas says "all evil relates back to suffering."[8] This is the absurdity of his ontological affirmation, since Black suffering is also an evil grounded in the particularity of race hatred perpetrated against Black people. And pain, as a byproduct of suffering, is an evil absurdity. But this assertion does not seem to apply to Black people in contemporary America nor during the four hundred years or more of Black suffering in North America. Thus, the Black Suffering Principle.

Black suffering, whether during slavery or in the current day—from daily killings and lynchings of Black males to the nearly forty percent of Black youth in America who now live in poverty—embodies the negativity of evil, not just symbolically, but concretely as well. How else can we describe the shooting in the back of a Black man, Walter Scott, when he was running away from police in Charleston, South Carolina? Or the severing of the spine of a young Black man, Freddie Gray, while shackled and handcuffed in a van driven by the Baltimore police? This is like a sick, sadistic act of evil, and yet it is not called evil or illegal. This was a type of "joy ride" or "rough ride," designed to kill a Black man through the lack of seat belts, of safety restraints, as well as through an apparent disinterest in the well-being of a young Black person. This is an act of torture,[9] as Jean Améry discusses—and it seems to me to be an act of evil. This is akin to what white people did to the young Black African freedom fighter Steve Biko, age 30, in South Africa, taking him from East London to Pretoria in the back of a Land Rover truck for 700 miles! And naturally, he died as a result, on September 12, 1977.

In Chicago, a seventeen-year-old Black teenager, LaQuan McDonald, was shot sixteen times by a white veteran policeman, an act symptomatic of the evil perpetrated against Black people by government-sanctioned vigilantes. Again, the murder of a Black male who was running away from the police is not considered suffering. The death of a Black male is not a death to be mourned. For me, this goes beyond the symbolism of evil and represents the personification of evil. Evil is not a symbol. Evil is an act of human intention designed to destroy another human being. "Black-on-Black" crime is also an evil, and one of immense complexity—an internalization of the ways of their colonizers. It is a self-hatred that causes pain and suffering to those whom we claim to love.

Black suffering goes intentionally unnoticed and unrecognized in our cities and towns and rural hamlets throughout America. It is called something else, given another nomenclature, such as "poverty," "joblessness," or "Black-on-Black crime." Let us call it what it is: Black suffering and the excess of evil. For example, the Baltimore riots that took place a few years ago were just a reflection of the hopelessness Black folk feel because of the years and years of neglect, police brutality, discrimination, racism, and injustice they have experienced and continue to experience. This experience is not just in Baltimore, but also in New York, Philadelphia, Atlanta, Richmond, San Francisco, and other large and small cities and towns throughout the country. My claim is that Black people are generally not violent; and if they are, they have learned it from those who founded this country with guns and swords—killing American Indians and slaughtering Black people through slavery, the auction block, and the lynching tree. Oh, and also through burning Black men and castrating them for public display. The spectacle of justice and righteousness was always a force in American religion and jurisprudence. I will say more about the work of acclaimed Black liberation theologian James H. Cone in a later chapter, especially his book *The Cross and the Lynching Tree.*

Black people are in spirit and in fact a loving people who deplore and abhor violence against the other. During the Baltimore riots, this was displayed beautifully all over the television screen when a Black mother of six recognized her sixteen-year-old son in a hoodie and face mask among those who had taken to the streets in protest. When the teenage boy made eye contact with his mother, she, in her pain and fear, began to confront and whip his behind in the street, in the public square, in broad daylight with cameras rolling from CNN, CBS, NBC, and other news networks. Everybody began talking about this event, which also was *prima facie* a spectacle, but one from which we all can learn. Yes, this Black mother loved her son so much that she risked everything to show him how scared for his life she was. Whatever it took to get him off the dangerous crowded streets, she would do it. But, more than that, while I was overcome with mixed emotions for the mother, I was also impressed by the behavior of her sixteen-year-old son. He never once raised his hands at his mother in disrespect and defiance. The whole time she was reflexively slapping him, screaming, yelling, and pounding him with her hands, he was trying to run, trying to get away from his justifiably angry and pained Black mother. I thought he was very respectful of her in the face of the public drama. Naturally, this was the one time white folks throughout the media said it was acceptable to beat your children in public and not be punished for it. Move over, Dr. Spock, Dr. Phil, and all the ivory tower scholars and pediatricians who call this type of action "violence against children."[10] The mother's actions and her son's response were both acts of love. Pure emotion. Acts of visceral reciprocity manifested in respect and fear. The mother's desperation for her only son, and the son's deference to his mother, despite the embarrassment of the public spectacle, were examples of the many faces and permutations of suffering experienced in urban America, with Baltimore as a prototype. This milieu of suffering is pandemic and characterizes a significant—that is, dominant— trope in Black life. Black suffering is everywhere, and it is institutionalized so much that it is unrecognizable to some who purport to write about it, and more importantly, to those who cause it. Again, this is the Black Suffering Principle, in which suffering is not suffering if it relates to Black people.

Black suffering, survival, and hope are reflected in the Old Testament Book of Job, a theme on which I expound further in chapter 9 of this book. The Job of the dialogues (chapters 3–41) is the symbol of unmerited suffering and the excess of evil.[11] He is the embodiment of the suffering of the innocent (none of us is completely innocent, but we are often more innocent than guilty). That is Job. But I think it is a reasonable postulate to assert that the Job of the prologue (chapters 1–2) is, symbolically, a white man, with all of his possessions of houses, land, oxen, and cattle. And the Job of the dialogues is experientially Black. Listen to the agony and pain. Feel the suffering. The suffering of a slave, the suffering of Fannie Lou Hamer, the suffering of Ruby Bridges, the suffering of Tom Robinson, the wrongly convicted Black man in *To Kill a Mockingbird*, the suffering of both Grant (the teacher) and Jefferson (the wrongly accused Black man) in *A Lesson Before Dying*. Listen to the agony and pain embedded in the language of the Joban text, "Even when I cry out, 'Violence' I am not answered; I call aloud, but there is no justice."[12] No justice! No justice, even when I cry out and call aloud. Is that not the exact phrase Black folk have been chanting loudly all over America—in New York, in Ferguson, in Sanford, in Baltimore, in Richmond, and in Charleston? All over America, the cry of the unemployed Black worker, the Black teenager, and the Black college student. It is also the cry of Job. Job's cry is our cry. No justice! Violence! No justice!

Another reality principle is the fact Black people tend to display an inexplicable love toward white people. Instead, the architects of the "no justice for Black people" rule are the violent ones. These are modern-day colonizers. The police. The Calvary. The "law and order" Brigade. These are the white church evangelicals Martin Luther King Jr. references in his "Letter from Birmingham City Jail" when he says:

> I have traveled the length and breadth of Alabama, Mississippi and all the other southern states. On sweltering summer days and crisp autumn mornings I have looked at the South's beautiful churches with their lofty spires pointing heavenward. I have beheld the impressive outlines of her massive religious education buildings. Over and over I have found myself asking: "What kind of people worship here? Who is their God?"[13]

These are also the "family values" Republicans who are sympathetic to white supremacists, as they have been since the mid-twentieth century. These are the Clinton Democrats who designed the "school to prison pipeline" legislation for Black youth. These are the "superpredators", to invert Hillary Clinton's claim, who mastermind Black suffering as a business practice and a political promise.

Black people have been suffering for hundreds of years, through chattel slavery, hatred and discrimination, racism, and all kinds of evil and violent atrocities. Therefore, I assert without equivocation or fear of the exegesis police—that is, the commentators and Bible scholars—that "Job is Black." Job is a metaphor and symbol of Blackness: "Even when I cry out 'Violence!' I am not answered; I call aloud, but there is no justice." He is parallel to the suffering that characterizes Black life on every socioeconomic and political level. Change has not come to America, contrary to President Obama's political slogan. Again, as a metaphor and in the social location of his suffering, Job is just as Black as James Cone claimed Jesus is Black. Similarly, rather than agreeing with the master's narrative, American Indians see themselves as the Canaanites, not the conquering Israelites that Black folk normally identify with, at least historically.

The apostle Paul, however, says that we have a type of justification in our faith. And in the Book of Romans, he states: "And we boast in our hope of sharing the glory of God. And not only that, but we also boast in our sufferings, knowing that suffering produces endurance, and endurance produces character, and character produces hope."[14] There is a difference between Job's response to suffering and Paul's response here in Romans. The latter is no doubt an expression of some type of eschatological hope—a hope not grounded in the real-life situations of the here and now. Boasting in hope and boasting in suffering while saying hope does not disappoint us does not ring true to the Black experience. Black people have indeed been and still are disappointed while also hanging onto some sliver of hope. But let us be truthful. Let us be real. There is a lot of hopelessness out there. Young Black people are addicted to selling and using drugs because the schools, family, church, and community have failed to ground them in hope. Black youths have developed a hopelessness that is, in fact, disappointing. Nihilism reigns supreme. Johnny Bernard Hill addresses this pathological condition in *Prophetic Rage: A Postcolonial Theology of Liberation*.[15] There is a suffering that tears away at the fabric of our faith. Yes, Black people do have character. For example, I think the sixteen-year-old Black boy in Baltimore had character because he did not raise his hands against his mother who was beating him on national television. Yes, he had excellent character—suffering produces endurance and endurance produces character, and character produces hope, according to Paul's theology.

I reiterate: Freddie Gray, the twenty-five-year-old Black man in Baltimore who was handcuffed, shackled, and thrown in a police transport van after being illegally arrested—died nearly ten days after his arrest and "rough ride" by police officers. He ended up with a severed spine. This death at the hands of the police was perpetrated by what Frantz Fanon calls "the enforcers of colonization." Fanon says, "In the colonies [Baltimore, Maryland; Sanford, Florida; Ferguson, Missouri, etc.], the official, legitimate agent; the spokesperson for the colonizer; and the regime of oppression are the police officer or the soldiers."[16]

The National Guard, the city police, and the state police spoke loudly in Baltimore as young Black people exploded with frustration, anger, and apparent hopelessness—a reaction to the police violence towards young Black males. This story of Black Suffering is so layered and complex with so many characters. It is an effusion of emotions and fears. It is a bursting forth of suffering and pain—an agony on the order of Job's suffering.

Let me be clear. There are those who say it is a shame for Black people to be rioting and looting in their own communities. This is also a gross fallacy, because Black people, on the whole, do not own these community buildings and businesses.

But in my view, the mayor of Baltimore should be commended and applauded for her wisdom in giving Black youths room and space to express their anger in the face of overwhelming police brutality and injustice. If she had not done what she had, I think those poverty-drenched communities would have felt even more hopelessness and the burning embers of the fire next time, a fire spoken of by James Baldwin that has been smoldering in the consciousness of Black folk for over four hundred years—a fire set ablaze by the racism and capitalism of a violent nation of duplicitous leaders, from Founding Fathers like George Washington and Thomas Jefferson, to Donald Trump and other modern-day politicians and vulgar capitalists from Wall Street to Main Street.

As human beings, we have all been born to mothers. Childbirth itself is an act of pain and suffering, despite the interventions of anesthesia and other painkillers. Mothers not only suffer during childbirth, but also as they watch their children grow. More often than not, this suffering is born out of love, and love itself is more an act of suffering and pain than one of blissful joy. This is a dialectic born out of creation, which moans and groans while bursting forth with new mercies and new joys every day.[17]

My dear mother, Carrie Anna Harris, gave birth to eleven children, one of whom died as an infant—not in childbirth, but from pneumonia and the lack of antibiotics like penicillin. In reality, the baby died from the lack of health care and the effects of poverty. I will say more about this in a later chapter.

Black suffering is laden with "paradoxes and incongruences,"[18] much like the suffering that is theologically construed as redemptive and unmerited. It is an "instead of" suffering, and yet our suffering continues almost unabated by the passing of time and the impact of Christian teachings and theological practices. Black people seem to be the most godly, religious, and spiritual people I know. And yet the suffering relentlessly continues.

Take the lynching of Black men and women throughout the South for decades. Mothers saw their sons crucified like Christ hanging on a cross from Maryland and Virginia to Mississippi, from Georgia to Louisiana and Alabama. We have experienced the spectacle of the crucifixion of Black people. Countee Cullen, in his 1922 poem "Christ Recrucified," writes:

> The South is crucifying Christ again
> By all the laws of ancient rote and rule:
> The ribald cries of "Save yourself" and "fool"
> Din in his ear, the thorns grope for his brain,
> And where they bite, swift springing rivers stain
> His gaudy, purple robe of ridicule
> With sullen red; and acid wine to cool
> His thirst is thrust at him, with lurking pain.
> Christ's awful wrong is that he's dark of hue,
> The sin for which no blamelessness atones;
> But lest the sameness of the cross should tire,
> They kill him now with famished tongues of fire,
> And while he burns, good men, and women too,
> Shout, battling for black and brittle bones.[19]

Women were lynched, too, as in Billie Holiday's song "Strange Fruit": "Strange fruit hanging from the poplar tree."[20] Black babies were ripped from the wombs of pregnant mothers and stomped to death by white men with hunting knives—this is what James Cone and Countee Cullen called the "recrucified Christ."[21] And let us not forget Emmett Till, who was crucified by two white men, J. W. Milam and Roy Bryant, and by a system of injustice and racial hatred reflected in the evil of slavery. That system is seen today not just in the South but all over America, from Florida and New York to Missouri and the Carolinas.

I reiterate, to the point of redundancy, that Black suffering is more than a "datum" in consciousness. It is constituted by something that exceeds singularity and is possessed of a plurivocity of data crystallized over time into the experience of Blackness, which by all accounts is tautological to pain and suffering. Again, Black suffering is not "similar" to the experience of color, as Emmanuel Levinas asserts, but it *is* the experience of color.[22] To be clothed in Black skin is the suffering experience of color. The color of suffering is Black. Both the language and the experience confirm that.

In Black suffering, the experience of color is fundamental. It is constant. It is ontological. It is causal. And it is this experience of color that gives Black suffering its singularly unique nature. That singularity is of experience, not of data. This means suffering in Black consciousness is inescapable. Every instance of life is color-coded in Black consciousness. Suffering is always present in mind, body, and soul. It is so present that it is "passivity." It is senseless, not simply sensorial. I agree with Levinas when he states:

> In suffering, sensibility is a vulnerability, more passive than receptivity; an encounter more passive than experience. It is precisely an evil. It is not, to tell the truth, through passivity that evil is described, but through evil that suffering is understood.[23]

Who else understands both suffering and evil more profoundly than Black people? This is not to diminish the suffering of others, nor to say, "My suffering is greater than yours." No, this is to say Black suffering is a constant reality that must be acknowledged today. It is not a past event. It is a present, ubiquitous reality. Given our history, to be Black is to suffer, similar to what the Bible describes as "the election of Jews." As Peter Ochs, the philosopher and Jewish Studies professor says, "To be elected by God is to suffer."[24] Is this not also the fate of Black people and the fate of Job? According to the biblical story, Job was wagered by God, elected specifically to be put up to the task of suffering at the hands of Satan. Levinas's dictum "All evil relates back to suffering," while confounding, forces me to assert its converse, namely, "all suffering relates back to evil"—which, for me, is symbolized by American chattel slavery, the ultimate paradigm of human absurdity and abject evil. For Jews, the Holocaust has no corollary in history because of the intense suffering perpetrated against them for no reason except hatred and evil. Unequivocally true. But I say the longitudinal suffering of the unending chattel slavery of Black folk is as constitutive of suffering and evil—or more so—than any other imaginable or unimaginable atrocity. More importantly, Black people are still struggling as a race of people to shake loose the manacles and shackles of their bondage, which still causes not only the slow but sure death of the body and mind, but also a burnishing of the soul. It is a miracle, beyond belief and explanation, that Black folk still have their sanity, are not all mad, and continue in the practice of their faith in a God—a faith that is questioned every day by issues of justice, love, and freedom.

Interlude: "Brothers of Randolph Street"

I continue with "Brothers of Randolph Street," a short piece of creative nonfiction about the life of Black boys. The ethical trajectory of this work points toward the truth of growing up Black surrounded by the pressures to make it from one day to the next. The piece is intended to demonstrate the theme of Black suffering that resonates in the everyday lives of young Black males as they face poverty in the home and community, failed public housing and schools, disinterested policy makers, drugs, and the overwhelming quest for acceptance among their peers. The story is intended to be a reflection on the Black pride, resistance, and hope that permeates Black life even amid suffering and moral decay. Hopelessness is a dominant trope in the struggle to negotiate life and death in urban milieus where only the strong survive. Black pain and suffering are evils.

"Brothers of Randolph Street"

They were brothers, but not of the same mother. Born in the same hospital and living a few doors from each other in the Idlewood Avenue housing projects, they grew up together. They all had the same father, Big John. They were spiritually connected, eating often from each other's tables and sleeping in each other's beds. Sometimes, they shared girls like they shared everything else. They were brothers in spirit and body. They wore each other's clothes, even down to the underwear, used each other's toothbrushes and deodorant, and smoked the same blunts and "roaches." As children and youth, they all went to Maymont, John B. Cary, or Clark Springs Elementary Schools, and then on to the notorious and low-performing Winford Middle School and "T. J." High School. This venerable and historic school bore the name of Virginia's and America's most honored governor and president, Thomas Jefferson.

White people would wince and cringe every time they heard the school's name disrespected and bastardized by young Black people as "T. J." The initials created an unjustified familiarity, a sullying of the venerability of Mr. Jefferson's name—a name as holy as the Bible and as revered as that of any Greek god. Move over, Zeus. Thomas Jefferson's shortened name had come to symbolize the school's Blackness and the warehousing of students for whom counselors and teachers had no college ambition—and from whom they saw no SAT scores to prove otherwise. The Black community's screed against and disrespect for Thomas Jefferson exposed the fact that Black people had come to understand the history books and Monticello tours were pushing a myth advancing the architects of American democracy. Thomas Jefferson was the master of a duplicitous life. Doublespeak. A slave owner who talked about equality and justice. He said education and slavery were two incommensurables, that freedom and a good education go hand in hand. Although he had no real love for Black people, not even Sally Hemings, whom he'd sexed from her age of thirteen or fourteen until he died. Almost everybody knew this sordid history. That was why the Black students would laugh and jape about the school's name.

In January 1787, Thomas Jefferson wrote, "Malo periculosam libertatem quam quietam servitutem," or, "I prefer dangerous freedom over peaceful slavery." As a slave owner and a slave trader, he was a Christian hypocrite, a white man about whom Black youth had little knowledge and no desire to learn anything more than what was taught in elementary school.

Allix, who never graduated from T. J., realized the school had become a symbol of low achievement and lack of success. It had become a metaphor for propagating a slave-like mentality. Allix, against all odds, had learned a little Latin on his own; and in a conversation about the school, he said to everyone's surprise, "Totum esse fraudi." He explained Thomas Jefferson was the chief of American fraud, which is why Black youth had kept his initials and changed his name. For most of them, "T. J." stood for "totally junked."

All of the Randolph Street boys attended "T. J.," but only one of them graduated—after being there for nearly five years. It was supposed to be a four-year program. Still, he graduated with perfect attendance on his diploma. This was a sign of stamina and sheer determination. The others had dropped out after getting in fights, carrying weapons to school in their backpacks, having sexual encounters in the bathroom, buying and selling drugs, and sleeping in class. It was not really their fault, because they lived among pimps and whores. Some of them had mothers who were addicted to all kinds of synthetic substances, including cigarettes and marijuana, and they had no Black teachers throughout elementary school, which was one clear measure for predicting whether Black youth will drop out of high school. All of them believed religiously they were in control of their drug use. Stupid naiveté. A sign of their deep addictions and lack of self-understanding.

At around twelve years old, even before puberty, they started having sex in the back alley behind the Baptist church on the corner of Randolph and Harrison Streets. Three of them had fathered children by the age of fifteen.

One day after church, one of the boys, Wesley, said to Reverend Jeremiah Brown, "Getting high makes me feel smarter. It clears my mind."

"Really," Reverend Brown said. "So why have you failed Geometry and English three times?"

"It ain't 'cause of that. I just can't stay awake in class. When I sleep, my mind is clear. I dream of good stuff." Wesley spoke with conviction and a tinge of anger. Reverend Brown's question had surprised him and nearly tripped him up.

"I can't talk to you," Reverend Brown said in disgust. "You look high and delusional right now. Your eyes are glassy, and your logic is twisted. Talk to me when you sober up tomorrow."

"Don't be using a lot of big words with me. You sound like my teachers, talking down and talking smart to me like I'm slow or something." Wesley spoke with sadness and a seething soreness.

"Hey, listen to me. My speech is your speech if you will listen and learn," Reverend Brown said. "I'm talking up to you, not down to you. I refuse to talk down to you or anyone else, because talking down to you is talking crazy and sounding like you sound. I am full of big words, man. It's my language that I am trying to bequeath to you. My language is your language. I give it to you as a gift of love. Take it and run with it."

"You so goddamn smart for not to know shit," Wesley said. He was mad because of his low achievement.

The next morning, Reverend Brown had breakfast with some of the same Black boys at a local diner. The place was musty and a bit dirty, but it was convenient, just around the corner from the church and the housing projects. These boys were always hungry. One of them, Allix, was a tall, lanky boy already sixteen years old and admired by the girls as a young, handsome sensation. That was his story. He loved to boast and brag about what he could do as a young stud. To hear him tell it, every girl was always looking at him, ogling with desire. He thought he was the shit, even though he had not yet fully learned to read on grade level. When his mother died, he became a man-child of the streets, lost to despair and a certain hopelessness. A teenage pimp. A drug dealer who smoked half of the weed he was supposed to be selling.

One day in late August, Allix stumbled into the little one-bedroom apartment where he lived on the edge of the public housing projects. He was lethargic and delusional, talking out of his head and mumbling a lot of trash.

"Allix, what's wrong with you? Are you all right?" asked his sister, Shaquita.

He let out a groan, soft and labored, almost inaudible. Then, all of a sudden, he collapsed. Shaquita looked on, helplessly smothered by fear and anxiety.

"Call somebody! Dial 911!" she yelled at the top of her lungs. Her phone had been turned off a few days earlier for not paying the bill. She felt naked and helpless without her phone. She blamed herself for using her phone bill money to buy a ticket to the Beyoncé concert.

It seemed like an eternity passed for the paramedics to arrive. When they did, a crowd had already gathered out front. Some in the crowd were scared because they had also smoked some of the same bad weed. Marijuana laced with rat poison and arsenic. It was a deadly concoction used to punish those who stole from Mr. Bentsen, the infamous and violent drug dealer in that part of the city's East End District.

When the EMT, nicknamed Stoney, got a close look at Allix's face, his hands began to tremble and sweat beaded upon his forehead. This was his younger brother who had spent a few hours just the night before telling him lies about the pretty new girl he was seeing and how she had made him feel loved as they did the "wild thang" all night long. Some of what Allix had said was true, but most of it was lies because he had been too drunk and high to maintain his virility. He'd thought he'd been doing something, but the girl was the queen of pretense. In his condition, it hadn't mattered because delusion had grabbed him by the balls. Plus, he was the kind of guy who appreciated a girl who lied to him about his sexual prowess. Because he, too, was a pathological liar, he recognized a lie when he heard one, but he hadn't been the least bit concerned. The lie had boosted his testosterone and his ego, which had been derailed by his inability to pass Algebra and Chemistry in high school. When Allix had turned sixteen, he'd stopped going to classes altogether and begun to hang out on Meadow and Cary Streets in the nip joints and in the alleys behind the church, the funeral home, and the corner store. At first, he'd only missed school a few days a week, and then it'd become more regular. And then school had fallen completely off the radar.

The school attendance officer had left message after message on his sister's phone, but Shaquita could not handle Allix. He was a big boy for his age, six-feet-four inches tall, weighing over two hundred pounds. After months of trying, she'd given him up to the wiles of the devil and to the street corners where he'd sold bottled water and drugs. The water was a cover, a decoy. After he'd seen the cash involved, he'd begun to label and bottle his own water called "The Elixir by Allix." Allix's elixir was a concoction of tap water mixed with a pinch of cane sugar and vanilla flavoring. Within a year, he was selling 10,000 twelve-ounce bottles a week for fifty cents each, grossing close to a half-million dollars on three street corners: Belvedere and Broad, Lombardy Street and Brook Road, and the corner of Hull Street and Commerce Road. The sugar was as addictive as opioids. Drinking this water had become a religion, a ritual more fulfilling than eating and more satisfying than sex.

"Man, what you putting in this water?"

"It's just water, man. H_2O, that's all. Really, that's it."

"I don't know. I ain't never seen niggas drink that much water before."

"Hey, you just suspicious of everybody."

"Better be glad it's water and nothing else."

"Well, come on, man. 'It's water,' all right! That water's got something in it, *something*."

"You know, some white folks been buying it lately and I think it's the FDA or the FBI working undercover."

"No problem. The law ain't got nothing to do with it. Everything we doing is legal. Just selling water 'cause people is thirsty. This is legit."

"For real, for real. I ain't never seen Black folk drink that much water before. And to pay fifty cents a bottle for it. You think I'm stupid or crazy?"

"Hey, this is God's water. It's holy water. Folk got more energy and more stamina than they ever had," Allix said.

"That could only mean one thing "

"And what 'one thing' is that?" Allix insisted on knowing the answer.

But there was no real answer to that mystery, not without soul searching. Not even Reverend Jeremiah Brown could help him. The Reverend had baptized Allix and his brother after rescuing Allix's mother, Lilly, and her six children from the homeless shelter downtown. When he'd first met the family, they were sitting on the steps of the church early one Sunday morning, almost an hour before daybreak. It'd been in early December. Richmond was cold and blustery at that time of year. The Reverend had gotten to the church early to check the old oil furnace and to make sure the boiler was working so by the time Sunday school started, the place would be warm and welcoming. That morning, as he'd opened the large sanctuary doors, he felt the smell of heat and his heart had relaxed as the shivers from the outside cold fled like frost vanishing in the rays of morning sunlight.

"Y'all must be cold," he'd said to the mother and her children.

Still shivering and stiffened by the wind chill, they could hardly respond. Their eyes told the whole story. Sunken and dark, they spoke of suffering and pain and hunger. They had only eaten a little milk and cheese over the past two days. The director of the homeless shelter had told Lilly he could only house them for five days; so when Saturday had arrived, he'd come up to their little room at the top of the stairs with the bad news.

"Sister Lilly, I'm sorry, but this is your last night here. We promised your room to another woman for tonight. You have to be out before midnight," he'd said.

Lilly had begun to sob, a light stream of tears pulsing from her eyes. She was afraid and frantic, wondering what she would do with herself and her five Black boys and one girl. Her children had four different fathers, all of whom had long ago abandoned them for new, more exciting experiences. She had no place to go except the church house and the people of God.

It had always been her salvation. The preacher had helped her and her boys a hundred times before. The deacons and the members weren't happy about it, often saying the pastor was spending too much time and money with folk who were always going to be poor and needy. They'd even quote the Bible and Jesus, saying the poor would always be with us.

"These folk are a drain on our church finances," Sister Hollister had said. "They don't contribute nothing but always want us to help 'em with something."

When Lilly had heard these harsh words, she felt sorry for herself and began to sing the old hymn she had learned in her little country church as a child:

Amazing grace, how sweet the sound
that saved a wretch like me.
I once was lost but now am found
was blind but now I see.

Through many dangers toils and snares,
I have already come . . .

Her voice had faded to a whisper as she'd wiped her eyes of tears and her nose of snot. Her boys, then eight, nine, ten, eleven, and thirteen years old, begged her to stop crying.

"Momma, don't cry. We gonna be all right," the oldest boy had said. She'd stroked him on the head, wincing and trying her hardest to heed his voice. But she couldn't stop. She'd been a bucket of water, a vale of tears and a mantle of sorrow. The pain and suffering had been etched in her face and in the somber sound of her pitiful song.

When Stoney realized that his brother was gasping for breath, he almost fainted because he knew they had smoked from the same stash. He was already feeling sick as he watched the vomit ooze from his brother's mouth. Most of the people in the crowd had developed an immunity to rat poison. They had been smoking it for so long, it was normal. It brought out the flavor and curbed the scent of cannabis. They felt Mr. Bentsen had been trying to kill them for years, but they had outsmarted him. The problem was Allix was young and new at this, and his body was weak because he had suffered from asthma as a child. It had only been a year since he spent three months in the intensive care unit at the Medical College of Virginia. Everybody thought he was going to die then. And then he'd gotten out of the hospital and started smoking weed again. He had a death wish, a rendezvous with the dark side of the moon. He also had a thousand friends doing the same thing.

Soon after, Allix was back in business. It was the combination of the water and the weed that was making Allix's business grow. He had a hundred times more followers on Instagram than the preacher did, and his customers were devoted. They bought water and weed every day and on Sundays after church, one could see the lines on the corners getting longer and longer, folks queuing up to buy a little water to quench their thirst and to ease their pain so they could run on a little while longer and live to see another day.

The following night, Allix was stopped by the narcotics officer from the Meadow Street police precinct.

"Sir, I pulled you over because your taillight was out."

"My taillight was working fine when I left home. I don't know what happened."

"Sir, do you have any drugs in the car? The car smells like marijuana. It's stinking up the street," the police officer said.

"I have a little weed. I'm gonna be honest, sir. Here, take a look."

"Okay, could you step out the car and put your hands over your head?" the officer demanded.

Allix got angry and refused to do it, so the police officer yelled and pushed him to the ground as he uttered expletives and racial epithets. And then, just that quick, there were four pops, like firecrackers. *Pop, pop, pop, pop.* Allix slumped over on the concrete street. Breathless. Dead. His hand clenched a bottle of water.

W. E. B. Du Bois and Black Consciousness: An Awakened Self

The brutality with which Negroes are treated in this country simply cannot be overstated. . . . For the horrors of the American Negro's life there has been almost no language. —James Baldwin, *The Fire Next Time*

In *The Souls of Black Folk*, William Edward Burghardt Du Bois provides a survey of the context and mentality of Black people in America during the mid and latter parts of the nineteenth century, beginning in 1861, as legal slavery is about to be confronted by the Civil War. The work reveals the apparent societal issues and racial ills that linger and spill over from the antebellum period, through Reconstruction, and into the "Jim Crow" era. Du Bois gives voice to the countless dark bodies[1] that have experienced evil, inhumane, and oppressive treatment. He delineates and interprets the self-consciousness of the African American in classic dialectical language. It is a two-pronged self-consciousness, which America imposes with denigrating interest on the Black Other, who is hidden behind the "veil." Du Bois explains with these searing and vivid words:

> The Negro is the sort of seventh son, born with a veil, and gifted with second-sight in this American world—a world which yields him no true self-consciousness, but only lets him see himself through the revelation of the other world. It is a peculiar sensation, this double-consciousness, this sense of always looking at one's self through the eyes of others, of measuring one's soul by the tape of a world that looks on in amused contempt and pity. One ever feels his twoness—an American, a Negro; two souls, two thoughts, two unreconciled strivings; two warring ideals in one dark body, whose dogged strength alone keeps it from being torn asunder. The history of the American Negro is the history of strife—this longing to attain self-conscious manhood to merge his double self into a better and true self.[2]

Self-consciousness is the acknowledgement and awareness of self in relation to the self and others. It is an aspect of humanness that helps to shape identity, perception, and truth about the self. The irony of the Negro's self-consciousness, as Du Bois describes it, is this self-consciousness does not have the Black self providing its determination; instead, it has an *other* who audaciously pretends and portends it knows the Black self. This perception, which is one of inferiority and ignorance, is forced upon the Negro while the true self-consciousness is suppressed. Like chattel slavery, this projected consciousness is a form of enslavement that leaves the Negro longing for Freedom. Freedom to be human. No matter its outer hue, the human soul desires expression as evidence of having meaning and purpose. The African American, at the point in history in which Du Bois writes, has been used as a revenue-generating asset for the slave master with no other major purpose. Like a farm machine or an animal. Like a plow, a horse, or a mule. A commodity.

As the Reconstruction period progressed, Black people sought education as an initiative for advancement in society. Along with education came the raw and ugly truth of the state of the social, economic, and cultural Black person in America. This truth stripped away the perceived ignorant bliss of the formerly enslaved. Du Bois gives an account of a young Black man named John who goes off to school to get an education. Before attending school, John is considered to be a "good boy" and a fine plough-hand by the "white folk," and he has genuine satisfaction with the world. He returns home from school, and everyone notices his persona has changed drastically. No longer is he the happy-go-lucky "good boy"; now, he has a sobering, disheartening outlook on life as a result of his education, which has prompted his self-conscious evolution and his understanding of the meaning and nature of evil as an act of destruction of the other, particularly the African American:

> A new dignity crept into his walk. . . . He looked now for the first time sharply about him, and wondered why he had seen so little before. He grew slowly to feel almost for the first time the Veil that lay between him and the white world; he first noticed now the oppression that had not seemed oppression before . . . restraints in his boyhood days had gone unnoticed or been greeted with a laugh. He felt angry . . . he clenched his hands at the "Jim Crow" cars. A tinge of sarcasm crept into his speech, and a vague bitterness into his life. . . . Daily he found himself shrinking from the choked and narrow life of his native town.[3]

This is what I call Brother John's awakening consciousness of the stark realizations of suffering in Black life. His newly developed anger is based on his knowledge of himself; he is now a conscious man, and he has feelings, dreams, and aspirations that should not be denied because of his skin color.

Du Bois makes references to the "veil" throughout *The Souls of Black Folk*, symbolizing the rift between the Negro and the other world that marginalizes and even obfuscates his existence. This "veil" is the issue of color and what it represents. This "veil" presents a two-edged sword that pierces the flourishing ideal of Black humanity. It is the dialectic nature of Black life. It is also proleptic and future oriented. The veil is the vision of hope for Black people. On one side is the oppressed, struggling to express the self being conscious of itself; on the other side is the oppressor, whose notion of superiority seeks to obviate the existence of the Other, to destroy Black life. This dynamic denigration and evil nullifies the progress of society. The fact unacknowledged by the veil is that Black and other people of color, and white people are interconnected on multiple levels. The suffering caused by the veil leads to frustration, regression, and confusion for Black people in general. And the damage inflicted on one group indirectly brings damage to the conscious other. The ultimate result is the deterioration of the human spirit, a spirit that white people do not quite seem to possess, as Frantz Fanon attests when he states that the white man struggles to be human.[4]

Self-consciousness is not a static phenomenon. One obtains knowledge about the self as lived experiences allow. As knowledge perceived as truth is received and processed, the self chooses to apply this knowledge, which may enhance existing awareness or cause one's awareness of the self to change. Du Bois demonstrates this idea from an educational perspective but also illustrates it in the religious context. He notes the religion of the Negro during this time is considered "sacred." He describes the charismatic atmosphere of the worship service and the music, which has great meaning as a "true expression of a people's sorrow, despair, and hope."[5] Spirituality was germane to survival during this period in history, as Black people looked to a God who would one day vindicate the injustice and oppression of their folk. They looked forward to the creation of another world, one free of hate, sorrow, and strife. This helped to shape the self-consciousness of the Negro by allowing them the understanding there would be a better day. This was hope. The Black church was the place of empowerment, business, and social gathering, as well as the "real conserver of morals, a strengthener of family life, and the final authority on what is Good and Right."[6]

The church existed on one side of the "twoness" of self-consciousness Du Bois speaks of because, as an ethical and axiological aspect of Black life, it was not valued by white people. The Black person cannot be her authentic self in the midst of Otherness, but can only peaceably exist as some misconstrued version of self. When can the Negro be? Du Bois quotes a black preacher: "*Dum vivimus, vivamus*," Latin for, "While we live, let us live."[7]

> But back of this still broods silently the deep religious feeling of the real Negro heart, the stirring, unguided might of powerful human souls who have lost the guiding star of the past and seek in the great night a new religious ideal. Some day the Awakening will come, when the pent-up vigor of ten million souls shall sweep irresistibly toward the Goal, out of the Valley of the Shadow of Death, where all that makes life worth living—Liberty, Justice, and Right—is marked "For White People Only."[8]

This is a cry for liberation so loud it seems impossible not to hear, but at the same time a cry so silent it, in fact, goes unheard. There is an aspect of hope for the Negro looking to a better day. This otherworldly perspective brings to mind the words recorded in Revelation 21:4—"And God shall wipe away all tears from their

eyes; and there shall be no more death, neither sorrow, nor crying, neither shall there be any more pain: for the former things
are passed away."

Du Bois concludes the self-consciousness of the Negro is bit-
tersweet. Bitter because it acknowledges others' devalued perception of the self and the oppressive battle of daily life. Sweet
because the Negro's innermost being informs him that he is the
embodiment of beauty, compassion, and a rich heritage. He is a
part of the foundation of America, gifted in ways unlike any other.
He is dark, he is strong, he is life. She is dark, she is strong, she
is life. They are dark, they are strong, they are life.

Hegel and Self-Consciousness

The German philosopher Georg Wilhelm Friedrich Hegel postu-
lates that self-consciousness is Desire. It is for itself and exists
only in being acknowledged.[9] With Notions serving as movements
of knowledge, self-consciousness is being-for-itself. In Hegel's *The
Phenomenology of Spirit,* self-consciousness is discussed as the
knowing of self in the "native realm of truth." It has "I" for its
object—the thing toward which a cognitive act is directed—and
reflects being of the world of sense and perception. It is essentially the return from otherness.[10] Self-consciousness is concerned with being-for-self and negates an "other."

Additionally, Hegel asserts the "other" is also a type of self-
consciousness. When speaking of consciousness that relates to
the world—sense-certainty and perception of self and others—
Hegel describes an immediate self-consciousness and an
immediate consciousness. The former has "I" as the absolute
mediation with lasting independence. This Hegel defines as pure
self-consciousness. The latter is consciousness that is not purely
for itself but for another. Hegel terms this immediate consciousness for another *thinghood:*

Both moments are essential. Since to begin with they are unequal and opposed, and their reflection into a unity has not yet been achieved, they exist as two opposed shapes of consciousness; one is the independent consciousness whose essential nature is to be for itself, the other is the dependent consciousness whose essential nature is simply to live or to be for another. The former is lord, the other is bondsman.[11]

This is the basis for Hegel's view of the relations between master and slave. His statement that the two are "unequal and opposed" is derived from the life-and-death struggle the philosopher describes, in which both lord and bondsman seek the death or negation of the other. This struggle involves the staking of one's own life; whichever side is able to do this has won freedom[12] and the one who loses is bound. Hegel contends the lord (master) is the side that has won in the struggle, making the other a bondsman by default. Using this awfully convoluted thought, Hegel posits one form of self-consciousness against another in a way that suggests one is of a lesser degree than the other.

However, during (and in the years since) the period of slavery in America, the master was (and is) capable of winning in the struggle for independent consciousness because that struggle was not (and is not) fought on a level playing field. The enslaved were disadvantaged, captured and taken to a strange land, and forced to work; and if any enslaved rebelled, death was their looming fate. There was no opportunity for the enslaved to fight fairly to achieve independent consciousness. As for the moral integrity of Black people, a so-called "superior morality" professed by the master allows him to put forth a dominating perception while the slave assumes one of peonage. This inequality, combined with the differing "essential nature" advanced by Hegel, is the essence of racism and white supremacy. When the master perceives and treats

the slave as "other," the slave is regarded as a "thing" over which
the master has power. In this process, unfortunately, the "other"
(slave) defers its own being-for-self (self-consciousness) and mim-
ics the thought of the master, which, in turn, negates the "other"
or "thing." This is the nature of oppression. By mimicking the master, the slave is acting with a false sense of self-consciousness that
is itself dehumanizing in nature. This is a moment of recognition
that, according to Hegel, is one-sided and unequal.[13] This inequality also constitutes dehumanization and requires conscientization
to combat it, as discussed in Paulo Freire's classic pedagogy of
the oppressed.[14] The actual self-consciousness of the enslaved
is unacknowledged, disregarded, and therefore "unessential." In
addition, a real sense of fear and powerlessness is ever-present
in the enslaved. And rightly so, given the evil and heinous acts
perpetrated against her by slaveholders.

The truth of the master's self-consciousness lies in the self-
consciousness of the enslaved. A strange and crazy notion. This is
not only an irony, but it is also an oxymoronic view. Nevertheless,
Hegel writes:

> The truth of the independent consciousness is accord-
> ingly the servile consciousness of the bondsman. This, it
> is true, appears at first outside of itself and not as the
> truth of self-consciousness. But just as lordship showed
> that its essential nature is the reverse of what it wants to
> be, so, too, servitude in its consummation will really turn
> into the opposite of what it immediately is; as a conscious-
> ness forced back into itself, it will withdraw into itself and
> be transformed into a truly independent consciousness.[15]

This strange and vexing language suggests until the master and
the enslaved have conciliation with the notion of self-consciousness,
they both continue operating in a misconstrued perception of one
another. Both, in a sense, are bound by each other.

In discussing freedom of self-consciousness, Hegel also discusses stoicism, skepticism, and unhappy consciousness. *Stoicism* defines consciousness as a being that thinks and holds something to be "essentially important"—or, true and good—only to the extent it thinks it is true and good. This is a reminder of the biblical text found in Proverbs 23:7, "For as he thinketh in his heart, so is he." The Notion of Freedom—or, freedom in thought—may not be the lived experience of freedom, although it is the quickest way to liberate self-consciousness.

Skepticism deals with the realization of self-consciousness's negation of the other. The freedom becomes a reality, negates the other side of determinate existence, and in doing so duplicates itself. It now knows itself to be a duality.

Unhappy consciousness is the consciousness of self as a dual-natured, contradictory being.[16] Hegel describes unhappy consciousness as "the gazing of one self-consciousness into another." [17] One self-consciousness—the Unchangeable, essential being—is looked upon by another—the Changeable, unessential being. The latter is the consciousness that is considered less important. The peculiar thought behind unhappy consciousness is that it is not yet aware of its essential nature—that is, the unity of both. There is an antithetical dilemma here because this dual-natured consciousness deals with individuality and the Unchangeable. The consciousness perceives them as a duality, but there is a oneness in their movement of which the consciousness is unaware. The Unchangeable sees itself as individuality and consciousness attained in its own self; but instead of trying to grasp this essence, it only senses it and falls back into itself.[18] The issue with unhappy consciousness is it finds itself desiring and working without realizing it already contains self-certainty. This results in the inward feeling of uncertainty and incompleteness. Relief and reconciliation are only provided for by a mediator who is a conscious being that connects the unessential consciousness to the Unchangeable.

The Spirit also plays a part. Hegel sees self-consciousness as a reality, whereas consciousness is certainty through reason. In the context of truth, self-consciousness is truth, but a truth that is not constant unless and until it reaches the Absolute. Hegel states the Absolute is the truth and truth is absolute.[19] When self-consciousness is juxtaposed with the Absolute, it is ever becoming.

The point here is self-consciousness is a temporary truth that seeks and has as its aim an absolute, but which is limited by its nature in attaining such a result. This is what Hegel refers to as cognition.[20] Even Hegel admits this is a topic worthy of debate. From a philosophical and theological perspective, truth is eternal, immutable, and divine. As John 8:32 states, "If you continue in my word, you will know the truth and truth will set you free." The argument here could be that truth is relative and can be given different meanings based on perception. Hegel's racist ideology does not allow him to understand this surplus of meaning. There is still a fascination with the Scripture found in the Gospel of John 18:37–38:

> Pilate asked him, "So you are a king?" Jesus answered, "You say that I am a king. For this I was born, and for this I came into the world, to testify to the truth. Everyone who belongs to the truth listens to my voice." Pilate asked him, "What is Truth?"

The Bible provides no record of a response.

Comparing Du Bois and Hegel

When analyzing W. E. B. Du Bois's description of self-consciousness of the Negro during the late-nineteenth century alongside Hegel's master/slave (lord/bondsman) dialectic, similar motifs appear that are indicative of a correlation between philosophical theology and lived experience. Hegel's master/slave dialectic provides an existential framework for the mentality of the master and slave, which aids in understanding the engagement and continual practice of chattel slavery in America. *The Souls of Black Folk* sets the stage for the reality Du Bois captures in the aftermath of the Civil War, the Emancipation Proclamation, and the Reconstruction period. Hegel first establishes how the master and slave came to be, in that the master won the life-and-death struggle of self-consciousness and became the free, independent, essential being.[21] The enslaved, who not only lost, but continues to lose, is seen as the "other" and is bound by the master. The self-consciousness of the enslaved is negated and takes on the master-imposed self-consciousness. A tension becomes evident here because the self-consciousness of the enslaved exists but goes unacknowledged. This is typical of racist white oppression. And what else do we expect? The enslaved sees himself and acts upon himself with the false self-consciousness. Meanwhile, his true self-consciousness is hidden even from himself. This is the veil.

Hegel's description is parallel to Du Bois's concept of the Negro's twoness [22] in that Du Bois speaks of a world which yields the Negro no true self-consciousness, but only lets him see himself through the revelation of the other world. What Hegel does is provide the *why* for this antiquated way of existing. The master seemed able to justify his position by the "staking of his own life" in the struggle of self-consciousness,[23] while the enslaved, in turn, concedes. And this makes the enslaved—or the now-freed Negro—inferior. Both authors provide the same oppressed state of human existence.

Du Bois's depiction is also dialectic in nature because while in an ideal world each person should be fully human in expression and existence, in reality, there is no concern for the Negro's expression. Because Du Bois focuses on the Freedperson who is no longer enslaved and shows even the Negro is legally free, there is still a form of bondage that followed them wherever they go. This, again, takes the form of the veil. The veil symbolizes the oppression and disparity experienced by the Negro. Du Bois also speaks of the Negro's hope that one day God will vindicate him and make things right.[24] This theodical view is prevalent in both Jewish and Christian thought, especially as expressed pre-Auschwitz and in the midst of American chattel slavery. The longing for the veil to be lifted is a longing for the souls of black folks' true self-consciousness to exist without strife.

Hegel presents his own view of this longing by discussing the three aforementioned approaches to the freedom of consciousness.[25] One route to free self-consciousness is by stoicism—to think it and be so. Another is skepticism—to be contradictory in nature. A third is the unhappy consciousness—the gaze of one self-consciousness into another. The self-consciousness of Black people described in *The Souls of Black Folk* is Hegel's "unhappy consciousness" because the veil of racism causes unhappiness by not allowing the self to be the self in freedom. This suggests an ostensible persona portrayed by Black people that covers up their oppressed humanity. Another aspect of the unhappy consciousness is its unawareness, or the fact that it does not recognize itself as having the same existence as the essential being.

There were (and still are) Black people walking around free, but they do not know their value or their worth, instead only knowing what the racially motivated white man has imposed for hundreds of years. Du Bois's illustration of the man named John shows us how John's self-consciousness evolved as he gained knowledge, and how his perception of himself and the world changed.[26] His world changed not in form, but in spirit. It was through education that the Negro had the opportunity to experience self-realization. This is what I term "Awakened Consciousness."[27] Brother John's transformation shows self-consciousness is not static. He is an example of Hegel's terminology of Notions,[28] or movements of knowledge. Notions have a direct impact on self-consciousness because they inform it of itself. They are truth in evolution. Du Bois also indicates there is a true self-consciousness of the Negro that longs to be free.

The connection between these two works lies in their display of human being interwoven to human, no matter the culture, context, or time. And as a science, philosophy is relevant to the dynamics of culture and anthropology. In chapter 6, I discuss Nat Turner—the ultimate Black freedom fighter—as the paradigm or prototype of a Black-awakened consciousness and the obviation of Hegel's "thinghood." Turner is the embodiment of both soul and self in the quest for freedom and selfhood. In a sense, his actions also turn the master/slave dialectic on its head, as they do thesis/antithesis. In Nat Turner, the real becomes *the* ideal and the ideal becomes the real. Turner's insurrection is a negation of death, especially if we understand slavery is tantamount to death—and that overcoming slavery is freedom and life, though it may lead to physical death.

Interlude:
"The Prison Visit"

Big Papa was big only in mind, not in form. He was as skinny as a beanstalk. His physical stature was bony and lean. He was tall, like a weed grown wild. Why this image came to mind, I can't explain. Nevertheless, I thought of my grandfather, Big Papa, as I saw the gaunt image of the young Black man walk through the metal detectors on his way to the visitor's waiting room. I don't know why such thoughts popped into my mind. Maybe it was because on that day, at that moment, I was trying to convince myself not to become sad. Not to cry. I wanted to be strong, to appear to be like steel. Hard as a rock. Stoic and detached. This was a federal prison. The Greenville Corrections Facility built on the edge of Sussex County and Greenville County in south-central Virginia—a few miles from the town of Waverly to the north and Emporia to the southeast. I could only think one thought: this is the death row prison in Virginia. It is the largest and most secure place of incarceration in the state and maybe in the entire southern region. It was only an hour's drive from where I lived, but it felt like it was as far away as the Gulag. The iron curtain.

It was too hot that August morning. It's already 102 degrees by eleven o'clock and the A/C in my car was in fierce competition with the sun's rays. The sweltering heat was pounding upon my face and the acrid air, still and silent, made me feel like an oven-baked casserole as sweat oozed from every pore in my body. It was steaming hot. Balmy. Sultry. So hot my underclothes felt sticky, damp, grimy, and drenched with perspiration. There was no escape.

The normally short, one-hour trip took over three hours that day because there was an accident south of Petersburg that snarled traffic for nearly ten miles. Cars and pickup trucks had emptied themselves of their passengers inasmuch as many had cut their engines off and were standing shirtless outside along the highway. There was nowhere to go as the police and firemen attended to those in wrecked vehicles. The rubberneckers made things worse and helped to turn what should have been a short trip into a whole day's journey.

I finally arrived at the prison after driving down the long, winding, isolated road. The structure looked bleak and depressing, almost devoid of human habitation. But that was a façade, an illusion of death and dry bones. The place was filled with black male bodies of all ages. It was a black nation, this incarcerated place. I walked through the visitors' entrance and inside there was a whole world of Black folk giving instruction and taking information. The women behind the tall counter were hefty and draped in their Virginia State correctional officer uniforms. This was my first time visiting this particular prison, so I was very inquisitive—almost nosey.

"Good morning, ma'am. I'm here to see—"

"You ain't here to see nobody until you fill out this here paper-work," she bellowed gruffly, cutting me off mid-sentence as she thrust a clipboard with a long questionnaire on it.

"Is that a cell phone you got there?" she asked. "Can't you see all these here signs that say, 'No cell phones allowed?'"

She stared intently at me like I had stolen something or committed a heinous crime as she motioned with her head and hands for me to go back outside and get rid of the cell phone. It was going to be a long walk to get back to my car.

"I thought those signs were for you and the inmates," I said half-jokingly and with a tinge of sarcasm. She was not amused. She was more than serious; I was messing with the wrong person.

She never said another word but her sign language, semi-otically led by her index finger, was clear and direct. It said to me, "Get out, go back through these same doors, and leave your phone, dollar bills, and everything except one key to your car. Leave it all outside."

There was a part of me that wanted to argue, to say her rules made no sense. I wanted to say I was feeling abused and oppressed. I was trapped in a building and in a system that was hauntingly and seriously designed to strip everyone who came through the front doors, the side entrance, or back doors like refuse. Trash. Execrable. I was a visitor, not a prisoner. She was a guard, not a prisoner. Or so I thought. And then I said to myself, "We are all prisoners." Me, the guards, the inmates—all of us are now locked up and locked inside this matrix."

As I headed back to my car, the weight of the system fell head-long upon me like a ton of bricks the moment that the barbed wire fences came into view. Rows and rows of gates and twelve-foot fences laced with razor-sharp wire messed with my psyche, my consciousness. I began to imagine how it felt to be caged in and to be encircled by bricks, mortar, fences, and walls without windows. My imagination was suffocating me to the point of anxiety. I was having a panic attack that had been building since I'd first gotten out of my car.

I was fixated on the high tower with prison guards carrying high-powered rifles. They were scoping the grounds. I felt threatened and afraid. They'd seen me a half-mile away as I'd driven onto the compound. The slave plantation. I was being watched, monitored, evaluated from a distance. I could get shot on my way into the building. Killed. Murdered. I was paranoid because of the recent shootings of black males, Laquan McDonald and Freddie Gray. I felt like holding my hands above my head as a sign of compliance and non-threatening behavior or action. I could imagine hearing the guard with the high-powered rifle one hundred feet above me in the tower saying, "Look out, he's reaching for a gun. He's got a weapon!"

"What happened?" the news reporter would ask the shooter.

"Well, I felt threatened when I first saw him get out of his car."

"But he was over two hundred yards from you on the ground, and you were one hundred feet above him," the news reporter would say.

"He looked like he had a gun in his hand. With his hands up, I felt that he was pointing the gun at me."

"You know that's irrational, don't you? You murdered him in cold blood."

"No, no, no. You don't understand. I really feared for my life."

"You feared an unarmed black man? A preacher of the gospel? Is that what you're telling me?"

"I—I . . . I guess so" he'd say as I felt my life slipping away in the name of fear.

Nat Turner:
Insurrection and Freedom

Oh freedom, oh freedom, oh freedom over me
And before I'd be a slave I'll be buried in my grave
And go home to my Lord and be free. —"Oh Freedom,"
Negro Spiritual

Then they utterly destroyed all the city, both men and
women, young and old, oxen, sheep, and asses, with the
edge of the sword. —Joshua 6:21

I had too much sense to be raised, and if I was, I would
never be of any service to anyone as a slave. —Nat Turner

Nat Turner is the putative symbol of liberation by any means
necessary, although he was not a violent man. Institutional
slavery is the symbol of suffering, evil, and greedy materialism,
and even more violent than concrete physical death. Nat Turner's

actions were a gesture of power, freedom, and justice against a repressive economic and political culture. Michel Foucault's notion that power "is above all a relation of force"[1] permeated the system of slavocracy. Nevertheless, Nat Turner's insurrection was also an act of love for his people, as well as a power move by the subjugated other. It was a social and political action, a statement of being human. It was an effort to reclaim and assert the humanity of enslaved Africans. It was tantamount to an "act of war" against a repressive and violent regime, designed to demonstrate the social ontology and hope for freedom of a whole race of enslaved people. Because Nat Turner purportedly could read and therefore possessed a deep spirituality, understanding, and knowledge, he also had the power to mediate the powerlessness of his bondage. His power—to plan, organize, and carry out a violent insurrection that resulted in the death of nearly seventy white people—caused an uproar in the slave economy and in the political landscape of Virginia and the slaveholding South. The Virginia State legislature quickly passed new laws forbidding Black people to congregate without a white overseer present, and they did much more to guarantee that such a freedom movement would never happen again.[2] And they were successful. No African American has ever done, before or since, what Nat Turner did.

When I think about the material in this chapter, I cannot help but hear in my memory the British rock group Pink Floyd's rebellious lyrics from their album *The Dark Side of the Moon* and its hit single "Money," a global critique of the violence of capitalism:

> *Money, it's a crime*
> *Share it fairly but don't take a slice of my pie*
> *Money, so they say*
> *It is the root of all evil today*[3]

These lyrics, like so many others, express the meaning of material culture in a way that foregrounds money and criminality in all things, including the foundation of slavery and the commodification of culture. In American chattel slavery, the slave's body was both the commodity (i.e., the product) and the producer of materials and money used in perpetuating and maintaining the system of oppression—the slavocracy.

The white supremacist logic embedded in American chattel slavery faced its most radical and cataclysmic rejection in the insurrection of Nat Turner. Turner has no equal in the quest for Black liberation because he rationalized slavery was equal to, if not worse than, death. Slavery, to Nat Turner, was indeed the sublation of life.[4] The antithesis to freedom. The alterity to being human and possessing self-consciousness. It was Dante's hell—albeit on Earth. It was evil and yet it was defended, supported, and practiced by the church and her Christian adherents.

The episodic nature of United States slave insurrections and their general inability to destabilize the economy of the slavocracy is highly correlative with two factors, if not caused by them: fear and the lack of resources. The desire to live regardless of circumstance—the desire to not die—is also a major factor that inhibited the majority of the enslaved in their desire to confront and fight an oppressive system. Looming in the mind of every enslaved person was the fear of being sold or separated from family, which for most was equal to or greater than the fear of death. Today, the family separation idea seems to harken back to slavocracy in the name of "law and order."

Nat Turner, however, possessed no such palpable fear. A sustained systematic theory and practice of violence was a necessary precondition to transforming the blatant dialectic materialism evident in the structure of slave society. An uprising by Turner and his peers required guns and other weapons of war—weapons the enslaved did not have and could not acquire. However, Black violence then and now is an imitation of white violence practices, which in America began with the conquest and destruction of

American Indians. Now, I am aware this thinking is partially a result of my own reasoning, romanticism, and idealism. Nevertheless, the issue remains one of consciousness, both because of and in spite of the commodified economic and political system necessary to sustain the institution of chattel slavery. However, this genuine condition of existence was not able to erase the ontological status of the enslaved in general—and particularly not that of individuals such as Nat Turner, Gabriel Prosser, and Denmark Vesey, who were possessed by a spirit of freedom that propelled them to become insurrectionists and freedom fighters.

Nat Turner is the archetype and symbol of resistance and insurrection in African American history. The philosopher Paul Ricoeur is partially right in saying "the symbol gives rise to thought."[5] Reasoned irrationality was a conscious act on Nat Turner's part. What I mean here is it was practically impossible to stir the consciousness of the masses of the enslaved to the point of revolt—especially since this consciousness was being mediated and mitigated constantly by the government's system of slavery and the individual shenanigans of dominating slave owners and masters. And yet Turner did exactly that, which was no easy feat. It was practically impossible. His action reversed the notion advanced by the architects of slavery—that the enslaved were docile and happy with their suffering. No, the enslaved were experiencing physical and emotional pain and suffering every day, and to claim they were happy about it constitutes an unimaginable evil.

The whole of history for Nat Turner consisted of the first thirty-one years of the nineteenth century and a subsistence in the geopolitical landscape of the slavocracy that existed throughout the American South, particularly in Southampton County, Virginia—just a few miles from where I was born. In this sense, wholeness is never more than the particular or the partial, contrary to the European concept of the universal.

Slavery on the plantation was to be Nat Turner's whole life,[6] yet he envisaged a life beyond the confines of slavery. His existential condition consisted of the dialectic materialism and racial hatred he experienced daily. This dialectic was a binary greater than Karl Marx's distinction between the proletariat and the bourgeoisie. It consisted not just of a class difference, but also a more fundamental ontological difference. Nat Turner grew cotton and tobacco, but he—like all enslaved people—did not reap the benefits of their labor. Slavery amounted to nearly 250 years of free labor—not labor like that experienced by Marx's proletariat, but hard labor that could result in death if the enslaved sought to learn to read, rebel, or run away in search of freedom.

The evil spirit and violence of American slavery and the colonialist mentality and politics of the European empires extended around the world, infiltrating every continent, including Africa. In fact, this white supremacist hegemony found representation in the twentieth century through the violent and repressive nature and practices of Jim Crow in America and apartheid in South Africa. For example, on September 12, 1977, a young Black and socially conscious critical thinker and freedom fighter named Bantu Stephen "Steve" Biko died in police custody in Pretoria, South Africa, after being beaten and brutalized by the architects of apartheid. Mr. Biko was terrorized and murdered while en route to speak to a group of students. He was killed by a system of oppression and injustice that was embedded in the consciousness of white South Africans. This was almost one hundred fifty years after the murder, hanging, and decapitation of Nat Turner, who was and is the symbol of the American Black freedom fighter, a symbol America has sought to eradicate from its history and blot out from its memory.

Nat Turner also epitomizes the prophetic revolutionary preacher who was discontented with the conditions of slavery.[7] Born October 2, 1800—the same year as John Brown—Turner was the most notorious slave preacher who ever lived on American soil. He was the embodiment of what Du Bois described as "a boss, an intriguer, an idealist."[8] Indeed, unlike any Black man before or since, Turner's consciousness of the dehumanizing and sanctimonious institution of slavery, coupled with revelations received from God, propelled him to seek freedom in the language that postmodernity has attributed to Malcolm X: "By any means necessary." He planned and implemented a revolt that killed nearly seventy white people before being captured and hanged in the Fall of 1831.[9] He was a self-made leader, preacher, activist, and intellectual. As a thinker and activist, he was extremely intelligent and religious, and seriously troubled and pained by the institution of slavery. For Turner, slavery was death, the sublation and negation of life and freedom. His proleptic vision was always of freedom on earth—freedom in the here and now, not simply in the hereafter, as the slave master and the white evangelical church taught systematically.

Nat Turner's messianic prophetism impelled him to plan and implement a strategy that could begin to liberate and free Black folk from a sustained and systematically evil form of human incarceration and bondage. While some white scholars[10] question and debate the cause and motivation for the Turner revolt, it is clear Turner was driven by his understanding of God and the need to be free. His efforts to "set at liberty"[11] the oppressed of Southampton County, Virginia, became the most dreaded and feared prototype of the struggle for Black freedom and recognition.[12] White people across the South began to fortify their efforts to guarantee nothing resembling the rebellion of Nat Turner would ever happen again. On a larger scale, American history and sociology have succeeded in vilifying Nat Turner and characterizing his physical violence as demonic—as if slavery were somehow nonviolent and Christian. No, Black people know firsthand the meaning of suffering and evil.

While Nat Turner's actions were the embodiment of liberation, countless other Black people embraced the liberation theme. Henry H. Mitchell points out resistance to slavery was a distinct mark of the Black preacher:

> Even under the constant supervision of Whites, and with the full awareness that there were Black informers, no Black preacher or exhorter dared preach on apparent acceptance of slavery unless he slipped in a few code reservations and encouragements to resistance.[13]

The violent revolt led by Nat Turner marked the turning point in the Black struggle for freedom and recognition. Turner's visions of blood in a battle between Black spirits and white spirits, in addition to other manifestations of the voice of the spirit he experienced, are symbols of his quest for liberation.[14] The visions could have been the symbolic expression of the conflict that existed between the existential reality of oppression and injustice as evidenced by slavery and the conscious desire to be free. Jungian psychology would suggest the "structured unconscious" played a role in the visions of Nat Turner.[15] Moreover, Turner's acts of violence were akin to what Frantz Fanon described as "a purgatory" through which oppressed people have to pass before they can achieve a fresh sense of identity.[16] As a psychiatrist, Fanon understood the effect of oppression and colonialism on the mental state, attitude, and actions of the oppressed and the oppressor. His understanding of the role of one's environment—especially in a racialized and oppressive context—far exceeded that of other well-known psychiatrists such as Sigmund Freud and Carl Jung.

Because the enslaved were politically, socially, and economically powerless, Nat Turner recognized violence was the only reasonable alternative to achieve liberation. In her essay "On Violence," philosopher Hannah Arendt says:

Power and violence are opposites; where the one rules absolutely, the other is absent. Violence appears where power is in jeopardy, but left to its own course it ends in power's disappearance. This implies that it is not correct to think of the opposite of violence as nonviolence.[17]

If Arendt is correct in saying the opposite of violence is power, then the methods of liberation practiced by Nat Turner and Martin Luther King Jr. were more compatible than opposed. In the American South in 1831, Black people were chattel in law (*de jure*), fact (*de facto*), and custom. They were considered inhuman and utterly—but wrongly—thought to be incapable of thinking and planning. Property is an inhuman entity. A commodity. So, according to the prevailing mindset, Descartes' maxim "*cogito ergo sum*"—not to mention any other self-affirming dictum—did not apply to the enslaved. The Enlightenment be damned! Therefore, the enslaved were thought to be absolutely powerless—unable to think, read, write, plan, or act. This thinking is demonstrated in Ernest Gaines's novel *A Lesson Before Dying*, when Jefferson's defense attorney describes him before the jury as a hog, an animal unable to plan. Nat Turner is the antithesis of this pervasive dialectic. He is the sublation of the intent of slavery. By contrast, in 1963, Martin Luther King Jr. could negotiate, agitate, collaborate, and openly speak against the prevailing political system. His possession of this limited power, achieved after a period of almost three hundred years, was a critical variable in the quasi-success of King's nonviolent method of liberation—a method not available to Nat Turner.

Nat Turner, known as "General Nat" or the "old prophet," also felt he was called for messianic purposes to free enslaved people. Henry J. Young, in his book *Major Black Religious Leaders,* argues David Walker's *Appeal* had influenced Turner in his liberation theology of action. Nat Turner claimed he had no recollection of a time when he did not know the alphabet. His ability to read was itself an act of subversion and freedom. Young explains the revolt by saying:

> Nat himself was not a violent man, but the situation of slavery, oppression, and racism forced violence upon him. He knew that violence was the only thing that would force America to take slaves' quest for freedom and justice seriously. Not only did Nat realize this, but God realized it as well. God spoke through David Walker in 1829 and warned America that violence and bloodshed would result if the slaves were not freed.[18]

Nat Turner's understanding and high level of consciousness compelled him to respond to the most vicious, violent, and hateful form of oppression and injustice to be perpetrated upon a people—American chattel slavery. He realized most white people had little respect for religious ethical arguments and moral appeals about human dignity, fairness, and justice for enslaved Black people. Only a radical and a cataclysmic action perceived to be beyond reason could convince the architects of a violent social order that violence begets violence. Nat Turner's actions shocked white people and forced them to acknowledge the antebellum South was not a sweet, peaceful place. Enslaved people were not happy and satisfied with their lot, as politicians and plantation owners often portrayed them when propagandizing the slavocracy. Through Turner's actions, "God was troubling the waters"[19] in tranquil, genteel, aristocratic Virginia. Young says, quite correctly, "The tragedy of violence that surrounded the Nat Turner revolt did not lie in the killings that Nat and his followers executed, but rather, it lay in the violence of slavery. The institution of slavery itself contained all sorts of violence."[20]

We will never fully know how many Black folk were killed by the evil and violent hand of slavery. Only in the eschaton, when the "sea shall give up its dead,"[21] will we begin to know and understand the extent of the violence suffered by enslaved Africans in the Transatlantic Middle Passage and the interstate slave trade. The European Enlightenment and the beginning of modernity are characterized by acts of terror, slavery, colonialism, oppression, and vulgar capitalistic materialism. After more than three hundred years, the mind of the American South is still struggling to change, still wrestling with the outcome of the Civil War and the Civil Rights Movement led by Rosa Parks, Martin Luther King Jr., and others. The evil acts of hatred continue as monuments to the Confederacy remain littered throughout the South, attempting to immortalize this gruesome, evil past. And so the Civil War rages on in Virginia and throughout the South.

In Panola County, Mississippi, a forty-one-year-old Black man, Garrick Burdette, was run over and killed by a carload of young white people in 2009. The police have essentially ignored the murder. During the same period, Johnny Lee Butts, a sixty-one-year-old Black man, was killed in the same county by a group of three white teenagers.[22] They too were driving the backwater roads of the Mississippi Delta—the same area where the state police had been instructed to shoot and kill Dr. Martin Luther King Jr. on sight. This, too, is the place of fourteen-year-old Emmett Till's murder for exercising his freedom of speech by purportedly saying, "Thank you, baby," to the wife of a white store owner in Money, Mississippi, after receiving his change for purchasing a soda. Those three words caused him to be hunted down like a dog—like an animal, like a slave—and beaten and bludgeoned to the point of pulverization. His mangled body was then restrained by a seventy-pound cotton-gin fan around the neck before being dumped in the Tallahatchie River to be carried by the currents to a place of no return. But by the providence and justice of God, his body turned up to be displayed by his mother to the entire world.

However, Nat Turner was not simply one of many. Regarding the Southampton County, Virginia, insurrection of 1831, he was the chief architect and strategist of an action that killed almost seventy white people, beginning with his slave master's family.

I reflect again *in medias res* upon Pink Floyd's *The Dark Side of the Moon* because of its symbolism, and because of the parallel semiotics[23] of the words in the album's title and the language of Turner's vision and interpretation of a solar eclipse that took place in the winter of 1831—six months before the now-famous insurrection. Turner interpreted many things in his environment as a sign of the impending eschaton. Also, in his actions to bring about freedom from slavery, he was performing the will of God, which was to "fight against the serpent."[24] Moreover, Pink Floyd's music once ruled the airways around the world, just as the British Empire and other European powers extended its long arm of colonialism into every corner of the globe: Africa, Asia, Australia, North and South America. In my view, Pink Floyd's song "The Wall" on their album *The Dark Side of the Moon* is a radical, avant-garde statement against miseducation, oppression, and societal ills:

> *Hey, Teacher, leave those kids alone*
> *We don't need no education*
> *We don't need no mind control.*[25]

The socially conscious music of 2Pac, Kendrick Lamar, Erykah Badu, and Lauryn Hill speak even more precisely to the particularity of Black suffering than that of Pink Floyd—for example, songs like "Changes," "King Kunta," "On and On," and "Lost Ones," respectively.

Some sources suggest Nat Turner interpreted the dark side of the sun as the Black hand of God moving across the universe. This phenomenon was also a sign that the reversal of things on earth was at hand. As an avid reader of Scripture and someone who pondered the deep mysteries of life and the meaning of God, Nat

Turner was a semiotician with prophetic tendencies. His understanding of biblical texts of reversal seen throughout the synoptic gospels—such as, "The first shall be last, and the last shall be first"[26]—prompted him to attempt to reverse the social order of Black bondage via violent revolution. Again, I reiterate the fact that the scale of Nat Turner's insurrection paled in comparison to the violence of white retaliation. Hundreds of Black people, both enslaved and free, were beheaded, hanged, and mutilated in the aftermath of Turner's uprising. Several thousand Virginia militiamen and nearly as many federal troops descended upon Southampton County to erase any semblance of further rebellion and to assure white people that the event was an aberration that would never happen again. After eschewing capture for more than six weeks by hiding on nearby farms and in the swamp near the Nottaway River, Nat Turner was captured, tried, and found guilty. By the end of October 1831, Nat Turner was hanged, then flayed and skinned in keeping with the evil character of the slavocracy. This act of terror was designed to make all Black people, free or enslaved, stand in fear, as Kenneth Stampp has written.[27] History repeats itself today when on social media we hear appeals to the fear factor from the highest levels of American government.

When Real Life Becomes the Ideal

Alterity (or otherness) is a production (or artificial construction) developed and institutionalized by the wielders of power and capitalism.[28] As a phenomenon, it is like the construction of race or some other hybridized form of a commodity, such as certain types of plants and animals. Michael Hardt and Antonio Negri describe alterity with precision and clarity, saying, "Alterity is not given but produced."[29] This same spirit and understanding are expressed by Edward W. Said in his book *Orientalism*[30] and Hélène Cixous in "The Laugh of the Medusa."[31] The production of

otherness is a deliberate and cynical act of consciousness resulting in the denigration of non-white humanity—and exemplified
poignantly in the production of the enslaved Black person and
the commodification of slave culture as the foundation of a free
labor economy. At least, that is the intent of otherness. And yet
Nat Turner refused to be commodified, although he was a product of the slavocracy and subject to the same process of othering
as all enslaved people were. For example, in Hegel's dialectical
schema, Nat Turner was the antithesis, "the absolute negation"[32]
of humanity as personified in and by the European. Blackness
and slavery were not simply the opposites of whiteness, they were
the continuation of an absolute difference—an identity produced,
constructed, and maintained by the white supremacist power
structure embedded in the Enlightenment. And yet, this construction was not absolute because Nat Turner—along with folk like
Denmark Vesey and Gabriel Prosser before him—confounded the
dominant anthropological and ontological process of production
by claiming their Otherness as an opportunity to assert selfhood
and overcome their intended denial of humanity. They defied the
negative dialectic of the "produced other" and asserted the self
as "the revolutionary other," a role truly capable of othering the
architects of Otherness.

Nat Turner was the symbol of the United States' project of
"othering," the enslaved being turned upside down and inside
out. The fearmongers now stood in fear. The architects of violence
were now its victims. And the sovereignty of the state vis-à-vis
white supremacy was confronted head-on with the sovereignty of
the individual self of Nat Turner—a Black sovereignty that existed
beyond the Christocentrism of white religion and anthropology.
Unlike Jesus, who was crucified for his politics, Nat Turner was
crucified for actually killing sixty to seventy white folks. This act
was unprecedented in the social imaginary of Black and white
people, both historically and proleptically. Nat Turner's 1831

insurrection subtends and subvenes the meaning of alterity in the consciousness of the radical Black individual because it situates otherness as the thesis, rather than the antithesis. Freedom is now the thesis. And the only axis to freedom—and not merely eschatological freedom—is through the struggle to bring it about via insurrection, the result of the personal pain and suffering of the preacher—Prophet Nat.

This idea brings me now to the philosopher Michel Foucault. For Foucault, sovereignty and royalty are necessary correlatives. Sovereignty essentially means power and control—a totalistic concept that exempts one from the exigencies and restraints of the law. The sovereign is in actuality above the law, and yet it constitutes the law inasmuch as the individual is responsible only to the self. No externality impinges upon the sovereign. This is a political and juridical understanding that is theologically attributed to God and God alone. In politics, the democratic monarch and the State are all but equal to God. During slavery, the slave master was a god and the plantation was a "state unto itself," where the master ruled and in the language of the Black Church "ruled and super ruled." By this, I mean the slave master's authority was unilateral, univocal, and without challenge, and his decisions were subject to no appellate authority. The master was sovereign, like a god. And the enslaved were powerless—or almost. The power of the enslaved rested in an awakened consciousness—a consciousness exemplified and symbolized by Nat Turner. Foucault seems to argue that power and sovereignty are constituted by acts of domination, or more precisely, perpetual subjugation. In my view, for subjugation to be "ongoing subjugation"[33] as Foucault argues, it must also be domination. Subjugation and domination are tautological in practice, if not in theory.

More importantly, for Nat Turner, power was not about domination, subjugation, or control. Instead, it was about freedom and liberation—about becoming a non-slave. Power for Turner was not even about violence or torture, but essentially and absolutely about the freedom of the body and mind. Conversely, power and sovereignty for the white slave master—that is, the monarch and the state—was and is about repression, subjugation, and control of the Black human body, mind, and soul.

Nat Turner and his comrades in arms symbolize Black people, and enslaved Black people in particular, who could not comfort themselves with assimilating into the hegemonic totality of the slavocracy, which by its nature and structure sought to "stamp out" or annihilate otherness as represented by the African. And Nat Turner is the excluded other, the essence of alterity in a system that tolerated only homogeneity among the enslaved and the absolute deification of the selfhood of the master—the "I," *cogito*, German *Ich*. Nevertheless, it is important to point out that Nat Turner was also the embodiment of what Catherine Malabou calls plasticity. He was respectful and obedient to an extent; he also ran away for a month or so and then returned to the plantation of his own volition. He prayed, sang, and preached; he believed in semiotics and other significations that led to the development of plans for the obliteration of slavery. So, in effect, the experience of slavery necessitated a brain's plasticity or adaptability, capable of explosion and creativity. Malabou states:

> The word plasticity thus unfolds its meaning between sculptural molding and deflagration, which is to say explosion. From this perspective, to talk about the plasticity of the brain means to see in it not only the creator and receiver of form but also an agency of disobedience to every constituted form, a refusal to submit to a model.[34]

Turner's brainpower could not be pigeonholed or segmented into a univocity that precluded change. It was indeed his brain that had him refusing to submit to the oppressive and dehumanizing nature of the slave economy and culture.

Nat Turner's Christology

Nat Turner's high Christology is evident in the language he used to respond to lawyer Thomas Gray, whose examination of Turner serves as the filter for much of what we know of the man. This is in keeping with Black religion's notion that Jesus Christ is God incarnate—that is, its belief in the materiality of God. For Black church folk, God (Yahweh) is Jesus and Jesus is God. The interchangeability of the language, of "God" and "Jesus," is still dominant in Black religious speech. Turner's question, "Was not Christ crucified?" is essentially asking about the "crucified God"[35] and the unmerited suffering of the cross. The rhetorical, matter-of-fact nature of this response conjures textual memories of Jesus's last statements from the cross. In Nat Turner's question, he conflated the seven sayings from the cross into a unified summary of his understanding of salvation and Christology. The reference to suffering and crucifixion of Christ is a deep and profound statement of faith expressed succinctly in Turner's words. Upon further reflection, however, I also interpret Turner's words not as a question, but rather as a declarative statement—a statement of faith highly correlated with Turner's perception regarding his fate. He is effectively saying that, as a Christian with deep spiritual roots and faith in Christ as sovereign God, he knows "Christ was crucified." By extension, he knows he, too, will be crucified—like Christ, and like Jefferson, a Black character in Ernest Gaines's novel *A Lesson Before Dying*.

Turner's understanding of the crucified Christ includes his interpretation of forgiveness and abandonment as reflected in Luke's gospel: "Father, forgive them, for they know not what they do."[36] It also references Jesus's words of dereliction and desperation: "My God, my God, why have you forsaken me?"[37] By the time of the trial, Nat Turner knew he faced the same "crucifixion" as Christ. His statement to the trial judge was all but saying, "It is finished."[38]

Nat Turner's cryptic response to the attorney's discovery question, "Do you have anything to say at this time?" was not only profound but revealing. Turner's rhetorical interrogative response, "Was not Christ crucified?" reveals not merely his consciousness, but a high level of self-consciousness. Turner had become a Christ figure in his mind and the minds of his followers, "his disciples." His reference to Christ's crucifixion without specific mention of the name "Jesus" suggests he had a vision of himself as the Black Messiah and Savior—the sacrificial lamb in the struggle for Black people's freedom. This was his cross, his lynching—a symbolic parallel made by James H. Cone—just as Christ was crucified on the cross of Calvary. Christ was the analogical figure that Turner used as a comparison, not David Walker, Denmark Vesey, or Gabriel Prosser. Christ.

Turner's Christology was not simply an expression of the crucified Christ as a symbol of death, but also of Christ's material body as subject to the political sovereignty of the state—a state imbued with a power, a might, and a readiness to wage war against any perceived or real human or inhuman threat. The sovereignty and power of the state are met with the sovereignty of Turner's self-consciousness, which is determined to extricate himself and Black people from the violence and self-negation inherent in the slavocracy. Turner's "visions of blood" and other semiotic references and interpretations portend the eschaton as the telos of freedom, while physical death is the sublation of hell on earth. Death as the sublation of slavery is grounded in hope in the resurrection.[39] "Was not Christ crucified?" is ultimately a statement of hope, in which death is the preferential option of the slave. This theology is inherent in the slave song quoted as an epigraph to this chapter: "Before I'd be a slave, I'd be buried in my grave, and go home to my Lord, and be free." The suffering and pain of slavery are beyond our modern imagination. Much of what we call suffering and pain is

a desire for more material stuff, which makes our lives devoid
of a true consciousness of suffering.

Turner's statement, "Was not Christ crucified?" is a testimony
to freedom and hope. It is death overcoming death. It is choosing
death rather than living a life of death under the daily violence
of slavocracy's repressive system. "Was not Christ crucified?" is
ultimately a call to freedom and suggests the emulation of Christ
is the same as death. The Roman Empire—that is, the Commonwealth of Virginia and its Southampton County government—will
always exercise its juridical and political power, as well as perceived might, to kill or murder its citizens, whether enslaved or
free, when they become a threat to the state's sovereignty. But the
power to obviate the sovereignty of the state resides in the individual, freedom fighter's self-consciousness. This pits one sovereign against another. The willingness to seek freedom at all costs
is evident in Turner's actions. This sovereignty of the individual
demystifies and decenters the power of the state and elevates Nat
Turner as individual and representative—as a symbol of the dis-
enfranchised enslaved people—to the level of the sovereign. This
is a transformation of nothingness into something—that is, into a
substantive human entity. It is a rebellion against "thinghood." It
is a person, a preacher, rising against the powerful perpetrators
of pain, not just getting in front of the text or preaching forward,
but getting in front of the Bible with a Black story of freedom and
revelation. A story that has all the elements of conflict, action, and
resolution, and as detailed as Aristotle's poiesis. And it is not fictive, but real. Now *that* is a story.[40]

Nat Turner's level of consciousness and self-consciousness
overcame the fear of death. More precisely, "dread and fear" were
no longer "lord" of his life.[41] Nat Turner turned Hegel's logic on its
head by avoiding the fear of death and by acquiring a mind of his
own, not through *work*—as Hegel's phenomenology maintains—
but through revolutionary action. Hegel suggests work creates

an alienated existence that leads ineluctably to a "mind of one's own."[42] He bolsters this logic by writing:

> Since the entire contents of its natural consciousness have not been jeopardized, determinate being still in principle attaches to it; having a 'mind of one's own' is self-will, a freedom which is still enmeshed in servitude.[43]

This language is as problematic in Hegel as it is in Paul's New Testament theology. For Nat Turner, servitude truncated and essentially obviated the enslaved having a mind of one's own. The slavocracy not only discouraged it but prohibited it in every conceivable way. There was and is no freedom in externally imposed servitude. The servant, the enslaved, is completely un-free in mind and body. The only way for Nat Turner and fellow enslaved people to become free was to cut off the head of the sovereign master, the false god, the Baal, the Beelzebub of the antebellum South. I am deeply troubled—though not surprised—by Hegel's notion that for the slave "freedom is still enmeshed in servitude." This is the evil and distorted language of the master. It is the master's logic and calculus; and in some strange way, this language reflects a deification and bifurcation of the self that exceeds the self.

Nat Turner's action is an obviation of the exterior essentialism of his character and the character of all enslaved people as predictable, happy, and docile. He rejected conformity to the construction of otherness as posited by the European and white American architects of alienation between master and slave, between the self and other. The irony here lies in the fact that the project of othering as practiced by slave owners is simultaneously an effort to create another in one's own image, thereby inflating the image of the self to the status of deity (God) while reducing the other to a negative social imaginary. Othering is never intended to result in self-consciousness or self-actualization in the Other. Nat Turner, however, achieved all the above in his self-determination to obviate his enslaved status and achieve freedom of mind, body, and spirit. He sought a holistic freedom in defiance of personal pain. His diachronic sensibility to the urgency of achieving freedom within a certain timeframe might have inhibited the degree to which his actions were successful. Nevertheless, the spirit of his effort was achieved by recognizing his freedom, which is the essence and meaning of *Geist*.[44] Spirit is freedom. In his actions, Nat Turner achieved ultimate freedom—not in the sense of Germanic Christianity's high Hegelian status, but in the sense of his extrication from the bondage of chattel slavery. This is the freedom of the body, mind, and soul. It required a cataclysmic action because the chasm—that is, the gap between slavery and freedom or master and slave— delimited the capacity of language to achieve any substantial transformation of the hierarchical binary of master and slave. The alienation between master and slave can only produce a deafening speechlessness! Only the action of insurrection could force a conversation among white people that at least made some individuals acknowledge the oppression and evil of the slavocracy. Of course, this conversation was self-contained and did not include the enslaved. That would be too humane, or too "human, all too human."[45]

The Master/Slave Dialectic

The only way to overcome the dialectic of master and slave is through the death of one, the other, or both. There is no achievable unitariness in the materiality of the dialectic between the master and the slave without the death of one or the other. I think Nat Turner understood this. There was no overcoming the representational understanding of the slave or the master. No matter how loyal, self-denigrating, and self-negating the slave was—and no matter how productive to the economy of the plantation and the slave system—he could still be whipped, decapitated, and sold at the sovereign and evil will of the master. So when Hegel writes "self-consciousness is faced by self-consciousness," it has come *out of itself.* This has a twofold significance: first, it has lost itself, for it finds itself as an *other* being; secondly, in doing so, it has superseded the other, for it does not see the other as an essential being, but in the other sees its own self."[46] His theorem reeks of negativity. The inability to see the other except as a form of reflection of the self is a strange type of "unconsciousness" rather than self-consciousness. In superseding the "other," it has violated self-consciousness and relegated it to mere consciousness, subjecting the other to being subsumed by the self. Hegel amplifies this by saying, "It must supersede this otherness of itself."[47]

The prevailing philosophical view of the interdependency within the asymmetrical dialectic of master and slave and the lack of reciprocity inherent in that relationship only serve to confound the question of identity. However, it seems the reflection of the slave in the eyes and mind of the master simply reinforces the master as master and the slave as slave. In relating to the slave as a "thing," the master is said to "inhibit his own self-consciousness,"[48] but this inhibition does not redound to the good of the slave. The telos is the same, ultimately—the intersubjectivity does not alter the natal relationship between the two. No new univocal relationship is achieved. The dialectic prevails. The Hegelian self-consciousness of the master be damned.

Finally, Hegel's ontological description of lordship and bondage or master and slave does not apply to Nat Turner or his followers. His description posits the master as pure self-consciousness grounded in an independence where nature is to be for itself, and the slave as merely immediate consciousness, or consciousness in the form of "thinghood . . . whose essential nature is simply to live or to be for another. The former is lord, the other is bondsman."[49]

This sounds more like political philosophy than phenomenology, especially as reiterated by the following words:

> The lord relates himself mediately to the bondsman through a being [a thing] that is independent, for it is just this which holds the bondsman in bondage; it is his chain from which he could not break free in the struggle, thus proving himself to be dependent, to possess his independence in thinghood. But the lord is the power over this thing . . . the bondsman, it follows that he holds the other in subjection.[50]

And yet, Nat Turner did "break free in the struggle" and loosened himself from the chains of slavery and bondage, if only for a moment. At age twenty-five, he first broke free by running away. Six years later, at age thirty-one, after being whipped like an animal, he again broke free by wreaking fear and terror throughout the South while conducting a killing rampage for Black freedom and human dignity. This was the penultimate act of freedom followed only by his physical death, carried out by the hand of the sovereign judiciary. Death is the sublation of self-consciousness, something Nat Turner possessed to the same or greater degree as the master. In Turner's actions, he turned the notion of the "thinghood of the bondsman" into a new independence constituted not by "thingness," but by a "consciousness existing *for itself,*" which is tantamount to lordship. Nat Turner overcame Hegel's essentialism as assigned to the master by becoming the master of his own fate, as well as the master of the fates of all those who met their death by his hand or the hands of those in his freedom-seeking army. Turner's actions have brought him a recognition unequaled in American and Black American history. Nearly two hundred years after his death, his struggle for recognition continues to be viewed as a milestone in the history and interpretation of injustice and evil in American chattel slavery.

7

Interlude:
"Plantation"

Talking, laughing, drinking, dancing, kissing, eating. People are friendly and happy in New Orleans, anesthetized by joy. Unspeakable, aesthetic joy. Ugliness, drunken, transitory joy. A troublesome joy.

There is a festive feeling in the air. It fills the nostrils with an intoxicating whiff of cognac and bourbon. All one must do is breathe and open one's eyes to the bright sunshine or the pelting rains blowing off the lake. It's the spirit of life where all the senses are stimulated by the simple fact of walking outside and stepping to the street corner—any street in the French Quarter. I love something about New Orleans. It is so different from Charleston, South Carolina, where I live. Too much suffering is there. Here, it's like a pleasant dream. A circus ride. A bubble. A time capsule of past *and* future. And just like that, in a flash, in the twinkling of an eye, I had an idea. New Orleans would be the next place I call home. I smiled and breathed in all the colors, sights, and sounds.

I was a long way from the bustling sound of the French Quarter, the music playing and the folks from everywhere dancing in the streets. From Royal Street to Bourbon Street, there is a panoply of places where music and musty smells dance the jig with each other and cause the spirit of carnival to pervade the air. It is a place described as one of three great American cities—New York, San Francisco, and New Orleans. Yet, the deeper my exploration extended into the city, the more suffering I observed. And the face of that suffering—like New York, San Francisco, Charleston, and New Orleans—is Black. Was my decision to come here too impulsive—decided spontaneously after a moment of aesthetic ecstasy? Did I really think I would escape the reality of the centuries of colonialism and enslavement just because I found a city that preserved many of the pre-enslavement traditions by merging them with the traditions of the French?

I passed a man on my way to the plush and posh Bourbon Orleans Hotel and just a few blocks from the famed Carousel Bar and Mr. B's Bistro—an old Black man who had cut himself, or somebody had stabbed him. He was wearing a blood-soaked sock on his right foot and what appeared like a gushing hole in his leg where his sciatic nerve ran from his butt down to his ankle. Pain was all over his face. He was hunched over and moaned and groaned. My mind rushed to the thought of a runaway who had his foot amputated for attempting to escape to freedom. No one was allowed to tend to his wounds—lest they be taught a lesson of their own. That was in the past. Or was it? I always think of the past in the present and I can predict the influence of the past on the future. Alas, just as so many enslaved people of yesteryear could not escape the chains of enslavement, I cannot escape the past, a past that keeps raising its ugly head.

As I came near, I asked, "Do you need a doctor?"

"I'll be all right," he said quickly.

I was a bit shaken and baffled by the happy and carefree scene in the middle of the day, and in the middle of the street with trumpets playing the sweet, jazzy, soulful blues sounds of the not-so-happy South. The incident also reminded me of the sorrow I felt in my spirit. In my mind, I thought it was a small sample of suffering and pain of the place we were headed to, the infamous Whitney Plantation of Louisiana.

The journey was only a short bus ride away from the cityscape. It took less than an hour to get there. The luscious foliage and the thick, bushy trees along the highway quickly gave way to miles and miles of sugar cane fields and the big antebellum plantation houses that dotted the hillside along the banks of the Mississippi River. This is the same river Mark Twain and Huck Finn talked about in their adventures—slavery, freedom, and nigger Jim.

The Whitney Plantation is a stone's throw from the Mississippi River. One can see it in the distances as one stands in front of the slave master's house. It is a small house compared to Jefferson's rambling Monticello estate or even his childhood home at Tuckahoe in Goochland County, Virginia. This Big House, the center of sovereignty, colonization, oppression, and greed, is modest in size and amenities. No fancy columns and ornate brickwork like with some of the more ostentatious mansions of Virginia and the Carolinas where tobacco was king and the flue-cured golden leaf was the mark of the majestic cigars and cigarettes flavored by the sweet aroma of the sugarcane imported from the plantations all along the Mississippi banks. The Mississippi River is America's most notorious river where the bodies of thousands of Black folk are interred from northern Minnesota to the Gulf of Mexico. It is an American trope, a symbol of the slavocracy transporting slaves, cotton, cattle, tobacco, and everything else from one plantation to another, as well as to markets all over the known world. Follow the Mississippi and one follows the tide of evil and hatred in America. I think of the riverboat accident in

Adventures of Huckleberry Finn when Miss Watson asked if anybody was hurt and the answer was, "No. Nobody hurt. Just killed
a nigger. That's all."[1]

In many ways, that type of thinking captures the spirit of
white America not only in 1850 but even today, over 150 years
later, where Black suffering continues to dominate Black life.

The Whitney Plantation is close to the main road. This surprised me because just a week earlier, I had visited the Tuckahoe Plantation in Virginia, and it seems to be more than a mile
off of River Road, sitting on a bluff high above the James River
that pales in comparison to the rambling, curvaceous, and mighty
Mississippi. Both rivers have come to signify how the commodification of the Black body was sustained for nearly 250 years of
chattel slavery. When the Atlantic slave trade ended and the Middle Passage dried up, the James and Mississippi Rivers continued
to propagate and facilitate the slave trade, as well as the horrors
and the torture of the slave auction block.

When I saw the small, metal cage used to hold the enslaved
for the auction on the Whitney Plantation, I felt the pain and fear
of death. I felt sick to my stomach. I could see it. It was a sickness unto death. There was sorrow in my soul. My spirit grieved
mightily. For some reason, though, I was compelled to take a
closer look, to step inside the torture chamber, the metal cage
where ten Black naked bodies would be held in place by chains
and shackles.

Then something happened to me. I call it my personal Pen-
tecost. I became unreasonably thirsty and considerably hot. I felt
a presence enter me and was filled with a spirit. Holy and otherwise, I not only saw the past in the present, I could also feel
the past the same way I felt New Orleans when I stepped onto
Bourbon Street. I felt the pain. I smelled the blood. The awful
scent of putrid human waste. The stench of sorrow and suffering
overwhelmed my nose and brought tears to my eyes. I heard the

cries of women and the cracks of whips. I tasted salty tears. My salty tears. I was enslaved, transported back into 1732.

The day I stepped into the cage was a day I would never forget. I could never be the same. Even when I left New Orleans, the images and sensations stayed with me and return to me in the strangest places and at the most inopportune times.

South Carolina was not the same after that trip. I found myself missing the New Orleans culture. Missing the food. Missing the music. Preparing to transition to New Orleans permanently, I thought I would stop by my alma mater to pick up some transcripts. As I was driving to the university, I remembered this old restaurant in the adjacent neighborhood. Martha Lou's Kitchen! That was it! Known for its good, old-fashioned soul food, but especially its fried chicken. Perhaps they had a New Orleans–inspired dish. If not, the fried chicken wouldn't disappoint. I decided to make the stop.

One could smell the bubbling grease in the parking lot before getting out the car. There were no baked foods on the restaurant's menu. After parking the car in the gravel lot, I walked in. When I pushed the door, it brushed against a silver bell and chimed.

I thought the bell would get someone's attention, but no one greeted me. I just decided to seat myself. After I sat down, I became unreasonably thirsty and considerably hot, the same way I'd felt when I'd stepped into the cage on the Whitney Plantation. That day I'd felt the past with every sense of my body. Then I knew.

It was happening again.

It was hot that last day of March and suddenly I was being told what to do as a plantation hand. That was the day I, too, had been sold down the river to the owner of a sprawling tobacco plantation. The rows were as long as the eye could see, and the fields were thousands of acres large. My name back then was Robert Lee, and the slaves all knew me. They were all calling me by name, but I was excited, telling them about my Ferguson,

Missouri, experience, and about Trayvon Martin, and the big rally I had attended down in Sanford, Florida. They'd all looked at me as if I were crazy. I also understood their bewilderment because earlier that morning, I had been in a breakfast meeting with a hundred Black professors and students from colleges all over the country.

Now I was back on the plantation slopping hogs and working in the fields. My mama and brother were also there. My brother, Luther John, was seldom seen with the rest of us because he was very light skinned and special to Master Breckenridge, but his wife despised my brother. Luther John had a real pair of cotton shoes and wore handwoven socks. None of the rest of us had socks, and our shoes were made on the plantation by the blacksmith after he had fitted all the mules and horses. For the most part, though, we were barefoot from about Easter to past Thanksgiving. We were always allowed to go to church on Sundays because the church was just a few steps from the Big House. We were real happy about that because Sunday was rest day. No picking cotton, no chopping grass, and no plowing the fields. The food was also plentiful in the master's house on Sunday from sunup to sundown. It was the only day we got our bellies full. I was always trying to get more to eat and sometimes we would steal a whole hog and cook it way back in the woods—about two miles from the Big House and then only when the winds were blowing south away from the house and across the riverbank. We were not always good at this because the direction of the wind could be tricky.

One day, in late October during the harvest, we had stolen a hog and barbequed it, and the smells of smoke and meat filled the air. For some reason, the winds shifted direction without us knowing it. We were dancing and carrying on a-plenty when somebody came busting through the trees on his horse. We knew immediately who it was. He always carried his six-shot pistol and whip everywhere he went. When he saw us eating, dancing, drinking, and parading around the tree stomps we had made for tables, he began cussing and fuming like a wild beast. "You goddamn niggers are worthless dogs. The wrath of God is upon you this very day!" he said with bloodshot eyes and the fury of Leviathan. There were about twenty of us that day, and the overseer Lee Winthrop was determined to find out who stole the hog from the master. It was a crime of high offense and could lead to death. He started with the old women, trying to get them to snitch.

"Lucille, you tell me who did this! Who stole Master's property?"

"Sir, Mr. Winthrop, I don't know nothing about that. When I got here, we was already picking meat from the belly. The tenderloin, I reckon."

He slapped her across the face and lashed her with the whip with a power as mighty as the East wind. She screamed as blood splashed from her face and neck. As he flung his arm back to strike her again, her youngest boy, Moses, yelled out at the top of his lungs.

"Stop! No, no! I did it. I stole the hog."

"No, you didn't. Don't do this, son," she cried and begged.

Overseer Winthrop, known as the evil executioner, hit the boy upside his head with his fist and then kicked him to the ground as everyone stood in fear rather than take the whip and gun from him and tie him to a tree and celebrate. There was enough of us to do it and get away with it. He could have disappeared that day. But it never happened. He took Moses before Master Breckenridge who lectured him on the virtues of hard work, honesty, truth telling, and the love and wrath of God.

"Moses, boy, haven't I been good and kind to you and the rest of my niggers?

"Yassar, Master."

"Don't I feed you good? You been getting your rations like the others."

"Yassar, I been."

"And you know God almighty don't want you to steal or lie. Is that right, boy?"

"Yassar. The fear of God is the beginning of wisdom." Moses could read the Bible.

"And the Bible says thou shall not steal or lie. I teach all my niggers the Bible as God is my witness. You got something to say for yourself, boy?"

"No sir, but Jesus was crucified is all I can say. And sometimes I get real hungry and weak in my knees. We all do. Lord know we do."

The master ordered all his slaves on the plantation to gather around the big oak tree on the coming Sunday after church and had Overseer Winthrop lock Moses in the cage until then. On that Sunday, the preacher read from Paul's letter to the Corinthians: "Slaves, obey your masters. This is the word of God. This is the will of God." After that, young Moses was stripped naked, tied to the big oak tree, and whipped with thirty lashes until blood oozed from every crevice of his smooth, lanky black body. The men, women, and children were all made to watch as Moses's mother sobbed and begged the master to stop the beating before he killed the boy. While she called on the name of God, Moses was left tied on the tree from high noon until sundown as the flies and ants tormented his bloodless body. He hung onto life until Monday at sunrise as his mother and other relatives prayed and called on God to help him. But, as the rooster crowed and the birds began to welcome the daylight, Moses gave up the ghost and died. He was only seventeen years old and had never left the confines of the plantation. There was little time to grieve as Master Breckenridge set the funeral for eleven o'clock the next day, a Tuesday morning.

The plantation church was full of slaves and the white families of both Master Breckenridge and Overseer Winthrop. The preacher, a short white man in his fifties, had done this ritual many times before because the Whitney Plantation was known to the slaves as the gates of hell, a death camp, a brutal and merciless place where evil was domiciled and the master was the Satan, though he thought of himself as God.

I was there in the crowd that horrible day, and I was an eyewitness to the gruesome murder of my black brother. Moses was my friend and big brother. We were just two years apart. I was fifteen and he was seventeen. We would chase rabbits, run after birds and butterflies together, and run around the yard near the Big House, but we could never go inside. It was forbidden by the slave laws and customs. Even if Master's children invited us inside, we could not go in the Big House; that mistake would get you an awful and terrible beating because it was too much like acting like white folks.

One day Miss Salley, Miss Abbey, and Master Sam had begged me to come in and play, but Miss Emma, the Big House cook, had overheard them and screamed at me. "Boy, you better stay out there, right there on the porch. Don't cross into this door, you hear."

"Yes, ma'am, Miss Emma," I'd said.

"Boy, don't you ever let Massar hear you say, 'yes, ma'am.' You must always say 'yessum.' You hear me talking to you? And, you must always say Massar in their presence.'

Any slave, child or grown, would be lashed and punished for speaking too much like white folks. Sounding proper or learned was grounds for merciless punishment. Lynching. You had to always keep your learning a secret and never let any whites know you could read or write. Like stealing food, reading was punishable by death on a cross. It was a high crime and an unforgivable sin.

I learned to read and write on my own. I remember one day when I was about seven or eight years old, I was helping the blacksmith unload some feed for the hogs and cattle and I noticed the letters on the bags. I looked at them and began to read. It said, "The Louisiana Feed and Seed Company, Baton Rouge." It just came to me and I blurted it out.

"Boy, you can read? You can read!" exclaimed the blacksmith as he hugged me so tight, I got scared. He was bubbling over with pride and fear too.

"I guess I can," I said.

"Don't you ever let Massar know you got the gift of reading, you understand, boy? Don't let none of these white folks see or hear you reading."

"Yes, sir. I'll pretend to know nothing."

"That's good, 'cause they'll hurt you. I seen it happen here once," he said, trembling as tears rolled down his face.

"A boy your age, black as the night and more handsome than the gods of Africa, slipped up and said, 'Yes sir, my mother told me to feed the chickens.' Do you know they castrated him and cut his tongue out so he would never speak again? I don't want nothing to happen to you like that, you hear?"

"You hear? . . . You hear? . . . Can you hear me? Wake up! Can you hear me?"

I noticed a Black lady hovering over me, her hands covered in flour and cornmeal, a rich concoction of her special Lowcountry batter for anything fried. I had fallen asleep in this little cinder-block hole-in-the-wall. Or had I left my body? The small space is no more than ten by fourteen-foot square area, where one can look directly into the kitchen and watch the shelling of peas and the stirring of boiling water saturated with sugar and butter as the rice slowly dropped into the pot. Seeing them cook must have triggered this experience. Unlike Gregor Samsa, the main character in Kafka's *The Metamorphosis*, I was not completely transformed, but I was transfixed. I noticed I was the only Black patron as she went to wait on other tables. Everybody else was white, gobbling up the fried chicken, pork chops, fish, and green lima beans. I overheard a white lady, who was already over three hundred pounds and looked as I imagined the school superintendent in Ernest Gaines's *A Lesson Before Dying*, complain about the small chairs as she placed her order of fried chicken, fried okra, and sweet tea. Pots and pans distracted my eavesdropping. The cook was an old Black lady with a readymade smile as she waited on the young white people. I felt slighted because I was essentially ignored, which is the typical way some black people treat other black people. This is a holdover from slavery and colonialism in America. The white people were delightfully smacking their mouths. One guy said, "These were the best collard greens I ever had."

"Thank you so much," the Black lady replied.

The whole time, I was completely ignored. I had to ask twice for a plastic cup for my Diet Coke. The can had been plopped on the small table as the server scurried to help another white person. The wall was filled with plaques and newspaper articles about the cuisine. A magazine called *The Saveur* proclaimed the cooks to be the best in the Carolinas, and the fried chicken to be the ultimate in delectability. The pork chop I had was a part of the leftovers from another day. It was tough and salty, and the cornbread tasted like a cake with cups and cups of sugar added. It was sweeter than the iced tea. I didn't learn that it was the fried chicken they were famous for until it was time to go. Even so, I felt like a stranger in the place. My vision of the past. My being present in the restaurant. My future in New Orleans. Too much was going on in my head. I just wanted to go home. Then, I remembered I had to pick up my transcripts. I considered procrastinating, but I had an appointment on Thursday that I could not reschedule.

It was late when I arrived on the campus. It was on a Wednesday. I could smell the aroma of fried chicken. I had to run all over the campus to pick up my transcripts. I'd forgotten how tedious this process was. I was transported back in time because the process of getting a copy of the transcript was unreal. I had to fill out a request form in one building and then take that form across the campus to the cashier's office and pay a five-dollar fee and walk that receipt back over to the registrar's office. They said, "Sir it takes three to five business days to get your transcripts."

"Ma'am, I'm sorry, but I need my transcripts today. I don't have that time to wait," I said.

"Those are the rules."

"I'm sorry to ask you to do this, but it would help me if I could get them today," I pleaded. "I drove down here today from out of town hoping to go back with my transcripts."

"Ah, ugh, ugh," she sighed with disgust and disdain. "Have a seat back out there."

"Thanks. I'll wait," I said without any hint of hubris. After I sat down, I became thirsty and considerably hot. I was exhausted. No, I was upset all over again.

8

Reading Toni Morrison:
Suffering and Hope

"A man ain't nothing but a man," said Baby Suggs. "But a son? Well now, that's somebody."

"I was talking about time. It's so hard for me to believe in it. Some things go. Pass on. Some things just stay. I used to think it was a rememory." —Toni Morrison, *Beloved*

I form light and create darkness. I make peace and create evil; I, the, Lord do all these things. —Isaiah 45:7

In order to crack open something in yourself to allow you to be aware of the presence of ancestors' spirits, you have to walk into nature with your emotional self, not just your intellectual self. —Malidoma Patrice Somé[1]

Tony Morrison's book *Beloved* has met acclaim from every corner of the world. But for me, it is a classic story of pain and suffering, and it conjures memories in the Black reader that, though beautifully told, are reminiscent of grief, struggle, and the experience of evil:

> "We could move," Sethe suggested once to her mother-in-law.
>
> "What'd be the point?" asked Baby Suggs. "Not a house in the country ain't packed to its rafters with some dead Negro's grief. . . . Can you beat that? Eight children and that's all I remember." "That's all you let yourself remember," Sethe had told her.[2]

Memory or remembering is a horrifying trope in the early pages of the novel. And the inability to remember, or the deliberate erasure of memory, is the result of enslavement and its vestiges that remain in the consciousness of Black folk's everyday life. The functioning of memory in the novel forces me to ask, "What is the experience of memory coming into consciousness?" And what about the impact of memory on one's sense of self? All of these deep questions of life ring loud and clear as Sethe and Paul D become reacquainted:

> "You can't leave right away, Paul D. You got to stay awhile. . . . Well long enough to see Baby Suggs, anyway. Where is she?"
>
> "Dead."
>
> "Aw no. When?"
>
> "Eight years now. Almost nine."
>
> "Was it hard? I hope she didn't die hard."
>
> "Soft as cream. Being alive was the hard part."[3]

The novel is laden with suffering and pain on the one hand, and a glimmer of hope and self-understanding on the other. There is also a strong questioning of selfhood and the possibilities the future holds. It is tempting for the reader to sentimentalize and think the novel is only about ghosts, sex, violence, and other themes. But to me, the novel reflects on slavery and the scars of the past in Black life. It is also about family, oppression, injustice, relationships, and moving forward despite the pain and suffering of the past. It is about how Black folk have been able to negotiate life against all odds. Additionally, the novel is about love, and negotiating and carving out hope amid the ubiquitous presence of suffering.

There is so much pain in *Beloved*. I can feel its every piercing arrow when I read it. It punctures the skin and makes the body ache. As I read, I can feel the welts from the leather straps beating against my back. I feel like Sethe when she says, "I got a tree on my back and a haint in my house. . . . I took one journey and I paid for the ticket."[4]

Memory can be destructive and dangerous because one never knows what it might dredge up. It is like playing with fire. If one gets too close or tells too much, memory can be destructive.

Conversely, it can be liberating and transformative, allowing one to face the demons. In this sense, necessities and grave dangers of therapeutic healing may also take place. Morrison is trying to provide the reader with a form of healing as burden sharing. Enslavement and its effects are not ever going away because the past is not going away; however, bridging the gap between past, present, and future seems to be a theme in the novel. Although there is a triteness to the eschatology seen in certain places, a palpable feeling of pain and sorrow is evident in these somber words: "Like kneading bread . . . working dough. Working, working dough. Nothing better than that to start the day's serious work of beating back the past."[5]

It took me twenty-five years to get through Morrison's now-classic novel. I simply could not read it. The story was too painful, too morbid and torturous. It was the hangings and the beatings—the abject indifference white people show toward Black life—that stopped me in my tracks. For years, I placed the blame on the writer rather than myself. "I don't like her writing," I would say. "It's too convoluted, too abstract, and too unclear." I made all kinds of excuses. They were genuine, authentic excuses for not being able to read the book. Then I would say there were too many gaps in the story. "The language is arcane. Cryptic. Esoteric. The characters are too enigmatic, too mysterious, and a bit too puzzling for me." Over and over again, a fog of skepticism and misunderstanding encircled me, baffled and stifled my every effort to turn the page.

But I was the problem. Her writing is awesome!

Now I understand it in ways I could not quite explain before. There are contrasting visions of love that run throughout the story—too-thick love. Sethe is alluding to love being excessive in relationality, and Paul D's concept of love is to love everything, but just a little bit. Never too much. The novel forces the reader to confront the question: In what context would a mother kill her child as the most loving thing to do? That's a terrible question, but that's exactly one of the most searing and sorrowful questions that bursts forth from the novel:

> "Why I did it. How if I hadn't killed her, she would have died and that is something I could not bear to happen to her. When I explain it, she'll understand, because she understands everything already. I'll tend her as no mother ever tended a child, a daughter. Nobody will ever get my milk no more except my own children. I never had to give it to nobody else—and the one time I did it was took from me—they held me down and took it. Milk that belonged to my baby."[6]

The horror of these words, the lingering memory, and the telling of this story, almost any story, requires a strength that is hard to muster. "This is not a story to pass on."[7] It is, in fact,

a ghost story, but it is also more than that. It is that because
the ruins of 124 will never be forgotten. Indeed, "remembering
seemed unwise."[8] And, as the novel states, "Down by the stream
in back of 124, her footprints come and go." Come and go. They
are so familiar. The word "familiar" is a ghost word. This is certainly a ghost story.

The story of *Beloved* is a story that haunts. The haunting is
there all the time, day and night. It is like a ghost, a "haint" that I
used to hear my father talk about growing up in Central Virginia.
My daddy had a lot of stories about ghosts. That is where I learned
that horses or mules could see haints. I remember him telling us
that his mother told him that when she was pregnant with him,
one day she was riding on a horse-drawn wagon and suddenly
the horse became agitated and unruly and the wagon flipped over
because the horse had seen a haint—a ghost. I heard other stories
of unexplained noises and curtains moving when there was no
one to be seen. So, I grew up hearing ghost stories as told by my
father. The other important point I want to make about Morrison's
Beloved is its cryptic, mystifying, and obscure ending:

> By and by all trace is gone and what is forgotten is not
> only the footprints but the water too and what it is down
> there. The rest is weather. Not the breath of the disre-
> membered and unaccountable for, but wind in the eaves,
> or spring ice thawing too quickly. Just weather. Certainly
> no clamor for a kiss.[9]

Wow! How dense is this symbolic language! These metaphors
and codes beg to be interpreted. And so as one who seeks to
interpret life and literature, I interpret this closing paragraph as
the denial of love and affection, as the language "certainly no
clamor for a kiss" suggests. Indeed, it may be a necessary denial.
More importantly, this story, this novel, is an interpretation of the
ghost story of America. In the end, it is about the haunting of the

whole nation by the many thousands gone—hanged, murdered, and buried under oaks and poplar trees, under green lawns and Astroturf, under ocean waters and creeks. *Beloved* is the story of the "haints" that haunt our nation from "sea to shining sea." While "[t]his is not a story to pass on"[10] as the closing trope of *Beloved* reiterates, it definitely is not a story to ignore. It must not be ignored.

The truth is, I had purchased the book in 1988, just after it had won the Pulitzer Prize for Fiction. Ten years later, by 1998, I had only gotten to page five or six. At that pace, I realized I would be dead and gone from this earth before I could finish the novel. I did not have this same problem with reading other books on suffering. There was something deep in my consciousness, buried in my psychic history, that blocked my ability to read about the suffering of Black people in Ohio during the mid-1840s. It is not fiction, though it is fictitious. It was almost like I was there. I, too, was enslaved like those who inhabited the beautiful yet horrifying Sweet Home plantation in Morrison's novel, that I have only recently finished reading. I could feel the agony and pain of those whose bodies hanged from the oak, poplar, and pine trees. The beatings, the hunger, the fear, and the longing for human dignity infuriated me to the point of paralysis. My brain would freeze, my lips would purse, and my teeth would grind to silence the rage in my soul. Reading should not be so hard for me—e.g., to read how the protagonist Sethe is beaten, whipped, and lashed by Schoolteacher—and yet, it was too hard for me to continue. The novel haunted me.

I had read Edmund Wilson's *To the Finland Station,* and I had listened to several Holocaust survivors while in graduate school studying humanities and philosophy. I was too naïve at the time to see that suffering and pain and the evil acts of humans against others have their home in race hatred. It was true for the Holocaust victims, and it is true for Black people. Nevertheless, I felt something. An uneasiness. An unhappiness with myself and the world around me. Maybe now I had come to realize Primo Levi's Auschwitz survivor was profoundly accurate in describing my dialectic dilemma: "Sooner or later in life, everyone discovers that perfect happiness is unrealizable, yet there are few who pause to consider the antithesis: that perfect unhappiness is equally unattainable."[11]

I have been unhappy all my life, and I am still unhappy about some things—things social, things political, things personal, things big, and things small. But when it comes to race and the evils of slavery and white supremacy, I think Primo Levi is wrong about me. I am perfectly unhappy about the evils perpetrated against Black people during and since slavery, and there is not a day that goes by when my purported happiness is not muddled by the memory of slavery's atrocities. This anamnesis, this deep symbolic reference, creates an unhappiness that, for the moment, reaches the level of perfection. There is a real gap in the consciousness of white people when it comes to Black suffering and the experience of evil. Evil is a lessening of being— a "fallen-ness." I am suggesting that—when it comes to Black suffering, epitomized by nearly 250 years of American chattel slavery vis-à-vis the Middle Passage, a prolegomenon to the evil and white supremacy that is the hallmark of modernity and the Enlightenment—scholars, both Christian and Jewish, are unconscious of the phenomenon, reality, and severity of Black suffering. Because it involves Black people, it simply does not register in their consciousness as suffering. It is recast as a form of something other than suffering.

Black suffering is an evil tragedy beyond the scope of the Greek tragedians. Sophocles and Euripides could not imagine the scope and duration of Black suffering. It is unlike the Jews' assessment of the Holocaust, represented in its most egregious form by the death chambers at Auschwitz. For Black people, God has never died—not during the evils of slavery, nor during the evils of Reconstruction or Jim Crow. Instead of concluding God is dead, another logic enabled enslaved Africans to sing the spiritual song, "Over my head I see freedom in the air. . . . There must be a God somewhere."[12]

The invisibility of God did not mean the absence of God and certainly did not mean the death of God. The shocking silence of God to Black suffering has not kept Black people from preaching, praying, singing, and believing in the justice and righteousness of God. The Black church is still a beautiful expression of the kingdom of God here on earth, and it seeks to mitigate against the forces of suffering and evil that permeate Black life. Blackness symbolizes suffering and pain, and yet the evil perpetrated against Black people is more than a symbol. It is an act. Paul Ricoeur's discussion of the symbolism of evil is akin to Descartes's discussion of *cogito, ergo sum*. They both fall short in the sense that Ricoeur's symbols are not the same as acts of evil and Descartes's "thinking" limits Being to the exclusion of acts, feelings, and other attributes of the body.

Du Bois's term "double consciousness" should be revisited to more readily identify with the language of today's Black community. Because the intention of language is critical to understanding, "double consciousness" may not be as easy to comprehend as, for example, the terms "dual existence" or "polyvalent reality." The objective of renaming would be to give a fresh perspective to the Du Boisian term in order to raise the consciousness of a people who may not otherwise know why their lived experience is accompanied by inequity and suffering in the face of integration and multicultural linguistics. Many young Black people who have no memory or lived experience with segregation, the Ku Klux Klan, and/or being called a "nigger" by white people often act as if white supremacy is dead or that it is a figment of one's imagination. This means there is no double consciousness in the Du Boisian sense.

Or more correctly, no consciousness at all regarding this suffering of Black folk. In fact, there is little to no understanding of the connection between Black suffering during slavery, the Reconstruction period, Jim Crow, the Civil Rights era, and today.

The suffering may, in fact, be different in the sense that slavery was evil, grotesque, and a violation of ones' total being. This was obvious, blatant, and pandemic. It was both seen and felt at every possible level of human existence. No one could miss it, no matter what narrative was being advanced. And, yet it was often ignored and sublimated by the leaders in society: professors, scholars, writers, theologians, pastors, teachers, plantation brokers and owners, and Jews and Christians alike. Poor, ordinary white people who did not have the money or the wherewithal to own the enslaved were also complicit in the maintenance of the slavocracy. This system was evil to the core, and in my view, there is a straight line between then and now—between the historical and the present day.

Today, the lack of consciousness also seems to characterize many Black people. This is inexplicable, and yet I must try to understand and explain it. I can only wonder what fog engulfs the minds of our people to the point there is such complicity with the status quo. This lack of awareness or consciousness will be explored throughout this book.

For example, in the context of suffering, the symbolism or significations of evil, are associated with the very concept. A theological rebuttal is needed to inject hope into this Draconian model. Symbols should move beyond giving rise to thought and give rise to action. The purpose of the action is to rectify or validate the symbol. The objective of action is to seek justice as a step beyond the symbolic to the point of transformation.

Hegel's master/slave dialectic gives a perspective of consciousness as it relates to the self and the other. He contends a certain self (the master) has won the battle of independent consciousness, while the other (the slave) has inevitably lost. Hegel views otherness as inferior, negative, and worthy of subjugation. He even introduces the term "thinghood" to describe the master's perception of the slave. Dehumanizing the other is a strategy that is designed to maintain a status quo of white supremacy (lordship) and captivity (bondsman). Contrary to the status quo, I believe there is an absolute positive element in otherness that is, at its core, part of nature.[13]

The good is seen readily in the basic nature of Black people who love others, care for the less fortunate, and empathize with the poor, the suffering, and the dispossessed. As I look around my environment, I see a lot of good: children playing, adults talking to each other, birds singing. I see young children running and laughing in open spaces; I see the construction of hospitals and homes; I see people trying to help one another in some small, almost insignificant ways; I see young people working together; I see a lot of good all round. We have good people doing good by performing many acts of kindness. Cordial people. People who are the symbols and signs of hospitality. This is the meaning of practicing Christianity. Only those who embrace and practice hospitality can lay claim to being Christian. Black people. Loving people. Gentle people. Black people are good people. Kind, helpful, and giving people. Long-suffering people. My favorite poet, Langston Hughes, often described as Black America's Poet Laureate, writes in his 1946 poem, "Roland Hayes Beaten":

Negroes,
Sweet and docile,
Meek, humble, and kind;
Beware the day
They change their minds!

Wind
In the cotton fields,

Gentle breeze;
Beware the hour
It uproots trees.[14]

The Experience of Suffering and Evil

Black suffering is layered in the experience of pain and torture—historical, physical, and psychological. The dominant element of racism and white supremacy is the trope that permeates each layer of this experience and can be said to constitute causality. Black suffering is grounded in the perception of Blackness as Other—Other, by which I mean an absolute and thoroughgoing alterity, one ascribed to inhumanity. It is the other as hated other. It is an unrelenting evil seen in the history of slavery, lynching, physical and psychological murder, and torture. Black suffering is grounded in the evils and the oppression of white supremacy and sovereignty—a hegemonic destructive ontology seen in every area of life. Yet, Black people continue to survive and to some extent thrive in the face of this universal hatred and evil. Black people are strong and resilient.

It was the Fourth of July, and I was walking down the tree-lined streets of Richmond, Virginia, the former capital of the Confederacy. I could not help but notice the American flags waving and the statues of Confederate generals and lieutenants buffeting the perimeter of Jefferson Davis Highway. I drive down this road, a major North-South corridor, almost every day, and I pass by schools with names like Robert E. Lee, Lee-Davis, and J. E. B. Stuart. These symbols of the Confederacy are reminders of the mindset of those who would rather die than grant enslaved people their freedom—a freedom that is claimed to be self-evident and sacrosanct on one hand and deniable to Black people on the other.

On July 4, 1776, the thirteen colonies unanimously declared their independence from the king of Great Britain due to tyranny.

This was the Declaration of Independence. It asserted that certain truths are self-evident, to wit, "that all men are created equal . . . endowed by their Creator with certain unalienable rights, that among these are life, liberty, and the pursuit of happiness." Moreover, the text states "mankind are more disposed to *suffer* while *evils are sufferable* than to right themselves." The signers of this Declaration of Independence, including John Hancock, George Wythe, Benjamin Franklin, John Adams, John Tyler, and Thomas Jefferson, were familiar with the language of suffering and evil, and still perpetrated a more heinous tyranny and despotism upon Black people—"deaf to the voice of justice and of consanguinity." The history of the United States of America is one laden with duplicitous laws, doctrines, and customs, such that Black suffering is not considered suffering and evil perpetrated against Black people is not considered evil. It is something else. The semantics change.

There are many overt signs and symbols of evil in American history and culture. The white robe and hood worn by members of the Ku Klux Klan are two of the most ominous symbols of terror and tyranny against Black people. They were worn by doctors, lawyers, judges, politicians, businessmen, and other white people from every segment of society. In the young adult novel *Stella by Starlight*, Sharon M. Draper writes, "Nine robed figures dressed all in white. Heads covered with softly pointed hoods. Against the Black of night, a single wooden cross blazed."[15] Nothing else needs to be said for the reader to know this language refers to the Ku Klux Klan. White robes. Hoods covering their heads. A burning cross. These are the implements of evil, terror, and violence. White supremacy. Hatred. Evil. Black suffering. That is what these symbols mean. And so does the Confederate battle flag!

If, according to the Old Testament prophet Isaiah, the creator of evil and woe is the same God who creates peace and good, the question is, "What kind of God is this who does all these things?"

From a theological perspective, God is in control of everything—good and evil. This Isaiah passage is unique in that it har-
bors language found only in this prophetic text. Nowhere else
in Scripture is evil blatantly and forthrightly ascribed to God—
Yahweh. Nevertheless, I would rather have God in control than
anyone else—any other deity and certainly no person who might
subject us to the feckless attitudes and fickleness of human personality. Dr. Robert Wafawanaka, an Old Testament scholar, says
even evil is not absolutely out of control, for it is under the reign
of Yahweh. Fittingly, ancient Israel, with a great sense of intro-
spection, did attribute everything good and bad to Yahweh. Con-
textually, Yahweh uses Cyrus the Persian king to bring peace to
exilic Israel (i.e., the Israel that had experienced the punishment
of exile). Conversely, he brings about evil and disaster for Baby-
lon as Israel's liberation and return to the homeland is about to
take place.[16]

God's divinity transcends the limits of human speech and
what we think about God. Theology can place no limits on God.
God is not confined to human semantics, to our words, to our
understanding. Our words are whimpering and wallowing in
weakness. Our language is limited by our human frailties.

Finally, I return to a dominant theme in this book, which is
American chattel slavery. While God seemed absent in terms of
intervening by siding with the oppressed, Black people kept praying, preaching, and singing to the glory of God. Against the odds,
these acts of faith kept alive the hope that freedom would come
in the morning. It has taken over four hundred years of sunsets
and daybreaks for freedom to begin to arrive. Yet freedom still
has not fully become a reality for most African Americans. Their
suffering continues in its morphed forms of oppression. Black
people, too, seem to adapt and adjust to its new, more complex
environments. Black folk's faith in God in the face of extreme evil
is indeed apocalyptic. Jewish apocalyptic literature, especially

Daniel, describes the Jews existing under persecution by empire, yet hoping for a better day when God would intervene to change their circumstances. Dr. Wafawanaka agrees, saying, "It does give a sense of hope despite the odds." Black people have been a hopeful people when all else has failed—hoping against hope. While my son Corey often says, "hope is not a strategy," I tend to think that it is a strategy and has always been one for the survival of Black folk. As I acknowledge Corey's statement as profound and practical in a time where Black people may seem too relaxed, without vision, and without a plan for progress, it is also critical we recognize that without hope, our suffering would indeed be a death sentence. It is with hope that we keep ourselves alive! In the face of laws, customs, and systems designed to create hopelessness, Black people remained and continue to remain hopeful.

Dimensions of Suffering and Hope

"Was it hard? I hope she didn't die hard."

Sethe shook her head. "Soft as cream. Being alive was the hard part."

"You looking good."

"Devil's confusion. He lets me look good long as I feel bad." —Toni Morrison, *Beloved*

God elects us and rejects us. Job is no exception, just as Jesus, too, was elected as the son of God and rejected as a representative of human material culture. We have nothing to do with our election by God. Job does not know what is going on, even though God has chosen him. God has elected him. And this election by God is both a blessing and a rejection—a curse.

We tend to locate our blessings in material culture. Our understanding of what it means to be "blessed and highly favored" is grounded in how much stuff we have. We have a Kardashian

complex, an L. A. mentality, where posh and glitter are the meanings of what we aspire to be and achieve—of what we understand
and consider a blessing to be. Blessings are considered things
like houses, land, luxury cars, fur coats, leather jackets, designer
brand shoes and suits, and all the accessories—from Ralph Lau-
ren to Tom Ford, to Cartier, Gucci, and other French and Italian
names, some of which we can barely pronounce. To say that we
are blessed and highly favored means we have money in our
pockets, jingling and jangling like gold and silver. We can buy
what we want to satiate the self. We can do what we want. We
can wear what we want because I am a supervisor, a foreman, a
clerk, a businessman. I am a college graduate. I have earned my
degree. I have a good job. Blessings abound. Well, that sounds a
lot like Job, does it not?

The Book of Job begins by saying how blessed Job was. He
had ten children—seven sons and three daughters. He had seven
thousand sheep, three thousand camels, five hundred oxen, and
five hundred donkeys, as well as many servants. Job had it going
on. He was balling and high rolling. Job was the man. The boss.
The chief. The shot caller. Then the scripture text says there
was a heavenly meeting where Satan was in attendance, and
the Lord asked him what he was doing there. "Where have you
come from?"

And then the Lord says to Satan, "Have you considered my
servant Job? There is none like him, a blameless and upright
man who fears God and turns away from evil." Notice the Lord
elects Job. Satan does not draft Job. The Lord God volunteers and
wagers Job. Satan then asks the critical question of God: "Does
Job fear God for nothing? Or is it because of his many blessings
that he is so faithful and fearful?"

Satan further says to God, "You have blessed the work of his
hands and his possessions have increased in the land."[1] In other
words, Job is "blessed and highly favored," in the language of

Black Church culture. We often say that phrase so cavalierly, so matter-of-factly, so thoughtlessly. This is almost a platitude in the Black church. It is infused in our music, in our conversation, in our language, in our speech, in our testimonies. But what does it mean? What does Job's story mean for us today? What does it mean to say we are blessed and highly favored by God?

To start, it means suffering is inescapable. In other words, your blessings are not about you. Rather, God has made all things possible. So if blessings are associated with blamelessness, as was the case with Job, then God is confident in wagering us against the devil because it is *not about what God has done for us*. It is about God being God. Therefore, suffering is a byproduct of blessings and God's favor. Suffering is not about sin and about being unable to follow one's own advice, as Eliphaz so slyly accuses Job. The debate between Eliphaz and Job concerns who is wise, who has stumbled, who has made a mistake, faltered, fallen from grace, lied, stolen, or committed adultery or some other sin. This makes Job angry and furious because he is, in fact, *innocent*, and yet he suffers. Suffering, innocence, blessings, and favor all tend to go hand in hand in this text. As a matter of fact, Job's suffering is directly related to his blessings, blamelessness, and favor with God. Because Job is in the favor of God—and because God is confident of Job's fear of God, confident of Job's veneration and love—God is willing to enter him into a contest with Satan. His blessings and favor have landed him in the jaws of Satan, where his suffering is severe, where sores have sapped his sense of sanity and swept seemingly all wisdom from his lips. Instead of praising God, Job is now cursing. Instead of rejoicing, he is cursing the day of his birth. Look at the scene here: Eliphaz scoots up beside him and says, in essence, "Can I have a word with you? You won't get mad if I tell you what your problem is, will you? You have been helping others who have stumbled. Now that you have stumbled and are guilty of some sin, you can tell me about it. You can't be innocent because the innocent don't suffer the way you are suffering."

Job gets increasingly angrier as "friends" Eliphaz, Bildad, and Zophar seek to explain more and more why he is suffering so. In this text, it is the innocent who suffer, the blessed and highly favored, because that is how the story is told. Job is blessed and highly favored and he does not understand why he is suffering. His friends don't understand because suffering, in their minds and our minds, is related to sin. And yet Job ain't buying that because he is, according to the narrative, innocent. This innocence almost turns into self-righteousness when he gets so perturbed, so impatient that he wants to confront God. He wants a face-to-face meeting with God so he can make his case. In chapter 23, he says, "[God's] hand is heavy despite my groaning. Oh, that I knew where I could find him that I might come to his [house]. I would lay my case before him and fill my mouth with arguments. I would learn what he would say to me. There an upright person could reason with him. And I should be acquitted forever by my judge."[2]

We need to be careful about what we ask. More importantly, a confrontation with God is more than a notion. It is too human of us to expect God must justify God's self to us. Look at what happens after Job gets a hearing from God. Instead of Job confronting God, God appears to Job in a whirlwind—a sign and symbol of inescapable power. "God accuses Job of ignorance and then sets about to prove it by peppering Job with questions."[3] God says:

Who is this that darkens counsel by words without knowledge? Gird up your loins like a man—I will question you and you shall answer. Where were you when I laid the foundation of the earth? Tell me, if you have understanding, who determined its measurements. Surely you must know.[4]

We do not set God straight as Job sought to do, asking for a face-to-face meeting with God as if we and God were equal. Job is mistaken! In the presence of God, the only thing we can do is keep silent. In God's presence, we become speechless. Wordless. Silent. Job is stunned not to the point of stuttering and stammering, but to the point of rudeness and silence. He knows nothing about what it means to be God, what it means to create something out of nothingness. He is a creature of God's creation, not the other way around. Job is pounded with questions of physics and astronomy. He is peppered with questions of oceanography and atmospheric science and speech:

> Where is the way to the dwelling of light. And where is the place of darkness? . . . Can you lift up your voice to the clouds, so that a flood of waters may cover you? Can you send forth lightning?[5]

> Then the Lord says to Job, "Look at Behemoth which I made just like I made you,"[6] and "Can you draw out Leviathan with a fishhook?"[7]

Friendship and Suffering

Life has one common meeting place for Black people and white people as well as all humanity, a destination that cannot be avoided—not by Plato, Aristotle, Paul, Silas, the minor prophets, or even Moses himself. As a matter of fact, Jesus also joined the saints and sinners alike at the commonplace of life's destiny. Death. That place where the wicked shall cease from troubling us, sorrow will release its crushing grip, and tears will cease to be. All of life, no matter how happy or sad—from preachers and pastors, to princes to potentates, to paupers and profligates—ends at the gate of death. The caravan of friends and foes, family and all others, comes together like the suffering and pain of

Job. The hard days of labor, the regrets of the night, the setting of the sun dim the light of day, and the curtains are drawn and the door is shut, never to be opened again. This is the negating finality of life's exuberance. Death is the denial of life! And for the Christian, the resurrection is the sublation of death. The denial of death's power.[8]

But in between, before this common destiny is reached, we have friends—friends like Job's friends Eliphaz, Bildad, and Zophar. Friends who seek to comfort us; friends who care and often mean well; friends who claim they will do anything for us. Like Job's friends who sat with him in silence, our friends have done and will often do the same thing. I know that Job's friends have been castigated and castrated by theologians, preachers, and biblical scholars alike for their lofty and predetermined views of God and suffering; for their sanctimonious explanations of the correlation between sin and suffering; and for their philosophy of retribution as a quid pro quo for sin and evil. Job's friends fail to understand the severity of Job's suffering is out of line with his sin, and Job cannot explain his innocence to their satisfaction. There is an asymmetrical relationship between Job's suffering and his human foibles.

When our friends think we are guilty of something, no amount of explanation will change their intransigent minds. But Job is innocent, and he still suffers. So the beliefs of his friends remain unchanged:

> Then Bildad the Shuhite answered, "How long will you say these things and the words of your mouth be a great wind? Does God pervert justice? Or does the Almighty pervert the right? . . . If you are pure and upright, surely then He will rouse himself for you and restore to you your rightful place."[9]

Hidden Hope: Beneath the Pain of Silence

Life itself is a series of suffering. No one escapes this often ugly and overwhelming reality. Certainly, there are different degrees of physical suffering and the mental anguish that often accompanies such suffering. Hospitals are full of patients—Medical College of Virginia (MVC), St. Mary's, St. Francis, Retreat, Henrico Doctors, Tucker Pavilion, etc.—and if one multiplied these by a hundred thousand, one would still not be able to number those who are suffering in physical pain. This is an ethical dilemma. This is our situation. This is our condition. It looks hopeless, dim, scary, and frightening. Sickness and suffering turn the life of the family upside down. They change everything. They make us realize how frail and tenuous our bodies and our lives really are. For example, when my father had a heart attack during my early years, I was devastated—stumbling and fumbling to find my way. My mother and all the rest of us were pitiful and painful in our sadness.

Because of God's wager, Job finds himself in a tough, even perplexing situation. On an ash heap on the outer skirts of town, his body is covered with sores. He is so emaciated, so gaunt, so strapped and strained by pain and suffering that the scripture text says his three friends—the three all-knowing homeboys, the doctors of diagnosis, the theologians and ethicists, Bildad, Eliphaz, and Zophar—do not even recognize him. Job looks so different, so shocking to their sight, so pitiful and so painful to behold that they became speechless. The Scripture says when the friends see Job, they sit in silence, unable to speak for seven days. Job meets their silence with his own. After seven days of silence, Job speaks first—not to them but to himself.

The language of the text is chilling and tinged with anger and disgust. But what does this mean for us today, when we have our own troubles, our own silent pain and sickness and sorrow, and we still must preach come Sunday morning? Where is the hope in all of this cursing and lamenting?

Job opens his mouth for the first time in this third chapter and curses the day.[10] He wants to get rid of the day of his birth. If that day could be eradicated, he would not have been born. But he is already born, and a curse is about the future, not the past. In fact, there is nothing he can do about what has already been done. Yes, he wants God's divine creation in Genesis 1:3 reversed. He wants God's "Let there be light" reversed. Job says, "Let there be darkness" upon the day of his birth because of his pain and suffering. Our hope is God is not listening to Job because Job is speaking so much like we speak. He sounds like we sound when we are mad and upset with God—when our pain overwhelms our preaching. The hidden hope here, too, is God ain't listening. Yes, our friends are listening. Our family can see and hear us in our pained state of mind. Everybody is frantic and upset because Job and I are talking crazy. But the day will not be taken back. The light will not be dimmed by darkness. God is the God of light and darkness—and light has overcome darkness. Job is ranting, cursing the day of his birth in stark, strong, searing, somber, earth-shaking terms.

But notice carefully. Read closely. Realize Job does not curse his parents for conceiving him and he does not curse God for allowing his birth to happen. Instead, he curses the day. The day. He is on the precipice of despair. He comes very close to cursing everybody, but he stops short of cursing God. His wife has told him "to curse God and die,"[11] but he still does not take her advice because he recognizes God is still God through it all.

Job does and says much. His suffering causes him to wish that he had never been born, but he never wants to end his life. He does not even entertain the thought of suicide anywhere in this text. Why? Because his life, your life, my life is not ours to take. "The Lord gives, the Lord has taken away. Blessed be the name of the Lord."[12]

On the Suffering of the Innocent

In the Scripture, sickness is now added to poverty—both of which constitute suffering.

Job's wife is furious because, in a sense, Job's misfortune is her misfortune. When she says, "Why persist in this integrity of yours? Curse God and die,"[13] this is Satan's echo. Satan has found a friend in Job's wife. Those who are close to us are the ones who often will prod us into doubt and suspicion.

Job does not curse God, does not speak ill of God despite his pain and suffering. His gratitude and love for God are profound and unwavering. Job realizes everything comes from God and everything is God's gracious gift.

Material prosperity, says Job, is not necessary to trust God. God is God despite our interest. And yet the enemy does believe that Job's piety and justice are tied to what he has or what he can get—to a reward. That is why Satan is more confident than he was the first time—because Job is not just poor now, but he is also sick. And because he is poor and sick, his suffering is magnified exponentially.

Black people have been poor, hungry, hated, powerless, and sick from every major disease known to man—afflicted by sores and sorrow. We, too, have sat among the ashes—spiritually, socially, and physically. The burning and lynching of the Black body for sport was an American pastime throughout the nineteenth century, right here in Richmond and throughout Virginia, at whose shores the *White Lion* arrived in 1619 carrying "twenty and odd" enslaved Africans. I wonder, also, about places like Lynchburg, Virginia. The name troubles me.

Too often, it is pleasure that we seek. It is the joy of life that we crave. We want to thrive and excel, to possess and to own all kinds of materials. We wish we were the greatest—with an abundance of material possessions, material culture, cars, houses, and land—you name it. And the more we have, the more we want and think we deserve. Our religion is based on what we can get, what we can possess, and how we can prosper. Prosperity has nothing to do with ultimate religion. Job's religion is indeed a disinterested one. He is not serving God for something. He is serving God because God is God, not because of a reward but because of his faith.

Our future is hidden and grounded in hope. God keeps our future hidden so we can have hope. Job curses his past; he curses the day of his birth, rather than his future. We do not know the future. It is a good thing the future is hidden from us. We do not know everything. Job does not know the whole story, but God does. God is a God of the future, making known the unknown. Because our future is hidden, we can run on a little while longer. We can deal with today and let God deal with tomorrow.

Interlude:
"Powell Street Station—
Purgatory in Paradise"

The incline has to be nearly sixty degrees from the bottom of Ellis Street to the top of the hill on Sacramento Street, a few blocks from Chinatown. He was walking from the Parc 55 Hotel at the corner of Powell and Ellis Streets across from the Bay Area Regional Transit (BART) Station in downtown San Francisco. John Henry headed north toward the wharf through Chinatown and past all kinds of great, delectable, aromatic eateries. Earlier, he had to abandon his morning workout to experience the natural terrain and topography of San Francisco. Normally, this walking does not provide for a great cardio workout, but his trek up Powell Street was a struggle to catch his breath. Not good for a forty-six-year-old.

The street is a symbol of the city with shops, hotels, pharmacies every few blocks and eateries every few feet. The homeless and the poor are embedded into the fabric of the city—looking

penniless and pitiful begging for a dollar, and sleeping in alley-
ways and on sidewalks. This is even more evident in Berkeley
just across the bay and a short train ride away. Berkeley, like San
Francisco, is truly a tale of two cities—one Black, the other white,
or one poor and the other richly bourgeois. John Henry knew this
because Asian and white people are everywhere. The Asian folks
both look and act White and are treated pretty much like white
Americans, with a sense of privilege and respect. On the other
hand, Black people are treated like what the French-Martinican
psychiatrist Frantz Fanon called the "wretched of the earth,"
like scumbags, like a burden, like those whom Mark Twain, the
beloved American writer, called "niggers" on every other page of
his classic novel *Adventures of Huckleberry Finn*. And even the
great W. E. B. Dubois referred to Black people as a "problem."

This was evident in the closing luncheon held by the Black
law students graduating from Berkeley. John Henry and his wife,
Abigail, attended the event because one of their sons, William,
was getting a law degree, the Master of Laws. The testimonies
of the Black students were palpable, heart-wrenchingly sad, sorrowful, and drenched with dramaturgy. On the other hand, their
stories were laced with hope, strength, determination, power, and
love. The sense of community displayed by the students brought
John Henry to his knees with melancholy and sadness. Time after
time, he was wiping tears from his eyes and snot from his nose
after being overcome with emotions.

"Stoicism be damned!" he said to himself. He could not con-
tain his empathy and sympathy for what Black people have to
endure in every walk of life, a life that continues to be a battle—a
war against the forces of suffering and evil. It may sound corny
or trite, but the "hills are alive" in San Francisco and at Berkeley
where the incline is so very steep that it will take one's breath
away. It is an uphill battle for Black people just to survive the suffering and the pain of racism in school, in the community, and in

the working world. That is if one is lucky enough to get a job in one's field of study. A master's degree is certainly no guarantee

Not only that, as he and Abigail were walking up the hill on Bancroft Way, John Henry also witnessed a white man yelling, screaming, and cussing at a group of Asian men who were all dressed in tight, slim-fitting black suits as they were walking up the hill toward the International House. They were alternating languages, speaking perfect English and Mandarin. The white man was visibly annoyed and frustrated.

"Go back to your own country, you piece of shit!" he said, gesticulating with anger.

He went on and on with his emotional tirade. "You are taking our jobs and causing unemployment here. Go back to your own country and leave us Americans alone!"

The Asian men looked straight ahead as if he were talking to the wind. They did not wince or wobble in their determination, not to even acknowledge his existence. The white man, too, was saying that it was an uphill battle, a steep incline for him to find a place to work. In America, he had become an "Other." No, maybe an "invisible" man. An invisible white man. An oxymoron, a psychic impossibility that was causing the white man to have a nervous breakdown.

John Henry had no sympathy or empathy for him because he was still privileged; and in spite of his paranoia or schizophrenia, he was still a white man in America who felt his privilege was slipping away from him or being snatched by immigrants. He had gone mad.

The day after Berkley's graduation, on Saturday morning, John Henry's family wanted to get breakfast at the world-famous breakfast spot, Brenda's French Soul Food Restaurant at 652 Polk Street, just a short half-mile walk from the Parc 55 hotel. However, if John Henry were to make a left out of the hotel lobby, he would head toward the wharf, but a quick right and a block to the west would put him smack in the Tenderloin District of downtown San Francisco. This is the flatland between Union Square and the Civic Center Office District. It was a long way away from the steep hills and boutiques on Powell Street where one sees and feels the high-dollar rent condos, the designer suits by Brunello Cucinelli, Oscar de la Renta, and Rolex watches that look too expensive to wear, or too dangerous. Too "in your face." "Tenderloin" is a strange name for a neighborhood. Semantic autonomy, deep-seated symbolism, and dissonance hover all over the terministic screen of the word.

For John Henry, the word *tenderloin* conjures up memories of the days when his father would roast or barbeque a whole hog on the Fourth of July. It was an all-night affair of festive stories and tall tales, myths and mythmaking, during a time when families were not so nuclear and segmented. John Henry lived together with cousins, aunts, and uncles sleeping on the floor, on the couch, or in a bed if one were lucky. This was the Black extended family. The African village. Unlike now, when everybody has their own rooms, phones, televisions, and computers. But the tenderloin of the hog was the sweet, soft underbelly that made for good eating. It was better than the meat of the ham, the shoulder, the ribs, and the places where bacon comes from. It was the pork belly equivalent of filet mignon. The word itself is worthy of reflection because tender, even without the loin, suggests satiating the palate. It's appetitive. It's sexual. But, it also implies an exchange of cash. To tender is to give something for something, to barter, to trade, to engage in a transaction. And "loin" in a red-light district in San Francisco has myriad connotations, meanings, and metaphors: sex, prostitution, bribery, as well as illicit and illegal action on the part of everybody in the neighborhood and beyond including the cops, the hustlers, the prostitutes, the gangsters, the thieves, the landlords, the bankers, and the homeless. The tenderloin is tasty and sweet to everyone. Everybody seems to be masters of their game, whether it's begging for food or money, or writing parking tickets for double-parked cars in a "no parking zone," or getting away with something pleasurable or shady. Something forbidden.

As John Henry, Abigail, and their sons, William and David, head to breakfast, they had to go through the piss-stained streets smelling of pungent vomit and stale clothes, worn by those whose bed was a sidewalk in front of a boarded-up building. Signs read "No Loitering" or "No Trespassing," and yet people were congregating everywhere. As they continued to walk against the cool brisk gale wind, on the corner of Taylor and Ellis, a man's beltless pants fell to his knees and his naked, wrinkled body was exposed to the searing San Francisco wind and the glares of passersby. He was unfazed by his own spectacle.

This is the place of legend and largesse. Strip clubs, diverse sexualities, and the poor from all parts of Asia line the streets where vacant and boarded-up buildings still make one feel lost and afraid in the urban jungle. John Henry made sure he made no eye contact with anyone. Looking dazed and straight ahead, he walked with brisk determination, trying to keep up with his sons who had said to their mother, "Ma, you need to stay close and not lag behind us."

Later, one of them said, "You could get snatched away and disappear in a moment if you get too far behind."

They felt like they were prey, almost like gazelles amid hungry cheetahs. John Henry had seen many times on National Geographic when a weak animal gets away from the herd, that animal better look out because in the wild, that is a dinner meal. A feast for friends. So they walked closer together, like the defensive line of a football team. And yet, John was distracted by the funky smells, the ugly sights, the sirens, the spectacle of a tale of two cities. The dialectic was confusing and nauseating. In a matter of minutes, they had gone from sleeping in a hotel room suite to walking among the seedy-looking streets peppered with liquor stores, quick payday loan stores, graffiti art, homelessness, and squalor. Yes, squalor. He thought he might catch a glimpse of the house where a famous book-turned-movie was written—Dashiell Hammett's *The Maltese Falcon*. He had no such luck; and anyway, this was not the time to let the mind wander too far from the task at hand, which was to get breakfast at Brenda's without getting mugged or shot by the police.

It was morning and the sun was shining bright.

After walking for thirty minutes, they finally arrived. Everybody knew they were getting close when a long line could be seen in the distance. As they neared the restaurant, the line was almost a block long. John Henry went in to put his name on the list.

"How long is the wait?" he quietly asked the lady at the door, receptionist and hostess.

"Oh, maybe an hour and a half. We're moving kinda fast this morning," she said rather matter-of-factly.

John Henry got back in line with his wife and sons. Sounding like a symphony, they asked, "How long?"

"Too long," he said. "The lady said that it will be an hour or longer before we get seated."

"Let's find someplace else," they said in a worn-out tone of syncopated harmony. In agreement, they headed back toward the hotel through the same stink-filled streets lined with litter, broken beer bottles, toilet paper strewn everywhere, and people of all colors and stripes talking to themselves. All of this was in search of an egg-white omelet and a glass of orange juice. Or was it whole-grain waffles and turkey sausage? They always became healthy eaters whenever visiting the Bay area. Strangely enough, John Henry's appetite never waned or wavered. The dirt and grime, the smell and swell of crime, and the abject fear that he felt never overshadowed his hunger and the goal to get a tasty, healthy breakfast.

They meandered through the busy, noisy, and clinic-filled streets in pursuit of happiness—French soulful breakfast on Saturday morning. And what a breakfast it was. Not because of the French toast, but because John Henry and his wife got into an argument about something he'd said previously about black suffering in a sermon. While he'd been giving the sermon, a Black woman and her mother had walked out of the church, expressing to Abigail a few days later that the graphic nature of John Henry's sermon had been too much for them to handle. He'd been describing the way white men murdered some black pregnant women in the South during the days of Jim Crow.

His wife had said, "I, too, was troubled by your example about the pregnant woman who had her baby cut out of her belly by a white man with a hunting knife."

"What? I was trying to describe black suffering the best way I knew how," John had responded. And then almost unconsciously his voice had elevated in anguish, "I don't understand Black people. Why is it that we don't want to hear about our *own* suffering?"

"We suffer enough. We suffer all week long, and so on Sunday, we want to hear about love, peace, and hope. We want to be encouraged," she'd retorted.

In disgust, John Henry had replied, "It's crazy that Black folk don't want to hear about their own suffering. They want the preacher to lie. To tell them something good instead of facing the reality of Black suffering. That's tragic."

This brief exchange had ruined their breakfast. His wife was not feeling his disgust and anger and thought his attitude was over the top. At some point, he had to kindly apologize for his disposition. While he didn't treasure talking about these things, he still felt compelled and driven to speak the truth.

He said to her, "I, too, am flawed. I, too, suffer. I, too, feel the weight of this hegemonic society. Some things need to be said because the real torture is how black people have been treated, me included."

John Henry lost that emotional argument, as he had many times before. The truth is he didn't want to make the six-hour flight back to the east coast any longer than it already had to be. What was supposed to be a celebration breakfast for their son's commencement had almost turned into a melee. It was a fight he clearly did not understand.

After breakfast, they kept walking along Market Street all the way to the wharf and waterfront where the crowds were larger and more diverse than they were at the Powell Street Station. Everyone was having fun, eating handpicked blueberries, drinking freshly brewed coffee, and tasting homemade organic ice cream. Even the poor could eat well.

After the morning in San Francisco, it was time to venture back across the Bay to Berkeley. Berkeley is the seat of public intellectualism in California and the center of free speech. Just down the street in Oakland, one finds the center of the resistance movement, the Black Panthers, and everybody who is trying to make their voice heard. It was overwhelming, the confusion of horizons John Henry and his family faced everywhere they went. Poverty, opulence, homeless people, and greedy capitalists all lived near one another.

In the heart of downtown San Francisco, the lines form early before the sun rises. By the time the four of them boarded the train to Berkeley, which was just across the Bay, the struggle to find a place for them all to sit was intense. John Henry said to himself, "I don't like riding the subway. Not in New York. Not the Green/Red Line in Boston. Not the BART in the San Francisco Bay area." He couldn't explain his propensity to staying away from trains and buses in urban America. He kept his distance from crowds and strangers. It may have something to do with growing up in rural, pastoral settings where the people were sparse and the iconic Ford F-150 pickup truck or the Chevrolet Impala was the sign of independence and upward mobility. He didn't know if that were true or not, but it used to be true, to some extent. "To some extent" because they were not upwardly mobile. They were the working poor. John Henry's family was either always struggling to make ends meet or going downhill. Incline/decline was the dyadic, the dialectic of life. The bifurcation.

He would see the same thing all over the land, where the urban milieu was saturated with people trying to "catch their breaths" or stay afloat, as the saying went. San Francisco was almost a perfect paradigm of Charles Dickens's dialectic, *A Tale of Two Cities*—a fusion of horizons. For some, it is the best of times; for others, it is the worst of times. Besides, the only train John Henry knew about was the Norfolk and Western, now Norfolk Southern, which stopped at a small depot in Ettrick, Virginia, on its way north to Richmond or south to Greensboro, North Carolina. As a matter of fact, he'd been a grown man before he'd even boarded a train, a short ride to Union Station in the nation's capital.

At the Powell Street Station in downtown San Francisco, the tattered, poor, and homeless abounded in staggering contrast to the landscape of upscale shops and restaurants. On the same streets, some leading retailers imposed their behemoth presence to satisfy the range of materialistic palates from the humble college student to the upper echelon of society. There was Saks Fifth Avenue, Louis Vuitton, Macy's, Target, H&M, and Walgreens. That drugstore was everywhere (I wonder what it means? Is it a metaphor for our sickness? Are we all addicted to consumerism—Starbucks coffee, Dunkin' Donuts, and diet cola? Sugar and salt?). People were hustling and bustling in every direction. Some in two-piece linen suits, designer shoes, North Face jackets, Adidas tennis shoes, and JanSport backpacks galore. The backpack was a sign and symbol of millennial convenience and plasticity. Men dressed in suits and ties, wearing their backpack like it was a part of their outfit. An accessory. No, it was more like a necessity, like a pair of socks, underwear, or a sweater. It was the new briefcase. The umbrella. The baseball cap. It was the sign of the times in the urban milieu.

As John Henry swiped his BART card to get on the train, the gate would not open. A buzzer sounded and he tried again to no avail. The attendant, sitting in the booth, looked annoyed and frustrated because she had to get up to see what's wrong.

"What's the problem?" she yelled.

"Ma'am, I don't know."

"Do you have enough money on the card?"

"Yes, I think so, I put $20.00 on it yesterday, and I only made one trip from Berkeley."

"Stand back so these people can get through."

"Listen, ma'am. I don't want to miss my northbound train."

"Sir, that's not my fault. You need to put more money on your BART card."

"What?" he said in amazement. "This is a scam."

"Just go over there to that machine, read the instructions this time, and add some more money to your card. Do you understand that?"

John Henry only smiled though he was frantic because time was not on his side and the attendant was annoyed that she had to get up to help him. He had already missed the 8:00 a.m. eight-car train. The platform sign read the next one, a five-car train, was coming in thirteen minutes. It took him ten minutes to read the instructions, use his debit card, and go back to the entrance and down the steps to the platform to board the train. He was out of breath and out of patience, not with the attendant, but with himself because he was his own biggest problem. John Henry was mad because he shouldn't have ridden the train in the first place. His son William had said it was the best thing to do. The cab or a ride share was what he should have done.

"Dad, I ride the train all the time," he'd said.

"Ok, I know, but I'm not a train person. It's not my style," John Henry had told him.

"Well, you can do it; just pay attention and observe everything," William had told his father as if he were a twelve-year-old child.

So, John Henry had followed William's advice reluctantly and with skepticism because John Henry was well aware of his own arrogance: driving a Mercedes coupe; dwelling in a nice apartment, working three jobs; vacationing in warm waters to get away from the arctic chill of winter weather. But still, he was not a snob. He saw himself as a part of the struggling middle class. He hated snobbish Black people because they didn't think white people saw them as "niggers" too. Furthermore, white snobs cloaked in liberalism and Southern hospitality really got under his skin. They believed they were so helpful, compassionate, and salvific.

"But the white conservatives are the worse," he thought to himself.

At the station, the rich mingled with the poor in a transient fusion of economic, social, and educational liminality. Outside of the Powell Street Station, some went back to multimillion-dollar homes while others went back to sleeping on the sidewalk. Some went to their six-figure salary positions while others returned to holding signs that read "ARMY VETERAN. NEED HELP. GIVE ME A DOLLAR" or "HOMELESS. NEED A MEAL." Was this because there appeared to be some "fusion of horizons?" John Henry was not sure if this were, in fact, a "fusion of horizons" or a confusion of horizons, where there remained one thing in common for everybody—the trains and the Powell Street Station, just one along the way from San Francisco to Oakland to Berkley.

Black Suffering and Struggle: In Silent Pain

Without words there can be no silence, yet the sheer absence of words is not silence. —Charles H. Long, *Significations: Signs, Symbols, and Images in the Interpretation of Religion*

Some of us who have already begun to break the silence of the night have found that the calling to speak (or preach) is often a vocation of agony, but we must speak. —Martin Luther King Jr.

Whereof one cannot speak, thereof one must be silent. —Ludwig Wittgenstein

And how shall they believe in him of whom they have not heard? And how shall they hear without a preacher? And how shall they preach except they be sent? —Romans 10:14–15

It is important for me to state that the Black preacher is grounded in a theology and philosophy of freedom and liberation that is much more practical than theoretical. As a preacher, the concept of "Silent Pain" resonates in my own life, as well as in the lives of those who have been in the bottom, or what I tend to call "the underside of culture"—from the Middle Passage to American chattel slavery, to Jim Crow, segregation, and beyond. So we are called to preach to human misery—personal pain and collective suffering. As a part of the community and the congregation, the preacher addresses pain and suffering out of their own pain and suffering. It is coming face to face with the painful frailties of the self that helps the preacher reach the people in their pain and suffering. This is the unique, special calling of the Black preacher, and it makes him or her a product of the people.

The preacher creates a critical consciousness by awakening those who have become numb to their pain and suffering. Theirs is a numbness that turns into nihilism and hopelessness unless the preacher intervenes with a word of hope via the sermon, the preached word, a word that must be heard, though some will resist hearing it—shutting up their ears, refusing to come to church, substituting all types of words and individuals for the preached word. But make no mistake about it. The preacher is compelled by their calling from God to help the people hear! Paul asks rhetorically, "And how shall they hear without a preacher?" How can it be? In other words, the preacher enables hearing—no. This is causal. This is fundamental. This is absolute. "How *can* they hear without a preacher?"[1] It's rhetorical, but the intended inference for the reader is this: without the preacher, there would be no hearing. It is the preaching of the word that enables one to hear what I do not want to hear and makes me do what I do not want to do.

In common speech, pain and suffering are indistinct. Bodily aspects of pain can express the meaning of suffering. Nevertheless, bodily pain cannot be shared. Most of the time, pain and suffering are metaphors for each other. In Scripture, Job displays the bodily aspects of pain and suffering. However, preaching is the weekly effort to provide meaning to Black suffering in an environment that devalues the meaning of Blackness. Preaching in silent pain—or, the agony of preaching—is a continued effort to reach the people and speak to transforming them and their condition of existence.

Silent Pain: A Metaphor

Let me speak about the meaning of revelation in my own life—a story about how God works. Three months before I graduated from Virginia Union University, I was called to serve as pastor of Mount Pleasant Baptist Church in Norfolk, Virginia. This call was beyond my wildest imagination. I had said to everybody who would asked me I did not want to be a pastor. That response was theoretical; because until a congregation unanimously calls you (or barely calls you) and offers you a very lucrative compensation package (well, it does not *have* to be lucrative), saying you do not want to pastor a church has no grounding in pragmatism, in everyday reality. Before you are called, your desire and understanding of the pastorate is merely an exercise in speculation and wishful thinking.

The Titustown neighborhood is in the northwest district of Norfolk, a quaint, quiet bedroom community on a busy thoroughfare between Hampton Boulevard and Granby Street. 934 West Little Creek Road. Mount Pleasant Baptist was Samuel DeWitt Proctor's great-grandfather's church—the Reverend Zachariah Hughes—where most of the people worked hard for a living, either in well-to-do white folks' houses or at the nearby Norfolk Naval Base, a monstrous example of American maritime defense.

As soon as I arrived at the church, I met my defining moment as a pastor, social justice proponent, and preaching practitioner.

There was a woman in the church, born and raised there, whose father was a deacon. One of her brothers was a deacon, and two additional brothers were trustees. The family was embedded in the church and community. The woman, Corine Braxton Brooks, had been trying to get the church—the church where she had been baptized—to understand God had called her to preach ten years or more before I had arrived as the young new pastor. The officers of the church had refused to budge or to act on her call to preach. Before my arrival, the pastors had dodged the issue as untenable and even unbiblical in their conservative, evangelical view. This was in 1976, and this issue of licensing Black women to preach was my painful baptism into the pastorate, church doctrine, and Black Baptist church politics.

After many Bible studies, prayer meetings, and deacons' meetings, I recommended to the deacons and trustees, the so-called joint board, that we should license Mrs. Corine Brooks to preach because my understanding of God was that God can call whomever God wants to preach—and that God is a God of justice and love. I cited the prophet Joel who says, "Then afterward I will pour out my spirit on all flesh; your sons and your daughters shall prophesy, your old men shall dream dreams, and your young men shall see visions. Even on the male and female enslaved, in those days, I will pour out my spirit."[2] However, that signature biblical text didn't really matter. Families were split right down the middle, and the all-male deacon board voted 8 to 3 to defeat the motion, to reject the very idea this woman should be licensed to preach the gospel. Additionally, the Tidewater Metro Baptist Ministers' Conference was against the idea in fact and in spirit.

As a Black twenty-five-year-old pastor and newly minted liberation preacher and teacher straight out of my classes, as well as using sources on Black theology and Baptist polity, I said to these leaders in the Baptist church that only the congregation had autonomy—not the deacons and trustees, who had been the status quo gatekeepers for many, many years. I told them I was going to be guided by the Holy Spirit and a higher moral authority, and present Mrs. Brooks's name before the entire church to see how the congregation felt about it. The deacons and trustees became furious with me for defying their advice and essentially obviating their vote and their misguided, hegemonic church authority. They felt they represented the views of the people, as if they were government-elected officials. The practice was such that no proposal or recommendation would ever see the light of day if the deacons didn't approve it and advance it forward. Many folks in the church know this story.

The church meeting was contentious and filled with suspense and high drama, like one of Tyler Perry's movies or plays. In the end, my preaching efforts forced the congregation to come to grips with licensing this woman to preach. And with seeing the issue as one of love, justice, and fairness—but particularly love, because justice and fairness are always forms of love. And I, as the pastor/preacher, could not be silent because preaching demands we speak, especially in the face of injustice, and more importantly, when the church confuses and equates itself with God.

As one of my first public acts as a pastor was to license a woman to preach the gospel against the will and advice of male leadership and female laity, this firsthand experience of advocacy and the struggle for justice form my point of departure in discussing women preachers from the perspective of the painful struggle to preach.

Their story is a reflection of silent pain. An individual's silent pain, the community's silent pain, the church's silent pain, and my pain, all wrapped up in one. This metaphor brings to the forefront how devastating silent pain and suffering is for Black humanity. No one goes unscathed. No one gets a pass. No one is free from silent pain.

Silent Pain Defined

Silent pain and suffering cannot be separated from the preaching life. They cannot quell, silence, or mute the preaching voice. In fact, silent pain for Black people is the birthplace of all substantive, transforming, and liberating speech. Although silent pain and suffering are not desired, not requested, and certainly not summoned by the preacher, they are always there. They are ontological traits for the conscious Black preacher. They show up when we wake up. They are part of life, challenges that ambush their target like debilitating predators. They do not respect persons in Black skin.

Silent pain is large and looming. It is dreadful and dismal. It is distressing. However, too much is at stake for pain and suffering to be allowed to silence the prophet and cancel the work of Jesus's suffering and dying on the cross at Calvary.

There is another side of silent pain that must be acknowledged and explored. This side provides us with some semblance of hope and respite. This other side of silent pain is our saving grace. It is in this place that we counterbalance the negativity and evils of society, change our disposition, and help transform the lives of those to whom we preach and minister.

The preacher has a mandate to use this awareness to create balance and sanity for the preaching life and to be engaged by the silent pain, rather than be constrained and restrained by its gripping hand. To be encouraged by it, not floored or knocked down by it. Really, to be empowered by both the silence and the pain.

Breaking the Silence: Preaching as a Vocation of Agony

It is a binding fact that preaching is a complex dialectical enterprise, much like life itself. Preaching is a joy and a sorrow, a high and a low, a constant struggle and a thankless achievement. And then it is more than that. Preaching is a calling unlike any other vocation. Granted, nothing is easy, although many things are made to look easy by the expert practitioners of their disciplines. The preaching gurus and griots often make it look easy to those on the outside, those in the congregation, those who have come to expect a marvel and a miracle whenever they hear certain preachers—Patricia Gould-Champ, Lisa Thompson, Charlotte McSwine-Harris, Demetrius Harris, Audrey Thompson, Deborah Martin, and Debra Haggins, to name a few. But make no mistake about it, these preachers recognize what a daunting task it is to actually preach the word of God, as does anyone who mounts the pulpit with perspective and Pentecostal purpose, holy fear, and fiery fierceness for the word of God. Preaching, as Martin Luther King Jr. says, is to "break the silence of the night," and to find that the calling to speak—that is, to *preach*—is often "a vocation of agony." The implication here is that it is difficult and virtually impossible to be silent, no matter how painful it is, when one has been called to preach to the silence and against the silence.

This is an awesome and awful calling—one from which many of us have sought to flee but to no avail. Like the prophet Jonah, we have tried to distance ourselves from God's calling by going in the opposite direction. That direction only suffices for a short while, because the call to preach persists. It endures. It allows no permanent escape because all efforts to get away from God are temporary and transitory. Ultimately, they are unsuccessful. The same holds for silent pain. It is inescapable for the Black preacher. It is like sin. One can only escape it through death. Preaching is the breaking of the silence, a silence many would want to embrace and many have embraced, but only for a season. To tackle silent pain, to confront silent pain directly, preachers have to continue the struggle to preach. Preaching itself is an obviation of the silence and a mitigation of the pain, although the suffering is deeper.

Jarena Lee: Black Women Licensed by the Holy Ghost

Realities such as the struggle to preach, societal resistance, the bifurcation and shattering of church and community norms, patriarchy, and hierarchy—even church monarchy and all the attendant barriers and roadblocks—come together in unison and almost univocal resolve against preachers. This is particularly true for Black women preachers throughout the nineteenth, twentieth, and twenty-first centuries. The Black Church and its leaders have struggled to embody the meaning and practice of justice and fairness when it comes to advancing Black women preachers in the church, and especially as pastors. We have a long way to go in making the church the headlight rather than the taillight, as Martin Luther King Jr. implored us to do.

Just recently, one of my associate ministers, Joy Carter Minor, a young woman preacher in the tradition of Anna Julia Cooper, lost her eighty-five-year-old mother in Moss Point, Mississippi. Joy is a licensed minister, seminary honor graduate, and preacher of the gospel, and she was asked by her family to preach the sermon for her mother's funeral. Everybody in her family agreed that as the daughter, Joy was the most spiritually and Holy Ghost-gifted person to fulfill this painful and difficult assignment. But as Mark Twain would say, "That ain't the wurst."

The pastor of the church where the funeral was to be held informed Joy and her widower father she *could not* preach from the church's pulpit. Instead, she had to deliver the eulogy from the floor behind a makeshift podium, behind an array of flowers that graced the pulpit and the front of the church. All the male preachers and pastors from far and near sat comfortably in the pulpit while Joy, on the day of her mother's funeral, was relegated to preach from the floor in front of the sanctuary. On top of everything else she was tasked to do that day, Joy had to endure this blatant public humiliation while hundreds of family members and friends sat, watched, and witnessed the Black pastor's and church's act of injustice and ignorance. This was church hierarchy and patriarchy in practice. This was the twenty-first-century in the United States, in the South, in the Black community, in the Black Christian and spiritual family, and in the African Methodist Episcopal church, a church founded by Richard Allen and embraced by the likes of Bishop Henry McNeil Turner and other stalwarts in the fight for justice and liberation. And yet, that fight still did not readily include Black female preachers, the daughters of Zion, the "Daughters of Thunder," as Bettye Collier Thomas describes these women struggling to preach the gospel.[3]

As it did for Tamar in the book of Genesis, pain should move us to action. And action should lead to justice, no matter how subversive. Sometimes the prevailing social system has to be bypassed or turned on its head. It must be disrupted, which is exactly what these women did to preach the gospel.

The earliest known Black female preacher, named Elizabeth, was born enslaved in 1766. She was a forerunner to Jarena Lee, Julia A. J. Foote, Harriet Baker, and a phalanx of other nineteenth-, twentieth-, and twenty-first-century preachers. Since Elizabeth's example, there have been no easy and pain-free claims for Black women seeking to preach the gospel. And yet, there has been no barrier wide, tall, or dense enough to mute the voices of those Black women preachers, gifted by the Spirit, who believed God called them to preach. Again, "Women imbued with the doctrine of holiness believed that no man or institution could sanction their right to preach, that this was the sole prerogative of God."[4] Nevertheless, the painful struggle to preach was felt at the deepest levels of human existence, often causing these women to choose between the call of the Holy Spirit to "go preach," and those forbidding and discouraging them to preach the gospel— their families, the established churches, and the church doctrines that oppressed women. The power of the gospel inevitably prevailed at great costs, personal sacrifice, and pain. It was a pain not too silent, but not too loud, either.

Having been a pastor all of my adult life, I'm surrounded by women preachers. My wife Demetrius is a preacher; my sister-in-law Charlotte is a preacher/pastor; and I have three first cousins—Jean, Carolyn, and Juanita—who are preachers. My cousins and I were raised in the shadow of my grandmother's house where singing, praying, preaching were a part of our daily spiritual diet. I say this to tip my hat in praise of those women who continue the struggle, who continue to be licensed by the Holy Ghost. These women realize the sacrifices made by the nineteenth- and twentieth-century Black women who chose to preach by any means necessary in ages of thick patriarchy and abject hostility from husbands, bishops, elders, pastors, and Black churches of every doctrine, denomination, and juridical order. In her sermon "Christian Perfection," Julia Foote says:

> We may be debarred entrance to many pulpits (as some
> of us now are) and stand at the door or on the street cor-
> ner in order to preach to men and women. No difference
> when or where, we must preach the whole gospel.[5]

This same spirit is echoed by Jarena Lee, who said, "If a man may preach, because the Savior died for him, why not the woman? Seeing he died for her also."[6]

Jarena Lee's bold, brave, and clear thinking as relates to preaching forged her way into ministry, which occurred in the most forward way possible. While watching a male preacher fumbling and struggling in the pulpit, searching for the right word and scrambling for clarity, Jarena Lee, by the power of the spirit, stood, interrupted the faltering preacher, and completed the sermon when he could not. This daring act of aggressive preaching, done against the wishes of her bishop, provided the impetus and evidence for her to be licensed by Bishop Richard Allen, who had previously disallowed such action. Jarena Lee identified with the struggle to preach and articulated the struggle to preach in her bold action. After receiving her call to preach, she said:

> I took a text and preached in my sleep. I thought there stood before me a great multitude while I expounded to them the things of religion. So violent were my exertions, and so loud were my exclamations, that I awoke from the sound of my own voice, which also awoke the family of the house where I resided.[7]

Wow! She was preaching in her sleep! Notice she said she took a text, though she was considered illiterate. Illiterate or not, don't forget to take a text. That's at least a sign that you're trying to preach, that you intend to preach. Lee also says in her autobiography:

> It was now eight years since I had made application to be permitted to preach the gospel, during which time I had only been allowed to exhort, and even this privilege but seldom. This subject now was renewed afresh in my mind; it was as a fire shut up in my bones.[8]

It was a difficult and dangerous enterprise for these women to stand up to those powers that surrounded them. Jarena Lee, Julia Foote, and others knew the call to go preach. Their efforts remind me of Peter and John in their bold preaching, as seen in

Acts. Peter and John embodied what I call preaching dangerously. Scripture records these words:

> So they called them and ordered them not to speak or
> to teach at all in the name of Jesus. But Peter and John
> answered them, "Whether it is right in God's sight to listen
> to you rather than to God, you must judge, for we cannot
> keep from speaking about what we have seen and heard."[9]

It is normal to gravitate toward that which poses no threat, no
harm, no perilous risk. Most of us do not want to cause any con-
troversy, so whatever the perceived road to safety may be, that
is the road we take. The reality is we safeguard ourselves from
whatever may be perceived and construed as dangerous. This
is a very rational, reasonable, and normative way to act. Anything else would be considered reckless and feckless behavior—a
weak, wrongheaded, and worthless way to act. We spend our
lives plotting and planning ways to avoid danger. Had not this
same Simon Peter vehemently and defiantly taken the safe way
out when Jesus was earlier condemned by the chief priests and
the very same Sanhedrin Council? The Scripture says:

> The servant girl, on seeing him, began again to say to
> the bystanders, "This man is one of them," but again he
> denied it. Then after a while the bystanders again said
> to Peter, "Certainly you are one of them; for you are a
> Galilean." But he began to curse, and he swore an oath—
> "Damn it, didn't I say I do not know this man you are
> talking about?"[10]

It seems to me we are calculating and cautious in our speaking if
we say anything at all.

Notice now in the scripture text, Peter and John were arrested
and brought before the court, the same court that had earlier
wrongly convicted Jesus. They were now standing accused of an

act that began with healing the lame man at the gate of the temple, the man who came daily to beg for money. Peter would have
been okay if they had simply said, "I have no silver and gold," and
stopped there. But Peter, speaking dangerously, said, "But what I
have I give to you; in the name of Jesus of Nazareth, stand up and
walk." The man had asked for money—not to walk, not to stand—
but money. So now this speaking and preaching about Jesus has
gotten Peter and John arrested and landed them in jail until the
next day. When the council saw the boldness of Peter and John, it
recognized they had been with Jesus, and the man who had been
healed was standing there with them.

When folk recognize you have been with Jesus, that is enough
to get you in deep trouble. Being with Jesus is a dangerous thing.
The antagonists conferred together and decided there was not
much Peter and John could say about the healing because everybody had witnessed it, so they called them back in and charged
them not to speak or teach at all in the name of Jesus. But Peter
and John answered them, "Whether it is right in God's sight to
listen to you rather than to God, you must judge, for we cannot
keep from speaking about what we have seen and heard." This
sounds like Jarena Lee and Julia Foote to me. They possessed the
identical defiant spirit as Peter and John.

Speaking and preaching dangerously means yesterday's
cowardice can indeed become today's courage. Instead of cow-
ering and capering to a compromise, Peter and John faced the
court with dignified defiance—dignified because they caused no
loud scene, no inflammatory or rhetorical acrobatics, no cussing and complaining about the verdict. They stood there quietly
with rugged determination and confident faith; they indicated
the prescribed silence was irrational and really impossible. Their
previous cowardly behavior in the face of Jesus's death had been
transformed into a courage almost beyond belief. Yesterday's fail-
ure had become today's triumph; yesterday's denial had become

today's determination; yesterday's dissing had become today's daring deed; yesterday's tepid tiptoeing around their association with Jesus had become today's testimony—powerful, defiant, and dangerous. "We cannot keep from speaking about what we have seen and heard."

Wittgenstein's aphorism is right: "Whereof one cannot speak, thereof one must be silent."[11] When silence is not an option, one has to speak. One has to speak, even preach, in silent pain. Just like one cannot easily stop a bird in the middle of its song, and neither can the testimony of saints be quelled or quieted in the presence of our adversaries.

Every morning recently, as spring continues to unfold and the joy of its speech fills the morning air with melodies—melodies more splendid and more beautiful than the sonatas of Bach, or the symphonies of Beethoven, or the beautiful saxophone playing of Branford Marsalis, or the trumpet of Miles Davis, or the strong voice of Jennifer Hudson, or the sultry and sassy sound of Rihanna—I hear the mockingbirds, the sparrows, or the blue jays giving a concert to the budding plants and the blossoming flowers, to the lilies and the daffodils. These concerts by the larks of the morning are testimonies to the goodness of God. The concerts given by the birds of the air are as glorious as the canvas painted by the lilies of the fields, the azaleas, the roses, the sunflowers. There is no restraining their testimonies. They speak as gloriously as the shining rays of the sun. They speak as clearly as the colors of the rainbow. They speak as loudly as the crashing sounds of thunder and lightning. When silence is not an option—not only do the birds sing a new hallelujah chorus as powerful as Handel's Messiah; not only do flowers paint a picture of the earth more beautiful than van Gogh, Picasso, Jerome Jones, or Adam Pendleton; not only does nature's bloom offer a loud testimony to the glory of God—but the preacher must also speak truth to power. When silence is not an option, one must declare, like the great reformer Martin Luther, "Here I stand, I can do no other, so help me God."[12] When silence is not an option, one must speak to the mountain and tell it, "Mountain, get out of my way!" When silence is not an option, you, too, must declare like Martin Luther King Jr., "injustice anywhere is a threat to justice everywhere."[13]

Long before Martin Luther King Jr., Fred Shuttlesworth, Fannie Lou Hamer, and Jeremiah Wright preached dangerously, there were Peter and John refusing to bow down to the Sanhedrin; long before Polycarp and Saint Jerome, there were Peter and John, preaching dangerously. Before Bishop Origen and Bishop Augustine, there were Peter and John, preaching dangerously; long before Nat Turner and Henry Highland Garnet, there were Peter and John. Long before Black Harry Hosier and the long line of slave preachers; long before Sojourner Truth, Jarena Lee, Clara Thompson, and Black women speaking out against patriarchy and paternalism, there were Peter and John. And yet long before Peter and John, there was Jesus of Nazareth, in whose name they preached dangerously. Jesus spoke healing to the lame man at the temple gate. Long before Peter and John, Jesus had already healed the sick and given sight to the blind; long before Peter and John, Jesus had raised Lazarus, telling Mary and Martha, "I am the resurrection and the life." Jesus had set the example of preaching dangerously by setting the captives free, proclaiming liberty to the oppressed, and preaching that the kingdom of God was at hand in him. Peter and John had been with Jesus and they could not keep from speaking of what they had seen and heard.

Sometimes, one may not want to speak because doing so may land them on the wrong side of popular culture, or even in jail. You may want to keep silent because you have been warned it might get you put out of your church or estranged from your family. It might get you tossed off the faculty, fired like Du Bois and Cornel West. You do not want to speak because the pain is too great, but the issues the Black preacher faces are even greater than the silent pain. They are too great to keep quiet, so we must break the silence and recognize preaching is a "vocation of agony, but we must speak." Ultimately, doing so might get you beaten and flogged, or crucified like Jesus Christ.

Preachers are called to be vigilant in the struggle to preach because of the many realities and distractions that tend to prevent Black people from surviving and thriving as a whole. The time has passed for us to be excited about a few reaching great altitudes. It is time now for the masses to experience what the Constitution has failed to provide Black people in a nation they have made possible with blood, sweat, and tears. If Black people are to aim for quality education, if Black adults are to show young people there is a way that is not paved with drugs, violence, and sexual promiscuity resulting in wayward, undisciplined children and struggling single parents, then we need to become employers of our people, providing salaries, health care, and healthful nutrition. Preaching is our opportunity to move life forward for Black people. Our preaching holds the possibility of creating a new world. Forward preaching is the only thing for us to do in light of silent pain. We must preach when pain is silent, and we must preach while we suffer.

Preaching in Silent Pain

We often think of pain and suffering as identical—and if not identical, then as closely related phenomena, as feelings directly related to the subjective nature of the self and particularly related to the human body. Indeed, we are all born through the gripping clutches of pain and agony, usually months after a sexual act of enormous joy and pleasure. From certain perspectives, pain is the dark side or the underside of pleasure.

Preaching, too, is thought to be a pleasurable experience. At least, the act of preaching almost has the same effect as the sexual act in that its biological and theological nature is an act of creation. As a preaching teacher, I find my students are sensitive and protective of their newly created "child," their baby, their sermon. They have given birth to this baby through some type of struggle, through personal pain and suffering. It is an agonizing enterprise in many respects, and metaphorically like childbirth, which I understand is both painful and pleasurable simultaneously. This newly created sermon, this result of praying, of a paradoxical dialectic and labor; this culmination of reading and study, this "offering" to God, the church, and the world community, is presented with exegetical notes; textual references; guesses at meanings; spiritual and divine interventions; theological, hermeneutical, and personal struggles—and then it is subjected to the keen, critical, and, hopefully, compassionate eye of the homiletics teacher who systematically begins to deconstruct and disassemble the student's holy creation. Their sermon. Their baby, often made with love, compassion, and prayer, is subject to painful unmaking and remaking. But the truth is, that's really how great sermons are made. They are formed and burnished by fire, by the pain and struggle of hard work, as well as strong faith in the grace and mercy of God. Sometimes, it is the *unmaking* of one's sermon that can result in its salvation, its life, its redemption at the hands of serious, compassionate critique that leads to rethinking and rewriting. Our sermons often have to be reworked, reshaped, and remade, which reminds me of the message from the prophet Jeremiah.

The Shaping Hands of God

The Lord told me to go to the pottery shop, and when you get there, I will tell you what to say to the people. I went there and saw the potter making clay pots on his pottery wheel. And whenever the clay would not take the shape he wanted, he would change his mind and form it into some other shape. Then the Lord told me to say: People of Israel, I, the Lord, have power over you, just as a potter has power over clay.[14]

We all are products of a commodified culture—quick to embrace the alluring and often lucrative and luscious ways of life. We are bombarded by a barrage of soundbites, from TV commercials about everything under the sun to deceptive political slogans, such as "Make America Great Again" or "Change Has Come to America." From the day we are born, we are molded and shaped—in our identity, in our personality, in our behavior, in resiliency. We do try to shape our children, to a large degree, by the same standards that have shaped us, and many of us are shaped by popular culture, entertainment, and the ways and wisdom of this world. Our young people love to listen to and mimic the profane language that seeps and surges through the songs they hear and sing. When they love to hear rappers talk about fondling and freaking, our youth are also indicating that profanity and degradation "don't mean nothing." Well, something is shaping the mindset of our young people and causing resistance to God, just as was true for the people of Judah during Jeremiah's time. All language matters, like Black lives matter. Language is our most formidable form of communication.

Whether it is Drake, J. Cole, Cardi B, or Jay-Z and Beyoncé—these are the idols of our youth, the spin doctors of our culture, the ones whom our children crave and love. Today, it is not just the youth who are shaped and shorn by the often-shallow things of the world. Everything shapes all of us—everything except for the most important and critical influence of all. We listen and take advice from every palm reader and soothsayer, every car salesperson and insurance person, every scientist and philosopher, every marriage counselor and drug counselor, every tax consultant, every lawyer and doctor—all shaping our bodies, our minds, our opinions, our practices, our words, our deeds, our beliefs, our thoughts, our ideas of right and wrong, our understanding of love and hate, and justice and injustice. Everybody is shaping us except God—except the word of God, except the will of God, except the voice of God, except the shaping hands of God. Jeremiah, the great prophet, was despised, denied, and "dissed" by the religious and political leaders of his time. Jeremiah felt God held kings like Jehoiakim in low esteem. Even Jeremiah's family turned their backs on him. Although he was warned by God[15] that he would face an uphill task, Jeremiah did not think it would be that painful. Nevertheless, almost everybody was against him. People were hostile to him and his preaching. He was unsuccessful and unpopular, and his word went unheeded by a "whole heap of folk." Eventually, he felt God had let him down.

In this scene from our scripture text, Jeremiah visits the potter's house because God tells him where to go. Jeremiah is a tough prophet, a prophet under siege, one who teaches us that God can make right what is not right. God does not necessarily turn the imperfect into the perfect, but God does turn it into something else. God is not overly concerned with perfection and flawlessness and faultlessness because God can transform the flawed, the faulty, the failed, the broken, the battered, the cracked, and the unbalanced—all that which is without symmetry and centeredness: "Whenever a piece of pottery turned out imperfect, he would take the clay and turn it to something else."[16] God, you see, is a "something else"-making God. The record is our witness! Come here, Shadrach, Meshach, and Abednego. Come, fiery furnace. God can take flesh and bones placed in a burning fire and reverse the laws of physics and chemistry to transform a fiery furnace into something else. Turning something into something else is not new to God because God is a God who can make right again that which didn't turn out the way God wanted it to be.

Some of us came here the "long way." Indeed, we are imperfect, cracked, and broken. Some of us have struggled to be treated with dignity and fairness; some of us have almost been broken by the turbulent winds that blow even in the churches—winds of indifference and denial, winds even of corruption and hate. You used to be this way or that, but God has made you into something else. God has reshaped you. God has reworked you from a shy, stammering stutterer to a strong stalwart standing firmly in defense of the gospel. God has taken our imperfections, our weaknesses, our innumerable flaws and failures, and turned us all into something else—preachers of the gospel—the John Chrysostoms, the Gardner Taylors, the Martin Luther Kings, the Jarena Lees, and the Anna Julia Coopers of the world.

The divine potter also has divine discretion. God is a discretionary God. God can change God's mind. The mind of God is not static:

> Then the word of the Lord came to me: Can I not do with you, O house of Israel, just as this potter has done? says the Lord. Just like the clay in the potter's hand, so are you in my hand, O house of Israel. At one moment I may declare concerning a nation or a kingdom, that I will pluck up and break down and destroy it, but if that nation, concerning which I have spoken, turns from its evil, I will change my mind about the disaster that I intended to bring on it.[17]

God's exercise of God's option to cause chaos in our lives—to uproot, to breakdown, to destroy—is withdrawn as a direct result of turning away from evil, of repentance. Israel's evil, her lack of justice and righteousness, her disinterest in the poor and the hungry—those things led to being uprooted and destroyed.

Beloved brothers and sisters, God is a God who can withdraw God's threat and revoke his promise all at the same time.

Not only that, God can do even more: "but if that nation, concerning which I have spoken, turns from its evil, I will change my mind about the disaster that I intended to bring on it."[18] Not only can God withdraw God's heart and revoke God's promise, but because God has a contingency plan that is dependent on the way we act, God can do something else. God can move from withdrawing God's threat to implementing God's promise. God is the architect of just change. God is the designer of divine discriminating discretion. God is the originator of free will. God can do whatever God wants to do—with me and with all of us.

God's hands shaped all of these forces and folk, all of these influences upon Judah, upon the people and land, upon kings and princesses. God's hands shaped the earth[19] and God's hands formed the mountains and the valleys, and made the rough places plain. And not just the mountains, God shaped the moon and the stars too. God formed us from the dust also. God's hands shaped our eyes and nose and mouth, our legs and arms, our knees and hips—and then after our bodies were shaped big and small, wide and tall, slim and trim, God's hands began to shape our personalities, our attitudes, our dispositions, our smiles, our joy and happiness. God's hands can shape a nobody into a somebody. God's hands can turn a pot-smoking, alcohol-drinking, drug-using, midnight brawler—a broken, dejected, messed-up parent or sibling—into a lover of the word, a teacher, a preacher, a doer of the word. God's hands can heal and help give hope. God's hands can work miracles in our lives, and God has done so through his Son, Jesus, the ultimate embodiment of God's shaping hands. Jesus on the hill of Golgotha, after being bruised and treated mean; Jesus, the Son of God, the Prince of Peace, the savior of the world; Jesus who says when he is about to die, "Father, into your hands I commend my spirit."[20] In God's hands, our pain is transformed into a promising proclamation.

Preaching Is When Silence Is Not Silent

Preaching in silent pain is at once a metaphor and an irony, two literary terms surrounded by the philosophical and the medicinal. It is a double-sided irony because while silence presumes speech, preaching is not presumption. It is speech personified, embodied speech, yet it is not without its own silence. By this I mean that preaching is a testimony to silence, and particularly a testimony to pain and to suffering in the Black community. It is a crying out, a yelling and screaming, if necessary, in response to Black people's pain and suffering. "It is an inverting of that which is endemic to Black life—suffering. It is doing what Jarena Lee, Julia Foote, and Maria Stewart did in prophesying as female Christian preachers."[21] Black preaching and pain are a result of systemic evil and hatred. Silent pain is pain nevertheless, and "preaching in silent pain" is an oxymoronic linguistic phrase that causes us to question the stringing together of these words and ask, "Is there such a thing as preaching in silent pain?" By all means! We know the pain is there; it cannot be fully ignored. To be Black is to be in pain every day. For example, my pain is unbearable some days, and my suffering is exacerbated by the fact I must preach anyway. Because I go on, some people naively assume I am not in pain. But my pain never goes away completely. It subsides, ebbs and flows, but when I go to sleep at night, it is there. When I wake up, it is there, weighing me down like a ton of bricks. Yet I must speak. I must preach.

This is also a metaphor because preaching is not really about silent pain; rather, it is about suffering—Black suffering, which is endemic to Black American life. To be Black in America and the world today is similar to being Black when Ralph Ellison wrote his classic novel *Invisible Man*. Very little has changed. The invisibility of Black people is a reality the Black preacher must always address, as is the persistence of their suffering. This is complicated by the fact that in America, Black suffering is *not* considered suffering—not physically, sociologically, psychologically, or theologically. It is considered something else by white America, and even by the Black preacher who refuses to see everyone around them is in some type of pain that has become suffering. After a while, persistent, catastrophic pain becomes suffering. If 250 years of slavery and millions of deaths—or "faces at the bottom of the well," as Derrick Bell describes them—is not suffering, then what is?[22] Those who are looking up at us from the bottom of the well and the floor of the Atlantic Ocean are expressing the phenomenon of Black suffering with the silence of death, a death brought on by the Transatlantic slave trade. Slavery was 250 years of silent pain and suffering.

Charles H. Long says, "The fact that silence presupposes words is what gives it this ironic twist. Without words there can be no silence, yet the sheer absence of words is not silence."[23] If silence is more than the absence of words, then preaching is more than the presence of words. Words alone do not a sermon make. Preaching has to be about something, something creative, something important, and something critical to Black life. As a pastor, I have become responsible to the community, not just to the Second Baptist Church. The position of pastor and preacher is a double responsibility in which silent pain is more pronounced and weighs more heavily upon the preacher's body and soul.

The Black preacher has to understand that pain is speaking the unspeakable. Pain is a scientific notion. Victor Anderson says, "We feel pain; we undergo suffering. We can't medicate suffering."[24] Pain is medicinal. Most doctors do not even know how to address one's pain, so we know the preacher "don't know," either. The preacher has to address suffering, which is something medicine cannot do. Pain and suffering are related but not identical. Any effort to make them the same, to conflate them, trivializes people in pain and diminishes the pandemic nature of Black suffering. It is only deep, systemic, and pathological pain that rises to the level of suffering. It is not the person who stubs their toe or has a toothache. Pain ameliorated or soothed by medicine is a type of pain that does not usually rise to the level of suffering. What pain and suffering have in common is they both exist and have a relationship with temporality, with time. They are transitory, temporal, and not eternal. Pain can be more transitory than suffering, even though suffering is what may be called "ongoing pain." Both phenomena involve intensity and endurance. A scriptural analog from Romans is, "Where sin increased, grace abounded all the more."[25] So, where pain increases, suffering abounds all the more; and where suffering abounds, preaching to this suffering must abound all the more. This means Black preaching—that is, preaching in silent pain—does not have the luxury of keeping silent, but instead must "all the more" address the suffering that engulfs the Black church and community. Preaching the gospel frees us to see a new way of looking at pain and suffering. Again, Paul says, "I consider that the suffering of this present time cannot compare to the glory that will be revealed to us."[26] We still await the revelation and its glory! So, more than struggling to preach, we have to struggle against the odds to preach and to survive as a people, as a church, and as a community. The gospel writer Mark speaks of Jesus preaching in silent pain and the preacher's struggle against the odds when he writes:

> And the crowd came together again, so that they could not even eat. When his family heard it, they went out to restrain him, for people were saying, "He has gone out of his mind." And the scribes who came down from Jerusalem said, "He has Beelzebub, and by the ruler of the demons, he casts out demons." And he called them to him, and spoke to them in parables, "How can Satan cast out Satan? If a kingdom is divided against itself, that kingdom

cannot stand. And if a house is divided against itself, that house will not be able to stand. And if Satan has risen up against himself and is divided, he cannot stand, but his end has come. But no one can enter a strong man's house and plunder his property without first tying up the strong man; then indeed the house can be plundered.[27]

There are times when we find ourselves at odds with the world and with everybody around us. It is not that we set out to be different, or that we make any special plans to be different, or that we have made any premeditated effort to be out of synchrony with our families, friends, church members, or leaders in society. But it does happen. Sometimes, we feel like we are all alone. As a preacher, I often feel out of synchrony with popular religious culture and in conflict with those who seem to have deified certain elements of tradition, elements that have had little or no significant impact on our liberation and freedom. At times, we feel alone because those around us seem to be so much a part of the status quo and so comfortable with "things as they are" while we are not.

I imagine this is how Rosa Parks felt in 1955 when her feet, body, and mind had grown so weary that, without malice aforethought, she took a seat on that bus in Montgomery, Alabama. When the white bus driver asked her to move to the back, she refused to be intimidated. She was not merely alone in her defiance. In 1955, a Black person could have been skinned alive, hanged from a tree, or lynched in any number of ways in Alabama for sitting on a bus while a white person stood. It was the *de facto* law, immoral and evil. Both Black and white people on that bus probably thought this woman was crazy. All of the Black folk on that bus had experienced the heavy and hateful hand of Jim Crow and the strong and stifling hand of the Southern tradition of hate and evil, masked by its façade of gentility and hospitality. They were likely baffled by the brazen behavior of this woman. In the twinkling of an eye, Rosa Park's bold resistance to the pressures of conformity overcame the expectation of torporific behavior, behavior tamed by time and trouble. She was like Jarena Lee who stood in the church and boldly interrupted the preacher and expounded upon his text because he "seemed to have lost the Spirit."[28]

There are countless examples of folk who have been at odds with the prevailing powers, from Socrates to Martin Luther King Jr. There are those among you reading today who feel alone, at odds with your families, with those in your workplace, or even with those in your clubs, groups, and auxiliaries—all because you are trying to do the will of God, trying to live right, trying to do right, trying to bring about justice and fairness.

I believe seeking to do God's will and practicing Jesus's teachings can put you at odds with your family, friends, and the world, as Jesus was at odds with the ways of the world. He was always struggling against those whose understanding of God's will conflicted with his own. As a matter of fact, throughout Mark's Gospel, we read of clashes of conscience and purpose between Jesus and the religious authorities, between a new spiritual and social order and the religious and social status quo. The Pharisees, scribes, and Herodians struggle to preserve their present state of religious affairs, and Jesus struggles to be himself—which puts him in constant conflict with the religious establishment.

I do not think his is a struggle *within*, but rather a struggle *against*. It is not simply an internal personal struggle, as perhaps Søren Kierkegaard experienced in choosing between his love of Regine and his love for God; it is a struggle of good against evil. It is not a struggle between two equal goods of differing personal interest; it is a struggle against principalities and powers.

It is a struggle against our tendency to lie; not our simple denial of the truth but, as Martin Buber writes, inventing "something in the place of truth."[29] This is a struggle against a lie, a struggle against spiritual treachery, because, as Buber notes, "in a lie, the spirit practices treason against itself."[30] People have their own way of lying, however innocently or maliciously. The Scribes, Pharisees, and other antagonists in Mark's Gospel tend to deny the truth. They do it through accusation, "through questioning in their hearts,"[31] through silence and conspiracy. Jesus faces a continuous struggle to be who he is, especially when the folk around him often fail to understand him. This story reminds me of our enslaved forebears who had to struggle just to stay alive. They had to struggle against the odds just to learn how to read and write.

This struggle for justice in society is also internal. The struggle against the forces of evil, against the prevailing religious and sociopolitical powers, against the establishment, against tradition, against any normative ethic or any established moral value, entails a personal struggle—an internal struggle against fear and loneliness, against pain and suffering. This is a struggle of the soul, a struggle of the conscience.

Black Americans have had to struggle against the odds in this country. From the slave ship to the battleship, from slavery to freedom, from the back of the white church to the brush harbor, from Jim Crow laws to the first Civil Rights bill, from the North to the South, from east to west, from GEDs to PhDs to no degrees at all, all of us have had to struggle. That is why I am bothered by those people who talk as if self-help is something new. Black folk have always struggled to pick themselves up while law and custom kept knocking them back down. My mother, father, grandparents, uncles, and aunts worked all of their lives, helping themselves and the members of our families in the process. I have sense enough to know I did not get to where I am on my own. I had some help from many people. To paraphrase poet Langston Hughes, "Life for most of us ain't been no crystal stair."[32] We have had it hard. Though the odds have been against us, through the struggle against evil and envy, against injury and ignorance, against injustice and indifference, against all that would keep us from doing God's will, all that would keep us silent—we have remained devoted, dedicated, and determined to speak and do what is right, just, and fair. Even if we must stand alone against those odds, we know we must be able to stand on the word of God.

What does it mean for us to struggle?

As we struggle, we need not allow others to define who we are. Our ontological status—our being, our "is-ness," the stuff of our existence—is not determined by what other folk are saying. Mark 3:20 says, "And when his family heard it, they went out to seize him, for people were saying, 'He is beside himself.'" People were saying Jesus was strange, that he was crazy. No doubt his relatives believed he was out of his mind and needed to be restrained. This is so much like the experience of Jarena Lee, Sojourner Truth, and Maria Stewart, who people thought were crazy because women were not supposed to preach. We can often deal with what people at a distance say about us, those who know us only from what they have heard. There was always much gossip and hearsay about Jesus. I can imagine people wondered what made him tick, how he could speak with authority and teach as no other teacher could. People were curious and probably talked often about his fellowship with sinners and tax collectors, his association with those on the other side of culture, those at whom high society sneered, who were the subject of gossip and jokes. People were also curious about his healing the lame. So, these people said he was beside himself, acting crazy.

When you strive with every fiber in your body and soul to do God's will, some folk will say you, too, are crazy, beside yourself. They will do everything in their power to restrain you. To silence you. I am sure Jesus felt some anguish, some silent pain, when even his family sought to restrain him because of what the people were saying, but that did not stop him from preaching and doing God's will. The will of God cannot be restrained; the embodiment of God's love cannot be restrained. The personification of his goodness, the grace that feeds the hungry and heals the sick, cannot be restrained. Jesus cannot be restrained. You cannot hold Jesus back; you cannot check his power; you cannot suppress the power of the Holy Spirit; you cannot shackle, bridle, inhibit, limit, or restrict Jesus. He cannot be restrained; and when his power overcomes us and we submit to his will, we, too, cannot be restrained.

Sometimes, when my heart is heavy and tears well up in my eyes, I struggle not to cry. But when I think about how good God has been to me, I cannot help myself. The tears just flow. Then, I know what the old saints meant when they sang, "I said I wasn't gonna tell nobody, but I just couldn't keep it to myself,"[33] or what the prophet Jeremiah meant when he said, "there is something like a burning fire shut up in my bones."[34] Even those who are closest to us cannot be allowed to define us nor restrain us from telling the truth or helping those in need. Jesus knew he was intimately tied to God. What the people were saying reflected their lack of understanding. It showed how little they knew about God's power. The people could only describe what they thought, felt, and discerned. What they described as being "beside himself" was a Jesus who *was* himself, demonstrating the attributes of God to both friend and foe.

In struggling against the odds, we should recognize good and evil are always in conflict. Jesus teaches us a lesson in logic in Mark 3:20–27 by showing the absurdity of the Scribes' assertion he is possessed by Beelzebub, the prince of demons. Think about it. If he were possessed by Satan, then he would be Satan, and Satan cannot cast himself out. To think such is absurd. Only good can cast out evil. The battle with Satan is a battle against wickedness, a battle of good against bad, of love against hate, of truth against lie, of justice against injustice. This is a battle not of Satan against Satan, but of Jesus against Satan. This is a battle of the will of God against the will of the world. This is a conflict with Satan by Jesus himself. By virtue of who he is, Jesus is always in conflict with Satan. He is always in a battle against evil, even when good is wrongly called evil. But we need not get discouraged, because good will always win out over evil. It may not always be evident, it may not be immediately understood, but it is ultimately so. Only God, through Jesus Christ, has the power to bind evil forces in this world. Satan and evil may be strong, but Jesus is stronger.

Struggling against the odds means sometimes your burdens are heavy. Sometimes, your feet are tired and worn. Sometimes, your friends and family may turn their backs on you. Sometimes, you may cry in the lonely hours of the night. But you are not alone, because Jesus has already struggled against the odds, and the odds have been overcome. He has struggled against evil and hate, against sin and death, against principalities and powers, and Jesus has overcome!

However, our struggle endures for the sake of the kingdom, the Black community, and the world at large. Silence has to be confronted and conquered. As preachers, we have to wrap our minds around silence to keep the embers of preaching burning, as preaching is the hope of the world. So while we must deal with silence, we must never be silenced. We cannot be silent. How else will evil and ugliness be addressed? How else will Jesus be lifted up? How else will folk know what the Lord has done for you and for me? My silence and my pain tried to convince me to keep quiet. And for a while—and in the spirit of Black religion—I said, I wasn't gonna tell nobody how the Lord blessed me, how the Lord saved me, how God woke me up this morning, how the

Lord heals me every day. I said to my suffering self that I was not gonna say a mumbling word. I said to myself, "James Henry, keep quiet"; but every time I tried to keep quiet, I felt like the prophet Jeremiah, Martin Luther King Jr., Joseph Lowery, and Ella Baker. There was a fire within me, a yearning and a trembling in my soul. Something within me that made me testify. Holler. Pray. "Thank you. Thank you, Jesus. Thank you, Lord. I tried, but I just couldn't keep it to myself. Pain, yes. Silence, no. If I don't speak, the rocks will cry out. If I keep silent, the wind and the waves will speak with a more awful and disruptive power and demand that the Lord be praised. Great is the Lord, and greatly to be praised. . . ."

The Un-Silent Side
of the Oppressed:
The Gift and Travail of Life

Woe to them who are at ease in Zion. —Amos 6:1

Some proclaim Christ from envy and rivalry, but others from goodwill. These proclaim Christ out of love, knowing that I have been put here for the defense of the gospel; the others proclaim Christ out of selfish ambition, not sincerely but intending to increase my suffering in my imprisonment. What does it matter? Just this, that Christ is proclaimed in every way, whether out of false motives or true; and in that I rejoice. Yes, and I will continue to rejoice. —Philippians 1:15–18

"So you dislike Negroes, Mr. Bellew?" But her amusement was at her thought, rather than her words.

John Bellew gave a short denying laugh. "You got me wrong there, Mrs. Redfield. Nothing like that at all. I don't dislike them, I *hate* them." —Nella Larsen, *Passing*

Everything related to silence finds expression in words. Silence presupposes words, and herein lies the irony. And so, in a sense, the Apostle Paul is profound and yet not so profound when he says the whole of creation groans and moans with sighs that are too deep for words.[1] If silence presupposes words, as Charles Long and Maurice Merleau-Ponty assert, then the irony of silence is such that speech and silence are, indeed, coterminous. They are both dimensions of each other. They are interrelated, such that all speech is surrounded by silence. And sometimes, just sometimes, it would be a blessing from the high God of the universe and the God of our ancestors for the Black preacher, for those who have something uninformed and silly to say, to keep silent—especially if what is being spoken is gibberish grounded in some form of self-serving carnival-like behavior. Occasionally, the preacher should not only let the surrounding silence envelop words, but also let the silence speak to silence. This means if the preacher is grossly unprepared to address the meaning and interpretation of the text and the social context of Black people who are in pain—if the preacher has nothing but hacks and hums to share with the people engrossed in human suffering—it is better, no, it is "more better," for the preacher to keep silent.

In the face of a society that dehumanizes Black people and murders them at will—as if we still operated under the stifling hand of the slavocracy—the Black preacher needs to be silent if he or she does not call this terrific and horrific reality into question. And if the preacher is not addressing these terrors in the sermon on Sunday, then the preacher is, in fact, silent, although while yelling and screaming and making noise that is more deafening and more deleterious than absolute silence. *This* is painful silence. It is not Black preaching. Its loud and boisterous sound can only justly be called noise, similar to the words of the prophet Amos, who painfully declares, "Take away from me the noise of your songs; I will not listen to the melody of your harps."[2]

Charles Long, the religion historian, asks in his book *Ellipsis,* "What more can be said after Buchenwald or after a flight to the moon?"[3] Well, a lot more can and must be said. The Enlightenment did not enlighten and the postmodern is not "post" anything when the suffering of Black people is just as palpable and pandemic today as it was one hundred years ago. Slavery has morphed into the mass incarceration of Black people. The lynching tree—a staple of Black life in the South—is now felt in every state, from the murder of Trayvon Martin in Sanford, Florida, to the murder of thirty-six unarmed Black males around the nation in 2015. The 2014 death of eighteen-year-old Michael Brown in Ferguson, Missouri, has increased activism against this epidemic of murdering Black people, but we preachers need to say more in the sermon to raise the level of consciousness in the Black church and community. There can be no silence. Preaching about these social, economic, and public health tragedies is mandatory. This means that silent pain is not an option! King was right in saying "preaching is a vocation of agony." The sermon must go forth. Preaching must go forth. Painful, yes. Silent, no! Long says:

> Modern Western cultures in the midst of their tremendous creativity and noisiness find themselves confronting an awesome silence—a silence that cannot be banished by the clamor of activity. It is the wonder and monstrosity of our deeds which has evoked this mood of silence.[4]

Long is right about this "mood of silence" provoked by monstrous and evil deeds, from slavery to Auschwitz, to racism, to white supremacy. But it is not enough to theorize about this. Long continues:

> The great language of creativity which we used to subdue and explain or to exploit the world has been placed in jeopardy; its mighty words are overwhelmed by the silence of the pauses between the words.[5]

Clearly, these omniscient "all-knowing" intellectuals of the West, capable of explaining away anything and everything with their "mighty words," have never been fully trusted by Black people. Suspicion has always been there although rarely verbalized or expressed. The language of freedom was also the language of oppression, hailing forth from the same Jeffersonian lips, the same duplicitous bodies writing long treatises on self-evident truths, equality, freedom, liberty, and justice for all, while at the same time, out of the same mouth, came hatred and evil.[6] The Black preacher, more often than not, refused to be silent in the face of this ugliness and evil. The preacher has often been the lone wolf among Black professionals in the fight for justice and fairness. This is because the preacher works for Black people in the community and church, and not for the power brokers and policy makers in corporate America.

Dr. King said it so eloquently over fifty years ago when he intoned that speaking and preaching is, indeed, a vocation of agony, an agony that must never be silenced.

In this vocation of agony, our new twenty-first-century mandate has to be a war on mediocrity in the pulpit, in the church, in our homes, and in our public schools, colleges and universities, and communities. We have to fight against the silent pain by speaking and preaching, encouraging Black people, and creating a spirit of questioning and excellence in our people throughout the world. The biblical story of Esther teaches about excellence and the subversive Queen Vashti.

An Invitation to Excellence

This happened in the days of Ahasuerus, the same Ahasuerus who ruled over 127 provinces from India to Ethiopia. In those days when King Ahasuerus sat on his royal throne in the citadel of Susa, in the third year of his reign, he gave a banquet for all his officials and ministers. The army of Persia and Media and the nobles and governors of the provinces were present, while he displayed the great wealth of his kingdom and the splendor and pomp of his majesty for many days, one hundred eighty days in all. When these days were completed, the king gave for all the people present in the citadel of Susa, both great and small, a banquet lasting for seven days, in the court of the garden of the king's palace. There were white cotton curtains and blue hangings tied with cords of fine linen and purple to silver rings and marble pillars. There were couches of gold and silver on a mosaic pavement of porphyry, marble, mother-of-pearl, and colored stones. Drinks were served in golden goblets, goblets of different kinds, and the royal wine was lavished according to the bounty of the king. Drinking was by flagons, without restraint; for the king had given orders to all the officials of his palace to do as each one desired. Furthermore, Queen Vashti gave a banquet for the women in the palace of King Ahasuerus. On the seventh day, when the king was merry with wine, he commanded Mehuman, Biztha, Harbona, Bigtha and Abagtha, Zethar and Carkas, the seven eunuchs who attended him, to bring Queen Vashti before the king, wearing the royal crown, in order to show the peoples and the officials her beauty; for she was fair to behold. But Queen Vashti refused to come at the king's command conveyed by the eunuchs. At this the king was enraged, and his anger burned within him.[7]

Unfortunately, mediocrity and marginality seem to be constants in life, expressing their twin characteristics more vividly in urban schools, churches, and communities. This doesn't have to be that way because the socioeconomic status determined by poor housing and low income are not the definitive predictors of achievement and success. For example, success in school is not determined by the cost of one's jeans or the name brand of your sneakers, but by faith and belief in God and oneself. It's not how much money one makes or in what neighborhood one lives, but rather how much one reads, studies, prays, travels, discusses, and questions things that make for excellence and consciousness in all areas of life. This applies to pastors, teachers, musicians, custodians, and students. Everything that has breath needs to be in pursuit of integrity and excellence. Everybody needs to feel if they believe, they can achieve. There is no time to be petty, like the superintendent character in Ernest Gaines's novel *A Lesson Before Dying*; we need to be like Grant the teacher, or Jefferson who learned to walk like a man fulfilling his aunt's desire that he not be perceived as a hog, an animal.

The problem with any excellence is it can become idolatrous. King Ahasuerus even turned his wife into an idol, which prompted her to say, "No," because she recognized the only decent content of any excellence is God.

Ester in the Old Testament tells the story of King Xerxes, whose Hebrew name was Ahasuerus, and his chief magistrate in court, Haman, who had "a grudge against a Jewish man named Mordecai."[8] Esther describes life in the Persian court with all of the splendor, glitter, and gold of the king's palace. "King Xerxes, or Ahasuerus, is ruler over 127 provinces, but he did not succeed in ruling his wife, Queen Vashti."[9] This is the scene. The king gave a banquet at the "Jefferson Hotel" for all his officials—mayors and governors, senators and congressmen; all the potentates were there, and they invited the sororities, the fraternities, the Greeks, and the Epicureans. The king displayed his wealth and power amidst pomp and circumstance for 180 days—an entire public school year. They had a party that went on non-stop from September to March. Dancing, drinking, singing. They were balling.

After all this dancing and prancing, partying and schmoozing, an even more lavish and grand banquet was held for seven more days "in the court of the garden of the king's palace." Oh, this was the bomb. My imagination helps here. There were white Egyptian cotton curtains and blue hangings tied with cords of fine linen, purple and silver rings, and marble pillars. This was royalty. The couches were made of gold and silver on a mosaic pavement of marble, mother of pearl, and colored stones. They served top-shelf drinks—tequila; Johnnie Walker Red, Black, and Platinum Label Scotch; Kentucky bourbon; El Dorado Special Reserve; Yamazaki 12-Year Old Whisky; Jefferson's Ocean Bourbon; Absolut Elyx Vodka; Hine Triomphe 50 Year Old Grande Champagne Cognac; and other vintage brands. They smoked Cuban cigars—hand rolled with flue-cured tobacco flavored by the heat of the sun and softened by the freshness of the morning dew. King Xerxes told everybody to drink as much as they pleased. There was no cash bar. Everything was on the house. The king ordered his staff to give everybody what they wanted, whatever would satisfy their hunger—leg of lamb, filet mignon, porterhouse, T-Bone steaks, lobster stuffed with crab meat and caviar, mushrooms sautéed in virgin olive oil, asparagus cooked in melted butter with a touch of oregano and sea salt. Move over, Julia Child, Wolfgang Puck, and chef Barbara Bryan. Move over, Big Mama. The king's chefs were unmatched in presenting a meal so delectable that no modern-day, five-star restaurant or top chef could match. This banquet hall made the Waldorf Astoria in New York, the Hilton in Paris, the J.W. Marriott in Washington D.C., and the Gaylord in Orlando look like small fried potatoes. On the seventh day, when the king had too much wine and was a bit intoxicated, he commanded the seven eunuchs who were his attendants to bring his wife, Queen Vashti, to him. And to have her wearing the royal crown, to show the people the excellence of her beauty. All of these things are indeed excellent; however, they are the wrong excellences. This is the problem. This is not the excellence we need. The content of your liquor cabinet or what's parked in your garage is not excellence. It's a limited excellence at best—and a false excellence at worst.

But Queen Vashti refused to come at the king's command. She said, "No," and this was the rebellious "no" that was heard around the world. The king was enraged, trembling in anger. The text says that his anger "burned within him."

Vashti teaches that we all have to come to a new awakened and critical consciousness about the meaning of excellence. Excellence is about understanding one's surroundings and social environment. Yes, Vashti was the queen, but she'd developed a new consciousness that said her life was about more than perfume and makeup, about more than being paraded in the public square as a thing of physical beauty. To say "no" to the king was rebellious, bold, and dangerous. This was the same spirit of rebellion seen in Jarena Lee and Maria Stewart, offered in response to those who'd tried to keep them from preaching. And this was the same "no" to slavery demonstrated by Nat Turner and some of his army. This was risky behavior. Sometimes, that is what it takes. As teachers and preachers, you may have to say, "No, I am not going to treat my students, my people, like they can't learn just because they live in the projects and receive Title I services." "No, I am not going to expect less from them because they are Black or Brown or poor." "No, I am not going to allow anyone to keep me from treating every student, every teacher, every assistant, every parent with dignity and respect." "And no, I am not going to disrespect myself by lowering my own standards of excellence." In Greek ethics, anyone striving for justice is excellent, a more excellent form of goodness.

The other thing we learn from Vashti's "no" is a "no" to oppression and marginalization is a "yes" to freedom and justice. Vashti said to her husband King Ahasuerus that she was not going to prance around before his drunken friends at the expense of her dignity. "No" means freedom for those who are oppressed. That was what Rosa Parks's "no" meant when she refused to give up her seat on that bus in Montgomery, Alabama, in 1955. "No, I'm tired of being treated like dirt." "No, I have a mind of my own." "No, I'm not going to give up my seat." Her defiance was heard around the world, and the nationwide modern civil rights movement began that very day in that small town in the Deep South. The Confederate flag flew atop the state capitol without shame as a sign and symbol of white supremacy, but her "No" meant Black folk never again would be docile and taken for granted. Never again would segregation in public transportation be the law of the land. Likewise, President Obama said, "No, I will not abandon the Affordable Healthcare Act, even if it means shutting down the government."

Esther 2:4 is the last time we hear anything from Queen Vashti. All we know of her is she was beautiful, and she said "no" before she vanishes from the book of Esther. And that is what saying "no" could mean. One can vanish from the face of the earth if not careful.

Like Rosa Parks's "no," Queen Vashti's "no" is a subversive and defiant "yes" to freedom and justice. It's not easy to go against the status quo. It's not easy to go against the power holders, the kings and princes of the land. It's not easy to stand alone in the fearless fight for justice, righteousness, fairness, and freedom. Yes, you may have to do it in your school, in your church, in the boardroom, and in the public square—but when you stand on principle and not policy, when you stand on right and not wrong, when you stand on justice and not injustice, when you stand on conscience and not careful calculation, you join the pantheon of prophets before you. You join the company of comrades who have been willing to say "no." Harriet Tubman and Sojourner Truth said "no" to slavery. Jarena Lee and Maria Stewart said "no" to those who tried to keep them from preaching. Fannie Lou Hammer and Barbara Jordan said "no" to corruption in politics. Martin Luther King Jr. said "no" to injustice and segregation. Queen Vashti said "no" to exploitation, and Jesus of Nazareth—my rock and my salvation, my shelter in the time of storms—said "no" to the Pharisees and the Scribes. Jesus said "no" to the devil, who showed and promised him all the splendor of the world. Jesus said "no" to every act of evil and hatred.

To advance this spirit of excellence and to move away from mediocrity is difficult and painful for preachers. In spite of their silent pain, the preacher must speak to the suffering that engulfs our congregations.

Sojourner Truth: "Ain't I A Woman"

To be Black in America is to be in pain, and to be a Black preacher is to be intimately familiar with pain and suffering. This is an ontological assertion given our existential reality of Blackness. It is not the pain, per se, that is destructive, but it is the silencing of the pain by the oppressive powers who hate Blackness that tends to destroy. There is no permanence to the silence of the pain; however, the pain *is* permanent, which is why its silence can never go unchecked. This becomes even more complicated when the Black preacher is a woman who is struggling against extraordinary odds just to exercise the gift of preaching. Again, this is why Black women from the first Black woman preacher—known only as Elizabeth who was born enslaved in 1766 in Maryland; to Jarena Lee, born in 1783; to Zilpha Elaw, born free in Pennsylvania in 1790; to Rebecca Cox Jackson, born free in Horntown, Pennsylvania, in 1795; to Amanda Berry Smith, born enslaved in January 1837; to the most well-known of all Black women preachers, Isabella Baumfree, better known as Sojourner Truth, born enslaved in Wester County, New York, around 1797—have borne the brunt of suffering.[10]

It was not unusual for women preachers like Jarena Lee, Zilpha Elaw, and Julia Foote to be criticized for being "too forward" in their preaching. And "forward" is exactly what these Black women preachers were. They kept moving forward by any means necessary in order to not be deterred by the systemic patriarchy that engulfed the church, the community, the family, and society. These Black women were able to imagine a world beyond the hegemonic biblical and societal texts they encountered on every hand. And not only that, they were able to forge forward, to preach sermons often challenging Christian practices and creating a world beyond the box into which society tried to put them. No matter how forceful and systematic the efforts, they could not be contained. They could not be restrained. They refused to be restricted and relegated to the realm of domination and demonization carved out for them by their detractors. We can all learn from the grit and determination of these women preachers, who were exemplars of strong faith and fighting strength.

In fact, the call to preach is a call against the pain of silence. The New Testament writer Paul says, "If I proclaim the gospel, this gives me no ground for boasting, for an obligation is laid on me, and *woe* to me if I do not proclaim the gospel!"[11] And Paul also says to the Philippians that it doesn't matter whether the preacher is pretending or speaking the truth, the gospel must be preached.[12] Preaching, then, is an affront to silence. Like marching and protesting, it is an obviation of silence. It is the inability to be muted by the masters of "morality" and "mean-spiritedness" that often masquerade as people of virtue—pretending to protect the church and the people from these Black women of thunder, these sisters of the spirit, these dangerous daughters of

Africa who respond to the call to preach by preaching out of season. To some folk, the time was never right nor will ever be right for Black women to take their rightful place in the seats of power, prestige, and practice of Black religion by becoming the preacher in the pulpit of the local church. The woman preacher as pastor, prophet, and pulpiteer is still resisted by some.

The journey of these Black women preachers and all women has been slow and painful; yet when it comes to preaching, they have met every doubtful "no" with a resounding "yes." These women preachers could not be "walled in" or "walled out."[13] It is evident that "women imbued with the doctrine of holiness believed that no man or woman or institution could sanction their right to preach, that this was the sole prerogative of God."[14] These women and others—such as Julia A. J. Foote, Harriet A. Baker, Mary J. Small, and Florence Spearing Randolph—believed they were licensed and ordained to preach by the Holy Ghost, the Holy Spirit, a higher power than the polity of the church. It was a sanction and "unction" from the cherubim and seraphim, from the council of heaven, rather than by the rules of Methodism or the oppressive doctrine of the church. Their understanding and interpretation of freedom and justice came not from the prophets Micah, Isaiah, Jeremiah, or Amos, but from God. From Adonai. From Elohim. From Yahweh. From the Holy Spirit and the spirit of their parents, their ancestors. They could hear the words from on high recorded in the Book of Revelation, "The spirit and the bride say come and let him who hears say come."[15]

Preaching in silent pain is the existential reality for the Black preacher today, just as it was for the women of the nineteenth and twentieth centuries. Today, while there are more women preachers, the record shows "female preachers were virtually written out of their churches' histories in the mid-nineteenth century—a silence that has been perpetrated ever since."[16] The invisibilization of women preachers is the result of the deliberate erasure of their existence from church records and similar methods of remembering. And yet there has been no enduring silence because the voices of women preachers today are heard around the world.

Though preaching in silent pain, broadly speaking, has been the dominant condition of existence for Black women, it also has been, and continues to be, a reality for *all* Black people. Pain and suffering is a gender-neutral phenomenon. The degree of silence is correlated to personality and commitment; nevertheless, the existence of silent pain, regardless of gender, is incontrovertible, unchallenged, and understandable by everyone who ever tried to claim to preach the gospel. Preachers and pastors know all too well that Sunday is a recurring event, just like the seasons of the year or the phases of the moon—just like night follows day, and summer follows spring, and sunshine often peeks through the clouds after the rain. I know some people self-medicate to mitigate the silent pain and to augment the already prevailing dialectic that exists in the personality, body, and consciousness, but I don't recommend that. The "medicine" of choice doesn't have to be alcohol or drugs—e.g., marijuana or cocaine. It could be pain killers prescribed by doctors and dentists, promiscuous sex, monetary greed, or hunger for attention and acceptance. It could be almost anything meant to soothe and satiate the self against the silence, against the pain. Against the agony of childhood trauma, the abuse by parents and pastors, the denial of complex feelings and unrequited romantic love. It could be a plethora of problems the preachers sublimate and submerge beneath their skin, causing eczema, hives, rashes, diarrhea, chronic obstructive pulmonary disease, irritable bowel syndrome, heart disease, obesity, asthma, etc. It is evident today that more and more preachers are finding pleasure in too much alcohol, cigar bars, smoking chambers, tobacco pipes, and vaping parlors. The pressure is high, and the pain is palpable. Silent, yet not so silent.

The pain is visible. You can see it in the eyes of the preacher. Glassy eyes. Eyes speaking of sadness and sorrow. Eyes crying out for salvation and hope. Eyes full of tears. Silent tears. Silent pain. Yes, silent pain, because too many preachers and pastors will not cry; instead, they sublimate their emotions. No matter how hard some are punched in the belly or the head, they get up stumbling back to the pulpit, bloody and bruised, as if in a fight with the gladiators, a fight with the universe, a fight with time itself. I speak of what I know, so I can't be silent. If I could not speak of the pain and suffering I feel as a preacher, as a father, a brother, a husband, and a pastor, I would have to be hopelessly silent. Ludwig Wittgenstein is right, "Whereof one cannot speak, thereof one must be silent." But I can't be silent. I must speak of the pain of being a pastor, of going from hospital to hospital praying for the sick and the dying, people whom I have come to know and love. It is a danger that I strive to avoid by keeping my distance, not getting too close to folk for fear I may have to suffer their loss and stand before their bodies uttering words that still make me nauseated: "Earth to earth, ashes to ashes, and dust to dust." Who is sufficient for such things? The preacher is tasked with a burden too heavy to bear, too hard for one weak, frail human to have to carry. And yet carry it the preacher must, no matter how heavy the burden.

Every time I think about my sons who currently live thousands of miles away from home, I am in silent pain. When I think about the racism both my sons endured while studying in prominent universities in New York and Boston, and while trying to work in law and film—two bastions of American institutionalized racism and white supremacy—I am overcome with silent pain and agony. Preaching is laden with agony, a "vocation of agony," but this truth is exacerbated by being a father to two young Black males who are always under assault. This is my pain, my experience; and if I could not speak about it, I would have to be silent. But speak about it I must, because I can't keep silent. Nevertheless, this is a pain and a silence that engulf me every day, every moment that I breathe. People tend to think I am strong because I often mask my pain by dealing with the pain of others. Sometimes I even pretend to be tough and hardnosed while constantly fighting back my tears. When I watched the blockbuster movie *Black Panther*, I felt strangely out of place because I was torn. On one hand, I was proud of the Black director's achievement, as well as of all the actors and actresses of color and their excellent performances. On the other hand, I was dismayed by the violence. As the movie ended, I was hoping the two Black cousins challenging each other to the death for a kingship, for a throne grounded in patriarchy and patronage, would come together in love and unity. Could they share the Wakanda throne? I left the movie feeling pained and sorrowful about how we systematically treat each other, thinking we must find a way to work together as a people. So, the movie made me cry in pain. And more recently as of this writing, the movie *Just Mercy* was even more painful for me to watch as these Black men were systematically banished to death row in the Alabama prison system. I thought to myself, as I fought back tears, "This is Black Suffering."

Wakanda has its secret weapon, vibranium, which has magical, miraculous healing powers. It can mend and repair catastrophic bullet wounds; it can help fly planes and do other miraculous feats—but when it came to keeping two Black brothers from killing each other, vibranium could do nothing. To me, this was a tragic reality.

Preaching in silent pain is very hard—hard to do and hard to hear. But it is healing and redemptive in its purpose. For too long, we have felt we are alone. In one sense, we *are* alone. "My pain is my problem," I have said all too often, because there is a feeling, a justified feeling, that there is no one to help us, no one to rescue us from the wreck.

Pain and Suffering Are Not the Same

Pain is bodily. Suffering is existential. Suffering is shareable, whereas pain is not. We preach out of pain and silence. Pain finds its expression in speech and in speechlessness—in the sermon (speech) and in the silence (speechlessness). Preaching in silent pain is, at its core, a paradox, an oxymoron. At a very basic and fundamental level, our pain is *always* both personal and silent. It is my pain, not anyone else's. It is not your pain, no matter how close you claim to be to the pained one, no matter how holy and anointed you claim to be, no matter how educated and how spiritual you are—whether you are a deacon, an elder, an apostle, a bishop, a saint, a sinner, or a board-certified doctor in anesthesiology, pharmacology, or neuroscience. To the best of my knowledge, I cannot feel your pain and you cannot feel my pain. We have no physical capacity to transfer our pain to another human being. Your heart attack, your aching knees, your sciatic nerve pain, your plantar fasciitis, your stress headache, your migraine, or your brain aneurysm—I can feel none of them, no matter how much I love you, or empathize and sympathize with you. This pain in my hip and in my arm is mine; you don't feel it. You can't. To say otherwise is a lie.

Preachers and church folk do lie. Ask Reverend Ambrose, a main character in Ernest Gaines's novel *A Lesson Before Dying*. He says of himself, "I lie, I lie, and I lie."[17] And he says to Grant about his aunt Tante Lou that she, too, lies about her pain every day, saying that she feels okay when, in fact, she is in pain. That's why, as patients, we all have to tell the doctor, the nurse, the anesthesiologist, and the pain specialist, how much pain we feel on a scale of one to ten. Or we have to circle a happy face or frowning face that indicates our level of pain. But pain remains personal and internal despite all of these professional people's knowledge, training, and understanding about chemistry, biology, medicine, and surgery. It's specific to your body, with no external or transferable elements to it. Pain can only be managed medically by doctors and nurses. However, it is not pain the preacher addresses. The preacher is compelled and called to address Black folk's suffering through preaching Christ. Black suffering is the critical issue the preacher must learn to interpret, understand, and explain.

So, as preachers, pastors, and ministers of the gospel, I encourage you to stop saying foolish, meaningless, callous statements—even scandalous, mythical, tragic, egoistic statements of malpractice. Statements like, "I know how you feel," or "I feel your pain," or "When you hurt, I hurt." This ubiquitous, omniscient "I" is blasphemous, pretending to be God. No, you don't know! That's posturing and perpetrating. It's "straight-up" false. It's lying in the worst form because it's a pretense toward godly empathy. Fake feelings. It's platitudinous and a gross misunderstanding of the difference between suffering and pain. Preach Christ and stop pretending to know what you don't know. Speak truth, which is to admit that as preachers, you don't know everything. Stop pretending to know and feel what you don't know and feel. Saying things like, "I feel my anointing coming on now." Just demonstrate it. Don't announce it. It's an unnecessary *pretense* toward otherness and even toward superiority to others. It's a *sovereignty,* which is always more about the power of the self than it is about the suffering of the other person. Indeed, *silence* may be the only compassionate response we can make to another's pain. Now don't misunderstand me here, because one's own pain—or the preacher's pain, or preaching in silent pain—is another simpler, yet more complex matter altogether. The Black preacher is called, as King says, to a "vocation of agony," a calling that, by its nature and its social geography, is one of pain and suffering.

I cannot help but think of the painful, pulsating words of the prophet Amos. He was not known for being a scholar or member of the elite class, yet his words ring loud and clear, cutting left and right to those who sit in seats of comfort. Amos was rural, a farmhand, a dresser of sycamore trees, a shepherd from Tekoa. Listen to Amos's silent pain, whose words express God's pain at those who do everything except preach justice and righteousness. Amos's words are searing as his struggle to correct comes from deep-seated and somber anger. Amos is one of the prophets who sees the connection between idolatry and the poor's oppression. He recognizes, as we should, that idols cost money, and the idolatry of the pulpit that focuses on the preacher is an immense contemporary problem. Note it is not the *word* I am talking about as idolatry, but rather the physical and material pulpit itself, located in the center of the sanctuary, elevated above everything else. It is elevated too often to the point of idolatry. Maybe even the Black church—built, torn down, and built again, bigger than it was the first time, with more flat screens and microphones for us to see and hear ourselves from every possible angle—is guilty of this self-absorption. That, too, is a form of idolatry, a form of economic oppression of the poor and glamorization of material culture—the elevation of the church building with the pulpit at the center, too often at the expense of the word of God, too often at the expense of the suffering poor and the oppressed.

Too often, the preacher is more prone to equate popularity with the gospel. Too many are unwilling to read and study to improve their preaching because the Black church is mesmerized by their performance. So many who attend seminary are not convinced of its import, reverting to whatever "works" to excite the people. Even those who graduate seminary are uncritical and often quick to abandon their educational achievement as not very useful. Many of our recent Virginia Union graduates have said to me, "I'm out of your class now; I don't have to hold myself and others to the same standard." And then there's the additional rejection of theology and methodology when the sermon is grossly inadequate, as folk will say, "I came to church to worship, not to demand excellence or to speak about issues of justice and righteousness." To that, I encourage us to hear the word from Amos:

> I hate, I despise your festivals, and I take no delight in your solemn assemblies. Even though you offer me your burnt offerings and grain offerings, I will not accept them; and the offerings of well-being of your fatted animals I will not look upon. Take away from me the noise of your songs; I will not listen to the melody of your harps. But let justice roll down like waters, and righteousness like an ever-flowing stream.[18]

Amos rails and rants eloquently against an empty religion, a religion devoid of social justice. His preaching is a type of personal suffering and pain, one he proclaims prophetically on behalf of the weak and the poor who have cried out to God for help with their situation of struggle and suffering under the hand of injustice. Not only that, as alongside this injustice lurks and looms the ubiquitous presence of unrighteousness. Injustice toward the poor permeated the law of Amos's time, and unrighteousness infiltrated the temples, sanctuaries, and worship services. These twin evils were offensive to God—and they were seen in services of worship, the pomp and circumstance of which is tantamount to idolatry and sacrilege to Amos. And I think that much of what we do today is equally odorous to God.

This scripture text is filled with doom and gloom, unimpressed by power and wealth, as well as certain practices designed by humans to impress themselves and each other. This is painful for Amos, and it's painful for me and you. It's hard for me to even say these words, and church folk don't want to hear them. Let's face it: we all but hate Amos and many of his comrades, and we are somewhat afraid to read these words in the Black church! These prophets say/write many hard and challenging things, but their words must be read in church. These words are scathing and scandalous. They are full of a searing, cutting-edge critique, tougher than anything I've ever said to a student at the end of their sermon and more direct than any sermon I've preached in the Black church. I'm too weak and puny to be such a prophet. We are too fearful, too afraid, too politically beholding, too Republican, too Democratic, too desirous of sitting beside Trump, I mean, Jeroboam II. We are too willing to collude, to bribe, to corrupt for personal gain—to wine and dine with the potentates and power brokers of the church, community, nation, and world.

There is a wide, deep gap in our religion and our lives. This is the gap between what we say and what we do, what we preach and what we practice. Justice and righteousness are not nouns, but verbs. We have to *do* justice and *do* righteousness every day. Our lives, our speech, our words, our talk, and our walk have to be in synchrony.

Amos is, indeed, a difficult biblical text for us to read and to hear. It's hard for the Black church to accept. We can "kinda" deal with the *thesis* in this text, but it's the *antithesis* that makes our feet tremble and our hearts palpitate. This is the embodiment of preaching in silent pain. The prophet is the preacher and the preacher is the prophet, and the prophet is saying this to his own people. Her own people are the subject of God's anger and disappointment.

Let me be clear here. The gift of Black preaching is the language of freedom and liberation burnished by the forced silence of the pain and suffering of the Middle Passage, centuries of African enslavement in America, colonization, and oppression. Preaching in silent pain is the only authentic preaching in America. This is Black preaching as a "gift" to the church. This preaching is, in fact, the other side of silence. It is the bubbling over of historic pain and the "coming to grips" with the unmerited suffering of the Black body. It is the expression of strength and hope "in spite of" the fetters and chains of hatred and evil perpetrated against Black people.

Preaching in silent pain is breaking the silence, replacing the veil of silence with the song of hope. This struggle is always present, as ubiquitous as the breath of life itself. And in some strange sense of self and understanding of the other, this preaching is original in its language and speech. It is unrivaled by the rhetoric of the dominant culture—that is, the privileged preaching of the historic perpetrators of silence and pain. Black preaching is the "rending of the veil," and at the same time, according to W. E. B. Du Bois and Charles Long, it is the creative experience of mitigating the negativity with cultural critique and a hope that is dimmed by injustice and oppression, but never extinguished. Maybe this is the real meaning of "celebration" in Black life and in Black preaching, and this celebration is both "critique and confession," both sorrow and hope. It is a new language used to express an enduring experience. A language no other speaker knows in the way the Black preacher knows it. It is not, for example, the rhetoric of Aristotle or the rhetoric of Augustine. But if Black preachers "drop the ball" by seeking to be popular and not prophetic—passive and not proactive, pensive and not powerful, wary of language laced and burnished by pain and suffering—then we, too, might as well be white evangelicals propagating or spewing out the same weak and wanton rhetoric of those who have colonized us and continue to offer soft support to oppression and injustice.

The One Joyous Thing That Matters

Some proclaim Christ from envy and rivalry, but others from goodwill. These proclaim Christ out of love, knowing that I have been put here for the defense of the gospel; the others proclaim Christ out of selfish ambition, not sincerely but intending to increase my suffering in my imprisonment.

> What does it matter? Just this, that Christ is proclaimed in
> every way, whether out of false motives or true; and in that
> I rejoice. Yes, and I will continue to rejoice.[19]

So much of what we concern ourselves with does not matter in
the least, and this is a difficult, almost impossible, lesson to learn.
In the grand scheme of things, so much of what concerns us, even
preoccupies us, has no real ultimate concern, and yet we think
and act as if it does. We are so human, and that is something so
real and expected of us. We cause much pain and suffering by
our focus on the nonessential, our focus on that which is ancillary
to being an effective preacher—the personality, the person, the
physical and aesthetic characteristics of the preacher.

Our interest in the human foibles and failures of the preacher
is natural and to some extent insurmountable, which means
overcoming the deep fissures in our faith is a struggle we negotiate daily. This struggle is the source of our envy and rivalry;
and while envy and rivalry are negative attitudes and behaviors,
they are not disqualifying traits. Black Preachers are undoubtedly
envious of each other. *Envy* is a noun and a verb. As a noun, it is
a feeling of resentment of the qualities or possessions belonging
to someone else. As a verb, it is a desire to have what belongs to
somebody else. Envy and jealously are enemies of somebody's
joy. And as preachers, we don't have time or energy for that. Do
what you do and do it well. Possess what you possess and possess
it joyfully. Whether your church is big or small, full or empty, in
the city or the country, be thankful and be grateful for what God
has given you and don't get caught up in envy, jealousy, rivalry,
and selfish ambition. But if you do—and you will—"it ain't gonna
stop nothing," because the gospel and the preaching of the gospel
are more powerful than all that.

As he writes his letter to the Philippians, Paul is in prison in
Rome while some rival preachers have used his imprisonment to

advance themselves rather than to focus on doing the right thing for the right reason. Some are preaching Christ from "envy and rivalry," and others out of "selfish ambition." Preachers can be petty, and personal pain can adopt the spirit of personal rivalry that takes advantage of the pain and suffering of others. Even in this text, we see some of the same attitudes and actions that manifest themselves today. While Paul is in prison, other preachers are spreading rumors that he is a "has-been," that this new reality is a sign his heyday has passed, that his effectiveness is diminishing, that his word is weak and his influence is waning. There is rivalry in and out of church. And while the church tends to promote much of this foolishness, most of the time, it promotes itself. We see it occurring in the church between those who are seminary-trained and those who are not. Some folks refer to the seminary as "the cemetery," suggesting it's a place of death rather than life and power. In a sense, this view is suspicious of learning and studying, implying the sermon can and should be divined rather than developed; that prayer and meditation are all you need to preach; and that if you stand up and open your mouth, the Lord will tell you what to say. All of this could be true, but the Lord expects us to do something for ourselves too. For example, we are called to read, study, pray, fast, meditate, exercise, eat right, and promote healthy and righteous living in ourselves and our churches.

The other side of this unnecessary dialectical view deserves some scrutiny too. Going to seminary and studying do not a preacher make. There needs to be no rivalry between those who have a master of divinity degree—or any degree—and those who don't. If you have a big church and no seminary degree, praise God! If you have a degree, praise God! If you have a small church in backwater Alabama or Virginia, praise God! The gospel is not about popularity or having a big church house. It's about lifting up Christ. Proclaiming Christ. No preacher is

perfect in any way. There is some semblance of envy and jealousy in the most humble and selfless preacher. There is rivalry
between pastors of one denomination and another, between
preachers in the same city and state. There are envy and self-
ishness and immoral behavior running rampant. There is lying,
stealing, deceit—you name it—and preachers have done it all in
betrayal of the gospel of Jesus Christ.

Here we have both the annoying side and the encouraging
side of the case of preachers—you can see the dialectics of the
preacher embedded in this scripture text: "Some proclaim Christ
from envy and rivalry, but others from goodwill. . . . Out of love
. . . Others proclaim Christ out of selfish ambition, not sincerely."
Clearly, some preachers use the name of Christ for cover or personal gain or selfish ends. It was true then and it's true today.
That's a given. We know and understand that. However, this text
begs to be interpreted. We can only ask: What does it mean?
What is the thing that matters? Now, that's relevant!

This is the miracle of preaching the word: Insincere, envious preaching also advances the gospel. Those who are enemies
of truth, those who hate others' successes, those who capitalize
on others' misfortune—their preaching still advances the gospel.
Even with the wrong motives, the gospel must be preached. It
will not be stopped! Listen to the scripture text, "Some proclaim
Christ from envy and rivalry, some out of goodwill and love.
Others preach Christ out of selfish ambition, not sincerely but
intending to increase my suffering." After saying all this about
the corrupt preacher and their attitudes and motives, Paul makes
this astounding, God-given revelation. It is a turn toward heaven
and a turn toward the love of God through Christ Jesus. Paul says
something informative and earth-shattering. Explosive. Some
preachers have bad motives, bad behaviors, bad theology, and
bad politics. Then in verse 18 of the scripture text, Paul says:
What does it matter? What does it signify? Then he answers

himself. "That Christ is proclaimed in every way, whether out of pretense, out of false motives or true; and in that I rejoice."

This is very anti-Docetist of Paul because the Docetists felt one could only preach if one were pure, holy and righteous. I know we still have some Docetists in the church and in our communities. Saint Augustine opposed the Docetist view; he realized we all are a mixed bag. Understand this: we don't preach the gospel; the gospel preaches itself. This does not mean we are let off the hook. We still have to do our best at all times and leave the rest to the grace of God. Our preaching should be in demonstration of the spirit. And our education should not abandon us in the pulpit and in church, as so many pastors seem to think and practice. The ubiquitous refrain that I hear too often among our recent seminary graduates is, "I am no longer in seminary, so I don't have to embrace any standard of excellence." This is a tragic reality that too many young preachers and pastors believe.

The power of the gospel is not contingent. The gospel is self-contained and self-surpassing. Get in front of the text. If you get behind the text, the text will pass by you. But if you get in front of it, I promise it will carry you with it. This gospel, this preached word, does not depend on the one doing the preaching. We already know ourselves; we know our weak and weary ways. We know we ain't worthy of this high calling. And this Philippians scripture text tells us in ways both revealing and not so revealing that this gospel's power does not depend on the motives, strength, frailties, feelings, attitudes, or behaviors of the one preaching. What matters is the gospel is preached. What matters is I ain't preaching James Harris. What matters is "I ain't qualified." What matters is I'm a nobody. Envious, yes. Selfish, yes. Ambitious, yes. But, it ain't about me, it's about the one who paid it all. It's about the one who forgives me and you. It's about the one who says, "Father forgive them, for they know not." It's about the one who says to Simon Peter, to James Harris, and to others: "Get thee behind me Satan." It's about the one.

Love Builds Up

Now about food sacrificed to idols: We know that we all possess knowledge. Knowledge puffs up, but love builds up. The man who thinks he knows something does not yet know, as he ought to know. But the man who loves God is known by God.[20]

A few years ago, the United States celebrated the 400th anniversary of Jamestown, the first English settlement in North America. But let us not forget that Great Britain was one of the architects of colonialism and domination of the "other"—often a hated other whose skin was colored black, brown, or yellow. As Black Americans, let us not forget our history and the role British imperialism played in the colonization of Africa, Asia, the Caribbean, and America, where cotton was king, and where those who picked the cotton for no wages and built Thomas Jefferson's Monticello and the University of Virginia were enslaved Black people. Let us not forget. Don't let the pomp and circumstance erase our memory of how stony the road has been for us and for the American Indians and others who were enslaved by the European empires. We have heard the president of the United States talk about democracy around the world, a democracy Black and poor people still have not fully experienced. We were enslaved in a democracy for nearly 250 years; and after that, we had to pay poll taxes to vote in the cradle of democracy. We were lynched and physically and mentally castrated in the land of democracy. Historically, American and British democracy means domination and subjugation of the powerless. Democracy is the language of the majority. It is a principle that, by its very nature, squashes minorities and quells dissenting voices, bullies the weak into submission, and engulfs the "other" into a univocity or universalism that obliterates their identity. That is the implicit meaning of the democracy practiced in the land—from federal government to state and local governments to historically Black colleges and universities and local churches.

Pope Benedict XVI "cited the words of a Byzantine emperor who characterized some of the teachings of the prophet Muhammad as 'evil and inhuman.'"[21] And yet he says he did not mean to malign Islam. Knowledge abounds in politics and religion. Knowledge abounds in Judaism, Christianity, and Islam. Apostle Paul says, "We know that we all possess knowledge."[22] Yes, we do. It was knowledge of atomic energy and nuclear physics that allowed the United States to be the only nation in the world to use the nuclear bomb against another country—shattering the bodies and buildings of thousands upon thousands in both Hiroshima and Nagasaki. The whole world knows this, and that's why other countries are asking themselves what they should do with their knowledge of how power is used to perpetuate itself and squash any semblance of rebellion. Should we believe that Goliath, the Leviathan, the Giant, is going to allow us "Davids" to be powerful? Today, even David has become a Goliath.

Paul is not an enemy of knowledge because there is goodness in knowledge. Knowledge itself is not the enemy, but knowledge, like anything else—like food sacrificed to idols, for example—can lead to idolatrous behavior. Knowledge devoid of faith is a type of idolatrous egoism. Knowledge devoid of love is a vile destructive force, capable of emasculating, destroying, and annihilating anything that crosses its path to power and domination. This is the same vaunted knowledge, the same boastful knowledge, and the same vain knowledge that allows our leaders to smirk and smile while talking about American democracy as they dominate powerless people. "We know that we all possess knowledge," Paul says. He is suggesting that this fact is not something to boast about.

Yes, we all have knowledge—but to boast about it is no virtue. By the way, Paul is not complimenting the Corinthians. This is more an indictment than anything else. Knowledge, rightly understood as a gift from God, is not something about which to boast. When we boast about our knowledge as if it were our own, all we are doing is proclaiming our ignorance. There is an irony here. The more you boast, the more "ignant" you sound, as my daddy would say. We all have to be careful, because a little knowledge is even more dangerous than a lot. Paul, like so many of us, is no enemy of knowledge. God forbid! Black people need all the knowledge we can get. But it's like power. Give some people a little authority (i.e., power) and it goes to their heads.

The more you know, the more you understand your limitations and finitude, and the more you should understand the infinite knowledge, love, and goodness of God. Yes, my beloved brothers and sisters—stay in school. Don't drop out. There is no place for you if you can't read, calculate, or converse with others. Don't hate. Don't be mad with "the man" because you don't qualify for the job. As long as they don't discriminate, they can't seal your fate. We should learn, read, study hard, stay in the library, burn the midnight oil, but don't forget that it's not knowledge that calms fears and curtails cravings. It's not knowledge that makes us say, "I am sorry," or "Pardon me." It's not knowledge that woke me up this morning and enabled me to keep on keeping on. No, it is not knowledge. It is not *gnosis* (i.e., "knowledge") that gives a person *exousia* (i.e., "power, authority"). It is not knowledge that provides freedom and liberation, because as Paul says about the food sacrificed to idols: "We know that we all possess knowledge." Knowledge puffs up, but love builds up.

Indeed, knowledge puffs up. It begs to be interpreted. It swells the conscious self. Knowledge focuses on the self, thus causing the self to create a negative and false pride. Knowledge inflates, makes us haughty and arrogant. It makes one falsely think too highly of oneself. This knowledge that puffs up is head knowledge—knowledge that has not made an axis through the heart and soul. This is knowledge that has not made the journey through experience—the journey through trouble and hard times, the journey through sorrow and suffering and pain, silent or otherwise. This is knowledge that has not traveled the long, winding road of headaches, nor the curvaceous and slippery slope of pain, despair, dejection, and rejection so many face. This head knowledge puffs up and makes us walk around like we have some power over others—indeed, often contempt toward others. White people over Black people. Men over women. This is puffed-up knowledge.

However, love builds up. In Christian ethics and theology—in practice in the church and the community—knowledge must always lead to love, not puffed-up pride. Love builds up; love edifies; love creates character and respect. Love creates justice. Love builds up strength in others and in the self by doing good for others. As a matter of fact, love is centered in the other, not the self. Love builds up the Black church and community. Love builds up the family, the school, the marriage, the children, the behavior, the attitude, the disposition.

Love is true knowledge and understanding. Love is the seat of power. Love is the parent of hope and the offspring of godly desire! When you build up those who have been beaten and torn down by the winds of indifference and the torrents of terror, those who have lost their hopes and dreams—that's true knowledge and love. True knowledge and love are bound together. They are married to each other with compassion and understanding. When you build up the self-esteem of your children and help adults achieve their goals and potential, that's love. When you build up your character so you treat the poor with respect and caring, so that you give your time to help somebody along the way, that's love. Paul made it even clearer a few chapters later, when he wrote, "If I speak in the tongues of men and of angels, but have not love, I am only a resounding gong on a clanging cymbal. If I have the gift of prophecy if I can preach and can understand all mysteries and all knowledge; and if I have faith that can move mountains, but have not love, I am nothing."[23]

Forgiveness and Disremembering Evil

> No longer shall they teach one another, or say to each other, "Know the Lord," for they shall all know me, from the least of them to the greatest, says the Lord; for I will forgive their iniquity and remember their sin no more."[24]

Out of curiosity, I went to Charleston, South Carolina, to see the church where the prayer meeting massacre had taken place. This was an evil so warped and gross—so reminiscent of how Black people were treated in the nineteenth-century South—that it almost defied imagination. And yet it did happen, right there in the heart of the city at a downtown Black church. The white-brick structure with its small steeple pointing toward the sky is the symbol and image of any Black church in America. Just a few steps from the street, it is surrounded by shops and other businesses. I wanted to walk up the tall steps and around the building to get a sense of the sanctity of the place. Its stained-glass windows spoke of worship and singing. I could feel the spirit of love and kindness that radiated from the building, the center of Black spirituality in downtown Charleston. After I read the marker on the front wall of the church proclaiming its history, I walked slowly down the steps and back across the street to take one more look at the church that had been grief-stricken by the murder of its members during a routine prayer meeting. This act of evil was symbolic of American racial hatred.

During the arraignment of South Carolina murderer Dylann Roof, family members of the nine Black people killed at Emmanuel AME Church all said to the judge, "I forgive him." This is radical love and radical hospitality. Black people are very forgiving of others, and less so of each other.

Forgiveness is not a changing of the facts of the past, facts that may have led to discord and distance. Forgiveness is a blessing that changes what seems to be unchangeable—the idea of the past. All of us who have a present also have a past. This past may be filled with all types of things, things suppressed and repressed. Things good and things bad. The things of lies, hatred, envy, and the things of evil. Painful, agonizing things; things sad and sorrowful; things with your mama; things with your daddy, siblings, spouse, lovers, and friends. Things with your enemies. This is not going to change. The facts of the past are the facts of the past. But the *meaning* of the facts (i.e., the things of existence) can be changed by the external (i.e., by God), and the name of this change is the experience of forgiveness, which is an act of transformation. Its power lies in the ability to make things new. To interpret in a brand new way this thing that has caused so much agony.

We carry grudges; we harbor anger; we hold onto the sins and weaknesses of others. We are like pit bulls and Rottweilers, tearing each other apart by our words and deeds. We chew on a bone until we have consumed its marrow—just eating away at anyone who dares to cross us the wrong way. It is so easy to do, so church-like, so old style, so lame and sorry for those who claim baptism and salvation. And yet it is such an apt description of our identity as deacons, ushers, choir members, missionaries, preachers, ministers, and teachers—human beings of all stripes and colors. It strikes me as a troublesome reality that we are so unforgiving, so interested in retribution or getting folk back for what we narrowly conceive as an act of disrespect, no matter how innocent, no matter how guilty. For example, I got angry for a split-second the other day. I was on my way to church on a busy road when I got caught by a red light. As soon as the light turned green, the person behind me started blowing the horn. I was perturbed. I was livid. I was mad. I wanted to get out and say something "nice" to that person, something equivalent to blowing the horn. But because I have been guilty of doing something similar, I drove off, in shame of myself, with sublimated road rage.

Not only are we unforgiving, but we are also not forgetful. Holding grudges is bad enough, but we also don't forget and don't let others forget what they have done to themselves and to us. We even say, "I forgive you, but I ain't gonna forget." Well, news flash: You are lying to yourself. Half of what you are saying is true, but it's not the half you think, because when we say, "I forgive you, but I'm not gonna forget," we are saying more than we believe. We are really saying we have not forgiven, and "that's why I ain't gonna forget and I ain't gonna let you forget, it either."

Our scripture text is an example of the opposite of what we think and do. The text is a perfect example of the divine grace of God. A God who "commits himself to a weak, stubborn, broken, and unfaithful people."[25] Israel's unfaithfulness to God is met not with punishment and anger, not with retribution and divorce, not with separation and eternal damnation, not with a formula for "sleeping on the couch" or being banished from the house altogether. Instead, Israel's unfaithfulness to God is met with— guess what—forgiveness. The text says, "No longer shall they teach one another, or say to each other, 'Know the Lord,' for they shall all know me, from the least of them to the greatest, says the Lord; for I will forgive their iniquity, and I will remember their sin no more."

What does it mean to forgive and to forget? This is the new covenant that ceases to privilege tradition. It puts an end to the glorification of the past. This new covenant is not like the old one established at Mount Sinai. That covenant has been broken. Covenants are made to be kept, but they are often broken; and when they are broken, God says forgive: "I will forgive their iniquity. I will forgive their sins."[26] God is a forgiving God. Forgiveness is a byproduct of grace and an attribute of love and mercy. Forgiveness is a part of knowing the Lord in your heart. It is a relationship with God that is stamped in the heart; it is written in the heart. It is stamped in the mind and consciousness of the people of God. Forgiveness is an attribute of God; and if we claim to have God in us, then we are compelled, called, and required by the love and grace of God to be forgiving. I will forgive their sins, their wrongdoing, their backsliding, their wickedness, their lies, their deception, and their greediness.

Forgiveness of sins is new, and it portends a future where everybody from the least to the greatest, from the youngest to the oldest, will know the love, grace, and forgiveness of God. This means God's law, God's word, has to get in us—not just on the outside, but on the inside. This is not an exterior thing, like a pair of shoes or a new set of nails or earrings. This new relationship has to be interiorized. It has to get in your heart and your mind, in your hands and your feet, in your eyes and your mouth, in your body and your soul. Then we can forgive one another as God forgives us of our sins. The text says, "For I will forgive their iniquity and remember their sin no more." God wipes the slate clean. Forgiveness and forgetting go together like the numbers one and two, like reading and writing, like love and marriage, like child and parent, like walking and talking.

God is an erasing God. God disremembers. God forgets about our sins. It's as if we pray to God, "Lord, forgive me for doing such and such and saying this and that," and God says, "I don't remember that. I forgot all about that." What are you crying about; what are you fretting over? God's knowledge of us includes God's divine capacity to forget about our sin—to remember our sin no more. Forgiveness and forgetfulness are close friends; they go together hand in hand. They include one another. They are each other's companion. Forgiveness includes forgetting.

I'm so glad that God forgives me, and God forgives you. When I've done wrong and don't even have sense enough to know it, God forgives. When others hold grudges and refuse to let go of our sins—our wrongs, our missteps, our lies, our addictions, our faltering failures, our disobedience, our stumbling drunkenness, our tendency to make ourselves look good at the expense of making others look like demons, our sinful acts, and our ugly ways—God forgives. And God refuses to remember. God is a God who chooses to disremember. God is a new-covenant-making God; God is a doing-a-new-thing God; God is a new-promise God; God is a God who fixes us up brand new no matter how broken, battered, and bruised we may be. God remembers our sin no more.

God disallows the consciousness of our sins in God's own anamnestic nature, in God's own self as a God who knows all, sees all, hears all, and understands all. God knows everything, even that which God forgets. In other words, God unknows that which God fully knows. By disremembering our sins, God deeply disallows God's own ability to remember. This disremembering, this forgetting of our sins and remembering them no more, is the love and grace of God. God says, "I will forgive your iniquity. I will forgive your sins and I will remember your sin no more." God has decided our sins are not worthy of remembering, our sins that are many—too many for us to calculate, and yet too few for God to remember. Our sins that are too egregious to be ignored by our families, friends, spouses, and community—and yet too insignificant to be remembered by God. God has other options to take. Our sins have been cast into the sea of forgetfulness, never to rise, haunt, and taunt us again.

God knows existence and iniquity have wounded us just by the daily grind of trying to survive. We are wounded by life's struggles and arrows. We are like children, daily experiencing the cruelty of a parent who is caught up in their own struggle for recognition and desire to dominate the small, weak, frail other. "We are like leaves soaking up the rays of the sun, glistening and shining like sprigs of grass and then in a flash, blown away by the rain-soaked wind of spring and summer."[27]

Suffering and Hope

Black Theology must take seriously the reality of Black people—their life of suffering and humiliation. This must be the point of departure of all God-talk which seeks to be Black talk. —James H. Cone[1]

"Come out dat do'way and shet it tight, fool! Stand dere gazin' dem white folks right in de face!" Ned gritted at him. "Yo' brazen ways wid dese white folks is gwinter git you lynched one uh dese days." —Zora Neale Hurston, *Jonah's Gourd Vine*

I'm sick and tired of being sick and tired. —Fannie Lou Hamer

My mother, Carrie Anna Jones Harris, died of colon cancer right before her sixty-fifth birthday. Nine months before that, my father succumbed to a massive heart attack. My family was devastated to the point of immobility, yet I had to preach,

Sunday after Sunday. I remember we never had health insurance because we were too poor to pay for it, and because my daddy was too proud to ask for help. Any government assistance, such as welfare, was outside of my parents' imagination. So when my mother got sick, she kept it to herself until it was medically too late to make a difference. She suffered in quietude and silence, which was her way. She never complained about her suffering and pain, or the many difficulties of living in poverty.

I remember during her last pregnancy, when I was seventeen years old, her pain and agony were palpable, caused by fluid retention and the ancillary effects of being pregnant for the eleventh time in twenty-five years. She never complained or expressed any contempt for our socioeconomic condition, nor for the injustices so evident throughout the land. The night she died, I cried myself to sleep, and to this day I regret that I was not there to provide her any care and comfort as she slipped away into the chilly hands of death. Then again, I was there. My presence with her and my father transcends physical location and place, such that they both are always with me.

My understanding of suffering and pain is shaped by the experience of being surrounded by suffering as a youth. We worked in the tobacco fields from sunup to sundown, year after year, to the point where I began to hate the whole enterprise and determined I would not be a prisoner of poverty and economic injustice. To be poor is to suffer in silence or in protest. It is to suffer hunger, poor health, and ridicule from the rest of society. I know the meaning of the *gratuitous amelioration* of suffering, and I know the searing pain of a toothache that lasts for endless days and nights because we could neither afford to go to the dentist nor the doctor unless it was a serious life-or-death issue. And my daddy was the judge of that since we had no health insurance and no money to spend except on food.

As a young seminary student at Virginia Union University, I first read James H. Cone's *God of the Oppressed* in 1975 during a Systematic Theology course. Cone was to theology as James Brown was to soul music—a godfather. He was a superstar among Black students and some professors, a fresh, defiant, loving, and radical voice in the Black church and in the theological community. He was eloquent and bold, and he would not back down from the arrows of criticism thrown at him from every direction—from Black and white preachers, pastors, and theologians worldwide. It was as if they said, "How dare he challenge our established and accepted heroes and norms in theology and history!" I was later chastised by some Black pastors for critiquing Cone and Wilmore in my 1991 article in *Christian Century*, "Practicing Liberation in the Black Church,"[2] in which I said the ivory tower theology of Cone consulted everybody except "Aunt Jane" and the people on the ground in the Black Church. Despite this critique, Cone created excitement and conviction in me. I never missed an opportunity to hear Professor Cone, whose words were as powerful as a freight train. My understanding of God and the Black experience would be forever enriched by his analysis of the theological enterprise—and, more than that, by his love of Black people. When I critique Black people, scholars and otherwise, it is never an *ad hominem*!

I began to incorporate the tenets of Cone's writings into my sermons and papers. It has never been easy for the Black church to face white supremacy and call it the demon that it is, but Cone gave some of us the courage to try to do it. Mac Charles Jones—or "Big Mac," as we called him—was the leader of the radical wing of students in our class and I was his little brother, both in age and stature. Mac was as huge as a Mack truck and just as powerful in his thinking and action. Our theology professor was a white United Methodist who completed his doctorate at Drew University and was considered liberal; however, he was challenged by Cone and all of us to rethink the inadequacies of a theology that was grounded in Americanism and Eurocentrism. Professor Cone, Gayraud Wilmore, and J. Deotis Roberts, our dean, provided us with a new interpretation and understanding—a more balanced explanation of the meaning of God and Black people's pain and suffering. Cone's opening bevy of questions in his chapter, "Divine Liberation and Black Suffering," is as timely today as it was forty years ago. Cone writes:

> The reality of suffering challenges the affirmation that God is liberating the oppressed from human captivity. If God is unlimited both in power and goodness, as the Christian faith claims, why does He not destroy the powers of evil . . . If God is the One who liberated Israel from Egyptian slavery, who appeared in Jesus as the healer of the sick and the helper of the poor, and who is present today as the Holy Spirit of liberation, then why are Black people still living in wretched conditions without the economic and political power to determine their historical destiny?[3]

The connection between suffering and the evils of society is evident. The wielders of power are the earthly architects of Black pain and suffering. The Black preacher feels this pain like everybody else. Preaching in silent pain has been the lot of the Black preacher from "before the Mayflower" to the age of Donald Trump.

During a worship service at Second Baptist Church in Richmond, Virginia, not long ago, I was visibly disturbed—shocked really—by a young lady and her middle-aged mother standing as I preached and walking out at a pace so brisk it appeared they had seen a ghost. Pain and anger were palpable in their countenances, their faces were visibly contorted, and the daughter's body language indicated her distaste for what I was preaching. The biblical text was from Job and I was speaking on Black pain and suffering. I had just read James Cone's latest book, *The*

Cross and the Lynching Tree, and was actually quoting from the text when these two people had stood and left the church. I was careful to correlate Job's pain and suffering with those of Black people in America, and even more careful to make sure I focused the sermonic discourse in textuality, as I am always committed to doing. I am the first person to admit Cone's book is hard and painful to read, but read it we must! It is the most compelling and descriptive theological explication and correlation of Black suffering to Christology that I have ever read. Cone makes his case in terms of classic liberation theology and provides searing insight every serious Christian, no matter their race, needs to understand if they want to overcome the illusion of a pietistic and evangelical religion that is endemic within the Black and white church, and society at large. On that day, as well as on others, I was preaching liberation in my silent pain, and Black people were offended, angered, and blaming me for even bringing up the subject of Black pain and suffering in the Black Church on a Sunday morning. A "blaming the victim" mentality was evident. The church prefers a pie-in-the-sky sermon against one that deals with social justice.

The next day, I received an excoriating correspondence saying my sermon was nonbiblical and outright blasphemous. To wit, the lady wrote: "Unfortunately, I had to leave in the middle of the sermon. I don't know if the sermon ended up on a good note because I just couldn't stomach any more of your 'preaching' that was going on."[4] And yet I, too, was in pain—preaching in silent pain. It is a fallacy to think, as so many do, that the Black preacher is not in pain. But they must preach. It is a silent pain that must not silence the preacher. Preaching is a rebuffing of the silence, but it is not an obviation of the pain. The pain remains even as the sermon mitigates against the silence. In this sense, preaching in silent pain is an oxymoron, a conflict of terms, a rhetorical fallacy.

In the book *God of the Oppressed*, Cone provides a theological framework of Black suffering:

> There is the experience of suffering in the world, and no amount of theological argument can explain away the pain of our suffering in a white racist society. On the one hand, the faith of Black people as disclosed in their sermons, songs, and prayers revealed that they faced the reality of Black suffering. Faith in Jesus did not cancel out the pain of slavery. But on the other hand, Jesus's presence in the experience of suffering liberated Black people from being dependent upon the historical limitation of servitude for a definition of their humanity. This *suffering to which we have been called* is not a passive endurance of white people's insults, but rather a way of fighting for our freedom.[5] [Emphasis mine]

There is something about this "call to suffer" that I vehemently reject because Black suffering is often caused by white supremacist ideology and actions rooted in hate, rather than being something to which "we have been called." Freedom, however, has always been an expensive thing, as Martin Luther King Jr. taught. And since the cost of freedom is often suffering, then suffer we must.

Forty years later, in his book *The Cross and the Lynching Tree*, Cone develops a poignant theological analogy of Black people's suffering and Jesus's suffering. Cone substantiates the ideology that suffering is highly correlated to Black life. Human agony and consequences have been, and still are, the order of the day for those born of a darker hue. Blackness is an enigma set upon the landscape of a Eurocentric society. The Middle Passage and the imposition of chattel slavery on Black people upon their arrival in America marked only the beginnings of Black suffering, yet a Black faith developed. And preaching in silent pain continues:

The sufferings of Black people during slavery are too deep
for words. That suffering did not end with emancipation.
The violence and oppression of white supremacy took different forms and employed different means to achieve the
same end: the subjugation of Black people. And Christian
theology, for African Americans, maintained the same
great challenge: to explain from the perspective of history
and faith how life could be made meaningful in the face
of death, how hope could remain alive in a world of Jim
Crow segregation. These were the challenges that shaped
Black religious life in the United States.[6]

The post-Civil War and Reconstruction periods gave rise to
the widespread practice of lynching to keep such an enigma
under control. Cone makes it clear that lynching was a form of
violence and terror, used to perpetuate fear, marginalization, and
the servitude of Black people:

> Lynching as primarily mob violence and torture directed
> against Blacks began to increase after the Civil War and
> the end of slavery when the 1867 Congress passed the
> Reconstruction Act. . . . White supremacists felt insulted
> by the suggestion that whites and Blacks might work
> together as equals . . . if lynching were the only way to
> keep ex-slaves subservient, then it was necessary. . . . [7]
> Whites often lynched Blacks simply to remind the Black
> community of their powerlessness.[8]

Like the crucifixions performed by the Roman government
during the first centuries, lynchings carried out by white supremacists in the nineteenth and twentieth centuries had the intention of bestowing dishonor and humiliation upon death—in this
case, upon the death of a Black person. This was something white
people orchestrated and apparently enjoyed. It was like going to

the county fair or the local carnival.[9] Again, Black suffering is not understood as pain and suffering by white people. It is something else, something outside their realm of consciousness. To think this way requires a deliberate sublimation of empathy replaced by an evil perverse pleasure. To take pleasure in the pain and suffering of another is a monstrous act of inhumanity:

> Both the cross and the lynching tree represented the worst in human beings and at the same time "an unquenchable ontological thirst" for life that refuses to let the worst determine our final meaning.[10]
>
> The crucifixion of Jesus by the Romans in Jerusalem and the lynching of Blacks by whites in the United States are so amazingly similar that one wonders what blocks the American Christian imagination from seeing the connection.[11]

The cross of Jesus Christ is seen as paradigmatic for Black suffering, as it became a source of power that helped establish the basis of Black faith.

Cone highlights the paradox of the cross, which is the motif of the crucified savior who suffered yet inspired hope. In a real sense, this shaped Black Christianity as an explanation of how Black people struggled against suffering in the world. But it still rubs me the wrong way as an inexplicable explainable. There is so much in Cone's theology that makes me feel hopeless and helpless at times. I am both troubled by the hatred of white racism and soothed by the love and hope that permeate Black theology.

Once exposed to the gospel of Jesus Christ, the enslaved interpreted and believed the meaning of the cross to be the notion that suffering is somehow connected to God's desire to bring liberation, victory, and justice to those who struggle because of their Blackness. The enslaved gravitated toward the message of the cross. The premise of this kind of faith could be deemed illogical when analyzing the condition of the subjugated Black person, but it also shows the perdurance of Black faith in a world of suffering.

Cone surmises expressions of faith and truth resonated through the arts. Both lynching and Christianity were so much a part of the daily reality of American society that no Black artist could avoid wrestling with their meanings and their symbolic relationship to each other.[12] Suffering Black people found a therapeutic outlet in singing, dancing, hand clapping, and shouting. Whether in the church house or the juke joint, the spirituals and blues proved to be vital and necessary components of the Black experience in America.

Cone also notes Lorraine Hansberry's award-winning play, *A Raisin in the Sun*, as a riveting depiction of Black life. An artist's motivation for expressing such compelling art was to cause all of society, regardless of race, to see the necessary truth and humanity of each other's existence. Cone also mentions how "the poet laureate of Black America," Langston Hughes, who wrote the controversial poem "Christ in Alabama," believed art is derived from life:[13]

Christ is a Nigger,
Beaten and black—
O, bare your back.

Mary is His Mother
Mammy of the South,
Silence your Mouth.

God's His Father—
White Master above
Grant us your love.

Most holy bastard
Of the bleeding mouth:
Nigger Christ
On the cross of the South.

Cone shows how Black artists during the Harlem Renaissance expressed the Black transvaluation of values, fusing their art with an affirmation of the ways of Black folk and a critique of the ways of white folks.[14]

When it came to singing, if white and Black Protestants sang the same song, they had different meanings. The interpretations of the words were based on life experiences. "Jesus Keep Me Near the Cross," "Must Jesus Bear the Cross Alone?," and other white Protestant evangelical hymns did not sound or feel the same as when Black people sang them because their life experiences were so different.[15] Cone provides examples of songs that were sung with passion and pain, such as "We Are Climbing Jacob's Ladder" and "Sometimes I feel Like a Motherless Child." When Mahalia Jackson sang the songs of Zion, Black folk felt something that could only be felt by Black people. When Aretha Franklin sang "Amazing Grace" or "Respect," there was a powerful connection felt by Black people who knew suffering firsthand. The music spoke to the raw emotions of pain and suffering. These songs provided a release because they allowed Black people to openly express their feelings without the ever-present danger of white people bringing them more harm. When Black people were challenged by white supremacy, with the lynching tree staring down at them, where else could they turn for hope that their resistance would ultimately succeed?[16] Cone gives a practical view of Black life by showing there were very few options available for Black people to overcome the oppressive society of America. Faith in God was their resolve.

Cone's observation of white theologians' silence and disregard for lynching has an indirect impact on Black suffering because white Christians continually failed to see the error in their ways. Lynching contradicted the gospel message. White theologians could have taken this opportunity to shine the light of truth on lynching in regard to the cross, which might have influenced white Christians to cease the practice. Cone also highlights the faith of Martin Luther King Jr. He points out that, like Niebuhr, King believed the cross was at the heart of the Christian faith. However, unlike Niebuhr, King had a keen awareness of the lynching tree's ugliness. Here Cone shows how King developed a dialectic between the cross as a symbol of God's love and the lynching tree as a horrific symbol of hate. This contradictory thesis and antithesis of a Christian society drew King to formulate a type of synthesis that God's love reconciled humanity through Jesus Christ. In the midst of suffering, King embodied the faith and courage to stand on the premise and promise of God's love, even with impending death closing in on him:

> Like Reinhold Niebuhr, whom he studied in graduate school, King believed that the cross was the defining heart of the Christian faith. Unlike Niebuhr, his understanding of the cross was inflected by his awareness of the lynching tree, and this was a significant difference. While the cross symbolized God's supreme love for human life, the lynching tree was the most terrifying symbol of hate in America. King held these symbols together in a Hegelian dialectic, a contradiction of thesis and antithesis, yielding to a creative synthesis.[17]

Cone summarizes King's life by saying, "King lived the meaning of the cross and thereby gave an even more profound interpretation of it with his life."[18] Unlike King, Niebuhr did not see the true bearers of the cross in America—those who were crucified by being enslaved and lynched.

This major theological disconnect can be seen as a component of the larger context of white America's lack of consciousness regarding the treatment of Black people. There exists such an ironic network of perspectives as consciousness relates to Christianity. If white and Christian, one is justified and entitled to carry out supremacist actions against Black people. Black pain and suffering are a struggle to be, a struggle to exist in freedom. This truth is ubiquitous in one aspect of Black suffering—the pressure that entails Black people to present a certain disposition among white people and then to display a different disposition amongst themselves. The human expression of being a Black person is unaccepted and intolerable for a good portion of white society. The pain and suffering of a repressed existence pull Black people into a spiral of objurgation. White people, free to display all dimensions of themselves, constructed and established a social system that does not provide Black people the same freedom and opportunity. The environment and context, in which reticence was and is the expectation, determined a Black person's conduct. Cone corroborates this two-sided way of life by bringing W. E. B. Du Bois's concept of the double-consciousness of Black people into the light of faith. Although some scholars view Du Bois as agnostic,[19] Cone asserts he was a man of deep religious faith:

> One cannot correctly understand the Black religious experience without an affirmation of deep faith informed by profound doubt. Suffering naturally gives rise to doubt. How can one believe in God in the face of such horrendous suffering as slavery, segregation, and the lynching tree? Under these circumstances, doubt is not a denial but an integral part of faith. It keeps faith from being sure of itself. But doubt does not have the final word. The final word is faith giving rise to hope.[20]

Du Bois viewed the Christ of the white church as not being the true Christ. Jesus was, according to the biblical narrative, living in Nazareth as a Black man would in America. In that sense, Jesus, like Job, is Black. Du Bois went so far as to say that if Jesus of Nazareth—who was despised, poor, persecuted, and crucified—came to America, he would be found among the Negroes and working people:

Du Bois elaborated on why the white Christ was not the biblical Christ: Yet Jesus Christ was a laborer and Black men are laborers; He was poor and we are poor; He was despised of his fellow men and we are despised; He was persecuted and crucified, and we are mobbed and lynched. If Jesus Christ came to America He would associate with Negroes and working people; He would eat and pray with them, and He would seldom see the interior of the Cathedral of Saint John the Divine.[21]

Du Bois's insight into Black suffering is integral because he constantly grappled with the study of theodicy in an attempt to understand why God allows the ubiquitous suffering of Black people. Cone cites Du Bois's literary work, "The Gospel of Mary Brown." It is a rendition of the story of Jesus written in a Black context, with Jesus's name here being Joshua. Joshua is Jesus's Hebraic name. At the end of the story, when Joshua is crucified, Mary cries out to God:

"God, you ain't fair—you ain't fair, God! You didn't ought to do it . . . you didn't have to make him Black. . . . And then you let them mock him, and hurt him, and lynch him! Why, why did you do it, God?"[22]

This is an appeal to God for a human response to Black suffering:

These questions, demanding God's explanation for Black suffering, sit at the nerve center of Black religion in America, from the slave trade to the prison industrial complex of today. Black religion comes out of suffering, and no one has engaged the question of theodicy in the Black experience more profoundly than Du Bois. Yet, he did not end Mary's gospel on a note of despair with Joshua's death on a lynching tree. "Mary—Mary—he is not dead: He is risen!" Joshua appears.[23]

Cone discusses an outcome of Black suffering in the death of Emmett Louis "Bobo" Till. Till, a fourteen-year-old boy from Chicago visiting Mississippi, reportedly whistled at a white woman and said, "Bye, baby," or "Thank you, baby." Nobody truly knows except the white woman who lied all those years and now admits it was a lie.[24] Four days later, Till was found shot in the head and beaten beyond recognition, his body thrown in the Tallahatchie River. Cone notes the Black response to the Till's "lynching" was unlike responses of fear and intimidation before it. This lynching spurred within Black people a notion of temerity:

> To a remarkable extent, the Till lynching would provide the spark that lit the fire of resistance in the Negro masses. . . . Black people throughout the country were outraged that white racists would stoop so low as to lynch an innocent child."[25]

Till's mother, Mamie Till Bradley, defied the paralyzing fear of white terror by allowing a viewing of his body for three days. This display of Black suffering is forever etched into the minds of Black people:

> She exposed white brutality and Black faith to the world and, significantly, expressed a parallel meaning between her son's lynching and the crucifixion of Jesus. She cried out, "Lord, you gave your son to remedy a condition, but who knows, but what the death of my only son might bring an end to lynching." It was as if she were pleading with God to let her son's death count for something. The two white men responsible were convicted of no crime. The lynching of her only son was indeed a very heavy cross to bear.[26]

Suffering is undoubtedly an element of human life, no matter a person's skin color, but Black pain and suffering have been experienced with a greater degree of insult added to injury. Black suffering is a result of white racism and hatred. The two white men responsible for Till's death, even after admitting to the federal crime of kidnapping, were not convicted. The insult of injustice added to the injury of Emmett Till's death. This is an instance of Black suffering that, like a record on repeat, plays out over and over again in America. The name and circumstance may differ, but each account arrives at the same destination of suffering, pain, and injustice. White apathy and disregard for Black suffering are elements that sit center stage in this oppressive culture and society. The same song of oppression played as the dance partners changed from slavery to Jim Crow, from being treated as chattel to being treated worse than animals.

Black people continue to suffer at the hands of white supremacy. There is strong resistance to allowing Black people to attain a sense of full humanity or the ability to materially flourish. Black people continue to cling to their faith as a means of hope, longing for the day when life will be better, even though it seems having faith in God would be difficult in these circumstances. "Why the suffering?" is the most relevant question to pose to an all-powerful God. An intriguing aspect of Black faith amid Black suffering is the profound ability Black people have to still believe in a God who will one day vindicate, even in this world filled with doubt. This is the hope that proclaims suffering is not a zero-sum game but, in fact, leads faithfully to a gain of victory and justice. This stretch of faith, according to Cone, required some degree of imagination to visualize beyond the current pains of life. Using a Pauline scriptural reference, Cone shows how this applied to the Till lynching:

> Suffering always poses the deepest test of faith, radically challenging its authenticity and meaning. No rational explanation can soothe the pain of an aching heart and troubled mind. In the face of the lynching death of an

innocent child, Black Christians could only reach into the depth of their religious imagination for a transcendent meaning that could take them through despair to a hope "beyond tragedy." For Mrs. Bradley, the voice she heard was the voice of the resurrected Jesus. It spoke of hope that, although white racists could take her son's life, they could not deprive his life and death of an ultimate meaning. As in the resurrection of the Crucified One, God could transmute defeat into triumph, ugliness into beauty, despair into hope, the cross into the resurrection. And so, like Paul, Mrs. Bradley was "afflicted in every way, but not crushed; perplexed but not unto despair; persecuted, but not forsaken; struck down, but not destroyed."[27]

Black Women's Suffering: From Ida B. Wells to Fannie Lou Hamer

Cone also discusses Black suffering from the vantage point of the Black woman. He begins the final chapter of *The Cross and the Lynching Tree* with a quote from journalist and suffragist Ida Bell Wells about the lynching of a woman named Eliza Woods of Jackson, Tennessee, who was shot numerous times and then hanged for all to see. Cone includes a portion of the song "Strange Fruit," written by Abel Meeropol and sung by Billie Holliday. The lyrics paint a cruel picture of America's South during the lynching era:

Southern trees bear strange fruit
Blood on the leaves and blood at the root
Black body swinging in the Southern breeze
Strange fruit hanging from the poplar tree.[28]

As we can see, Black women were not exempt from lynching's terror. If white people thought it warranted, Black women were hanged without any deference to their gender. Cone describes one of the most grueling accounts of a lynching against a Black woman. In Valdosta, Georgia, in 1918, Mary Turner, who was eight months pregnant, protested the lynching of her husband, Hayes Turner. Turner had been lynched simply because a white mob could not locate the Black man they actually sought. Because Mary Turner strongly vowed to seek justice, the sheriff decided to arrest her and give her over to the same white mob that lynched her husband. They stripped her down, strung her up by her feet, and drenched her with gasoline. While she was burning to death, someone took out a knife and cut her stomach open. When her unborn infant fell to the ground, someone stomped it to death.[29] Ugly crimes of this magnitude went unpunished—and pain, suffering, and injustice went unrequited.

From the lens of Black women, Black suffering was similar to that experienced by Black men, but there was a slight distinction. Cone identifies Black women as the "oppressed of the oppressed." He quotes womanist theologian Jacquelyn Grant who removes the "maleness" to see the suffering experience of Christ as equal to the suffering experience of Black women. She identifies the interpretation of Jesus Christ today as the experience of the poor, Black woman. However, the thought of "Christ as a Black Woman" has been disregarded by male theologians; as Cone suggests, it needs further theological development.[30]

Cone references another womanist theologian, Delores Williams, who brings another observation to light about Black women throughout American history. She discusses how Black women have played the surrogate role to white men, white women, *and* Black men. This has meant being white men's concubines, white women's mammies to their children, and Black men's supporters and sometimes protectors. Black women have even stepped into the role of being surrogates to lynching. There are accounts of Black women being lynched when a white mob is unable to locate the Black men. In these cases, as historian Patrick J. Huber says, the Black women were "collateral victims."[31]

Cone continues by noting there was also equality in the treatment of Black men and women, as they both were tortured, beaten, scarred, mutilated, burned, shot, and whipped. When Black men were lynched, they were the husbands, sons, brothers, uncles, and cousins of Black women, who had to carry on without them. This included raising fatherless children and attempting to manage financial resources in a racist, misogynistic culture. The Black woman was not only familiar with struggle and suffering. There were also instances when, unfortunately, Black women suffered and Black men did not. Rape was a heinous, violent crime considered to be "more bitter than death."[32] This is another example of Black suffering that has an ironic note to it. Black men were seen by white people as beasts that lusted after white women and would take one for their own if given the chance.[33] Black men were killed when accused of raping a white woman in a misguided attempt by white people to maintain the white woman's dignity and honor. White men felt they had to protect their white women, regardless of the absense of justice. However, since the time of chattel slavery, Black women were raped and sexually assaulted by white men. If a Black man made the audacious attempt to protect or defend a Black woman, he was faced with either torture or death as the consequence. This was another example of suffering—the unfairness of Black men being unable to protect Black women in the same manner as their counterparts:

> In the white imagination, the image of Black men was transformed from docile slaves and harmless "Sambos," to menacing "Black beast rapists," the most serious threat to the virtue of white women and the sanctity of the white home. The image of Black women was changed

from nurturing "Negro mammies" to salacious Jezebels, nearly as corrupting to white civilization as Black men. As Theodore Roosevelt said, "the greatest existing cause of lynching is the perpetration, especially by Black men, of the hideous crime of rape—the most abominable in all the category of crimes, even worse than murder." On the other hand, Black men's assertion of their right to protect their daughters, sisters, wives, mothers, and other women from unwelcome advances from white men could bring down the full weight of Judge Lynch.[34]

The image of white women being pure and virtuous and Black women being loose and sinful has distorted the view of Black women so extensively that the residuals of this perception still linger today. Black women endured the loss of men in their lives and also lived under the constant threat of their children being in danger of white mob violence. Cone discussed the paradoxical concept of suffering as it relates to the faith of Black women:

> Such suffering created a deep religious paradox for Black women, challenging their faith in the justice and love of God. A free Black woman named Nellie, from Savannah, Georgia, expressed the spiritual agony Black suffering created for her faith: "It has been a terrible mystery, to know why the good Lord should so long afflict my people, and keep them in bondage—to be abused, and trampled down, without any rights of their own—with no ray of light in the future. Some of my folks said there wasn't any God, for if there was he wouldn't let white folks do as they do for so many years.[35]

The faith of Black women gave them the courage to fight, patience when they could not, and the hope that whatever they did, God would keep them "from sinking down."[36]

Ida B. Wells, Fannie Lou Hamer, and Billie Holliday are a few
of the Black women in history who addressed Black suffering
in America during the days of lynching and segregation. Cone
begins with Ida B. Wells, whom Frederick Douglass referred to
as "Old Man Eloquent." As lynching continued in America, Wells's
struggle against it evolved into a crusade. She expressed its injustices in a newspaper called *The Free Speech*. She wrote with
fervor, delineating the fact that "Our country's national crime
is lynching." Cone adds that her fight against lynching was so
radical and uncompromising that many anti-lynching advocates
in moderate organizations like the National Association for the
Advancement of Colored People and the National Association of
Colored Women shunned her.[37] One event that sparked Wells's
attention was the lynching of three Black men in 1892, one of
whom was a companion. Wells questioned the main reason for
lynching, as it had been known to be the punishment for rape.
Cone notes Wells conducted research that showed rape was, in
fact, only given as a reason for about one-third of lynchings. In
most of those cases, these claims referred to consensual sexual
acts, while in others, the claims were often false.[38] Wells determined white people were intolerable of Black people competing
with them in any area, whether it was economically or socially.
Cone adds that, in Wells's view, white people despised Black people for being considered equal:

> Nothing more detested whites than the idea that Blacks
> were equal to them. "You don't act in a way to make white
> persons feel that you don't know they were white" . . . Any
> word or body movement that was *perceived* to be insuf-
> ficiently deferential, like standing upright and looking a
> white person in the eye, could get a Black beaten or killed.[39]

This is an important piece of the Black suffering puzzle
because it reveals the truth of a white person's mindset of evil

and superiority. White people attempted to eliminate the threat of Black people competing for resources and status by keeping them oppressed. America's system was designed to keep Black people at a lower social level. Wells attributed her progress toward justice to her faith in God. Cone shares her theological view, which was similar to Martin Luther King Jr's, showing that the meaning of the cross is living in a radical, unconventional, and sacrificial way in order to disrupt the wrongs of the world, even at the risk of loss of life:

> For Wells, faith in the God of Calvary was not an excuse for passivity. She rebuked those who patiently waited on God to save them from injustice. When she disguised herself and risked her life to visit twelve condemned Arkansas prisoners who had survived the massacre of nearly three hundred Blacks in Elaine, Arkansas, 1919 . . . she asked them "Why don't you pray to live and ask to be freed," after which one of the prisoners said, "We never talked about dying anymore."[40]

The boldness and austerity Wells displayed was a great example of the struggle against suffering during the lynching era. Like Du Bois, she and other Black women shunned white Christianity as the true gospel. Cone highlights legendary jazz singer Billie Holliday and her rendition of "Strange Fruit" that shook America to its core. Her sorrowful, soulful, melodic chords dispelled the ignorance of the blatant disregard for Black suffering at the hands of white America. The song forced white Southerners to wrestle with their cruelty, and it was so convicting that some radio stations banned it from being played. Her powerful, poignant sound expresses the agony and the horror of Black suffering. Cone discusses how "Strange Fruit" captures the great contradiction in Southern culture and the religion that defined it. As one white man said, "Lynching is part of the religion of our people."[41] Cone questions white religion, asking, "How could the white Christian community reconcile 'blood on the leaves and blood at the root' with the blood on their consciences?" He includes the following descriptive words from the song: "Here is a fruit for the crows to pluck," like the "the dogs beneath the cross" in Jerusalem where Jesus was crucified. "Here is a strange and bitter crop."[42]

Additionally, Cone pays homage to Mississippi sharecropper Fannie Lou Hamer, noting she was a great civil rights leader who sought justice for Black people. She, like Wells, also relied on her faith in God and Jesus Christ in her struggle against suffering. Her fight for freedom and justice was grounded in her view of the cross. Her hermeneutic was centered around the stance that bearing a cross, as Christ did, automatically renders one a candidate for death. She held her religious convictions in high regard and lived out a faith that sought liberation for oppressed people. Jesus, in her opinion, was the means to liberation. Cone notes Jesus's death on the cross was the example Hamer used as an ethical paradigm "in the freedom struggle."[43] Hamer gave an account of an encounter in suffering during her speech to the 1964 Democratic National Convention in Atlantic City. She told the story of her attempt to vote, as well as register and Black people to vote, in Mississippi, which resulted in her being beaten and jailed. She asked the listeners rhetorically, "Is this America?":[44]

They whipped her body but they did not whip her soul. The cross gave her courage to keep fighting what womanist scholar Angela Sims, reflecting on the "ethical complications of lynching," calls an "ethics of resilience." The truth of what she said about Jesus was defined by its practical results. And if today, like Fannie Lou Hamer, "I cling to the old rugged cross," it is because I have seen with my own eyes how that symbol empowered Black people to stand up and become agents of change for their freedom.[45]

Hamer's legacy is an example of a Black woman who endured and conquered. As Cone suggests, "Black women transformed America through their suffering."[46] Cone acknowledges the sacrifices Black women have made throughout history, sacrifices that served as bridges for Black people to endure the raging rivers of struggle. Black women's willingness to sacrifice for their families at the cost of their lives reveals their incredible tenacity. Cone emphasizes that the cross indeed sustained Black women and their resistance to succumbing to the ills of an unjust existence. The faith Black women had in God gave them the courage to face harm in their efforts to move toward liberation and justice on this side of the River Jordan.

Cone reiterates the importance of the cross to Black people. He indicates it exists as a treasured symbol because "it enthroned the One who went all the way with them and for them. The enslaved African sang because they saw the results of the cross—triumph over the principalities and powers of death, triumph over evil in the world."[47] He also adds a vital thought as it relates to Black faith during struggle—namely, that bearing the cross is a necessary action for gaining freedom. Cone poses the question: What is the meaning of this unspeakable Black suffering—suffering so deep, painful, and enduring that words cannot even begin to describe it? Only the song, dance, and the shout—voices raised to high heavens and bodies swaying from side to side—can express both the wretchedness and the transcendent spirit of empowerment that kept Black people from going under as they struggled against great odds to acknowledge the humanity denied to them. Black faith emerged out of Black people's wrestling with suffering. They struggled to make sense out of their senseless situation, and in the effort, related their predicaments to similar stories in the Bible. On the one hand, faith spoke to their suffering, making it somewhat bearable; on the other hand, suffering contradicted their faith, making it an unbearable burden. That is the profound paradox inherent in Black faith, the dialectic of doubt and trust in Black people's search for meaning as they "walked through the valley of the shadow of death."[48] God was the one reality white people could not control and whose presence was found in unexpected places, doing surprising things. "God may not come when you want, but God is right on time" was a faith declaration frequently repeated in Black churches in troubled times. As was, "Making a way out of no way."[49]

There is a biblical hermeneutic of liberation throughout Cone's work. It shows Black theology seeks a spirit of liberation, to create the liberated self through Jesus Christ. Just as Jesus exposed the truth and disrupted the norms of the oppressive and unjust status quo of first-century Palestine, Black people must continue to struggle against suffering in order to disrupt the same oppressive and unjust cultural structures in America. I am troubled by certain elements of the cross that appear too evangelical and too explanatory of Black suffering. To me, Black suffering is a result of the social evils and human hatred against Black people as a whole. Frantz Fanon so eloquently states the issue in his epic works, *The Wretched of the Earth* and *Black Skin, White Masks*. He says Black people love white people, and white people struggle to be human.

ENDNOTES

INTRODUCTION

1. Robert Redfield, interview by Anderson Cooper and Sanjay Gupta, *CNN*, April 9, 2020, https://tinyurl.com/y8ht4dfa.
2. Magic Johnson, interview by Anderson Cooper and Sanjay Gupta, *CNN*, April 9, 2020, https://tinyurl.com/y8ybqpdc.
3. Valerie Montgomery Rice, interview by Fredericka Whitfield, *CNN*, April 12, 2020; see also Lekeisha Jarrett and Khadijia Tribie Reid, interview by Frances Weller, "African American physicians dispel myths about people of color and COVID-19," *WECT News 6*, April 15, 2020, https://tinyurl.com/y7jbab24.
4. Michael Paul Williams. "Police, Two Naked Men and Two Different Outcomes," *Richmond-Times Dispatch*, Aug. 31, 2019, https://tinyurl.com/ve52ptk.
5. See Michel Foucault, *Discipline and Punish: The Birth of the Prison* (1975) and *Power/Knowledge: Selected Interviews and Other Writings 1972–1977* (1977); Michelle Alexander's *The New Jim Crow: Mass Incarceration in the Age of Colorblindness* (2010).

CHAPTER 1

1. See Franklin D. Roosevelt, "Four Freedoms Speech," accessed March 17, 2020, https://tinyurl.com/sz84z8a, and https://tinyurl.com/rncontk.

2. Langston Hughes, *The Collected Poems of Langston Hughes* (New York: Vintage Classics, 1995), 281.
3. Hughes, *The Collected Poems*, 249.

CHAPTER 2

1. See Søren Kierkegaard, *The Sickness Unto Death* (New York: Penguin Classics, 1989).
2. On this line of thinking, I am indebted to my longtime friend and brother, ethicist Walter Fluker, who used this language in our discussions on Emmanuel Levinas and Emil Fackenheim in Richmond, VA, July 20, 2015.
3. Kelly Brown Douglas, *Stand Your Ground: Black Bodies and the Justice of God* (Maryknoll, NY: Orbis Books, 2015), 15–16.
4. Long made this analysis during a lecture at Virginia Union University, Spring 2009.
5. See for example Emil Fackenheim's writings and the works of Jean Améry, especially *At the Mind's Limits: Contemplations by a Survivor on Auschwitz and Its Realities*, trans. Sidney Rosenfeld and Stella P. Rosenfeld (Bloomington: Indiana University Press, 2009).
6. "Auschwitz 'accountant' jailed over Nazi killings," CBS News, July 15, 2015, https://tinyurl.com/skmzfym.
7. This movie, though a representative depiction of Black life on a plantation, was nevertheless, written and directed by a white man, Quentin Tarantino. Additionally, the character and role played by Samuel L. Jackson was the epitome of Black self-hatred and the evil effect of slavery.
8. Emmanuel Levinas, *Entre Nous: Thinking of the Other* (New York: Continuum Books, 2006), 79.
9. Améry, *At the Mind's Limits*.
10. Dr. Benjamin Spock was an American pediatrician and psychoanalyst who wrote the best selling book, *The Common Sense Book of Baby and Child Care (1946)*
11. Philippe Nemo, *Job and the Excess of Evil* (Pittsburgh: Duquesne University Press, 1978).
12. Job 19:7.
13. Martin Luther King Jr., "Letter from Birmingham Jail," in *The Radical King*, ed. Cornel West (Boston: Beacon Press, 2015), 127–147.
14. Rom 5:3–4.

15. See Johnny B. Hill, *Prophetic Rage: A Postcolonial Theology of Liberation* (Grand Rapids, MI/Cambridge: William B. Eerdmans Publishing, 2013).
16. Frantz Fanon, *The Wretched of the Earth* (New York: Grove Press, 1962), 3. I have taken the liberty to call the aforementioned American cities "colonies" to suggest colonization or postcolonialism continues to be evident in our postmodern society.
17. See Rom 8:22.
18. James H. Cone, *The Cross and The Lynching Tree* (Maryknoll, NY: Orbis Books, 2011), xv.
19. Countee Cullen, "Christ Recrucified," first published in *Kelley's Magazine* (October 1922); reprinted in *Countee Cullen: Collected Poems*, ed. Major Jackson. (c) 2013 Amistad Research Center, Tulane University. American Poets Project (Library of America).
20. Billie Holiday, vocalist, "Strange Fruit," by Abel Meeropol, recorded April 1939, Commodore, A-side on *Classics in Swing*, 1939, 78 rpm.
21. Cone, *The Cross*, 93.
22. Levinas, *Entre Nous,* 92–94.
23. Levinas, *Entre Nous,* 92.
24. Peter Ochs and Eugene Rogers, "Election and Incarnation" (lecture notes, University of Virginia, Charlottesville, VA, January 1, 2002). I have been a graduate student in several seminars taught by the University of Virginia Professor of Modern Jewish Studies Peter Ochs. The specific seminar of this reflection was titled "Election and Incarnation" and taught by Ochs and Eugene Rogers in 2002.

CHAPTER 4

1. W. E. B. Du Bois, *The Souls of Black Folk* (Chicago: A. G. McClurg, 1903), 11.
2. Du Bois, *The Souls of Black Folk*, 7.
3. W. E. B. Du Bois, *The Souls of Black Folk*, 105.
4. Frantz Fanon, *The Wretched of the Earth* (New York City: Grove Press, 1963).
5. Du Bois, *The Souls of Black Folk*, 87.
6. Du Bois, *The Souls of Black Folk*, 88.
7. Du Bois, *The Souls of Black Folk* 93.
8. Du Bois, *The Souls of Black Folk*, 93.
9. G. W. F. Hegel, *The Phenomenology of Spirit*, trans. A. V. Miller (London: Oxford University Press, 1977), 110–11.

10. Hegel, *Phenomenology of Spirit,* 105.
11. Hegel, *Phenomenology of Spirit,* 115.
12. Hegel, *Phenomenology of Spirit,* 113–14.
13. Hegel, *Phenomenology of Spirit,* 116.
14. Paulo Freire, *Pedagogy of the Oppressed* (New York: Continuum, 1992).
15. Hegel, *Phenomenology of Spirit,* 117.
16. Hegel, *Phenomenology of Spirit,* 126.
17. Hegel, *Phenomenology of Spirit,* 126.
18. Hegel, *Phenomenology of Spirit,* 132.
19. Hegel, *Phenomenology of Spirit,* 47.
20. Hegel, *Phenomenology of Spirit,* 47.
21. Hegel, *Phenomenology of Spirit,* 114.
22. Du Bois, *The Souls of Black Folk,* 7.
23. Hegel, *Phenomenology of Spirit,* 114.
24. Du Bois, *The Souls of Black Folk,* 90.
25. Hegel, *Phenomenology of Spirit,* 126.
26. Du Bois, *The Souls of Black Folk,* 105.
27. This term was first used among our faculty at the Samuel DeWitt Proctor School of Theology, Virginia Union University, by Professor Miles J. Jones in our discussion of the school's mission during a faculty meeting in spring 1995.
28. Hegel, *Phenomenology of Spirit,* 104.

CHAPTER 6

1. See Michel Foucault, *Power/Knowledge: Selected Interviews and Other Writings 1972–1977,* ed. Colin Gordon, trans. Colin Gordon et al. (New York: Pantheon Books, 1980), 89.
2. Alexander, *The New Jim Crow,* 28–44.
3. David Gilmour, vocalist, "Money," by Roger Waters, recorded June 7, 1972–January 9, 1973, Harvest, track 6 on Pink Floyd, *The Dark Side of the Moon,* 1973, vinyl.
4. This information is redacted from James H. Harris, *Preaching Liberation* (Minneapolis: Fortress Press, 1995).
5. Paul Ricoeur, *The Symbolism of Evil* (New York: Harper and Row, 1969).
6. Turner is generally described as a prophet in Stephen B. Oates, *The Fires of Jubilee: Nat Turner's Fierce Rebellion* (New York: Harper and Row, 1975); F. Roy Johnson, *The Nat Turner Story: History of*

the *South's Most Important Slave Revolt with New Material Provided by Black Tradition and White Tradition* (Murfreesboro, NC: Johnson Publishing, 1970); and Eugene D. Genovese, *Roll, Jordan, Roll: The World the Slave Made* (New York: Vintage, 1976).

7. Some sources say Turner and his party killed fifty-five white people, others say sixty. See Johnson, *The Nat Turner Story*, and Herbert Aptheker, *Nat Turner's Slave Rebellion: Including the 1831 "Confessions"* (Mineola, NY: Dover Publication, 2006).

8. See Du Bois, *The Souls of Black Folk*, 135.

9. See Aptheker, *Slave Rebellion*, 38.

10. Henry H. Mitchell, *Black Belief: Folk Beliefs of Blacks in America and West Africa* (New York: Harper and Row, 1975), 33.

11. See Luke 4:18.

12. See Axel Honneth, *The Struggle for Recognition: The Moral Grammar of Social Conflicts* (Cambridge, MA: MIT Press, 1996).

13. Mitchell, *Black Belief*, 33.

14. See Aptheker, *Slave Rebellion*, 136.

15. C. G. Jung, *Psychological Types*, eds. and trans. Gerhard Adler and R. F. C. Hull (Princeton, NJ: Princeton University Press, 1976).

16. Frantz Fanon, "Violence and Liberation," in *Self and World: Readings in Philosophy*, ed. James A. Ogilvy, (New York: Harcourt, Brace, Jovanovich, 1981), 339–45.

17. Hannah Arendt, *On Violence* (Orlando, FL: Harcourt, Brace, Jovanovich, 1970), 56.

18. Henry J. Young, *Major Black Religious Leaders, 1755–1940* (Nashville: Abingdon Press, 1977), 56.

19. Cain Hope Felder, *Troubling Biblical Waters: Race, Class, and Family* (Maryknoll, New York: Orbis Books, 1989).

20. Young, *Major Black Religious Leaders*, 58.

21. Rev 20:13.

22. Nicole Krasavage and Scott Bronstein, "Are Victims Falling through America's Hate Crime Data Gap?," CNN, updated March 23, 2013, https://tinyurl.com/w7kc3qq.

23. Semiotics is essentially studying signs and wonders.

24. See John Simkin, "Nat Turner Rebellion," Spartacus Educational, accessed March 21, 2020, https://tinyurl.com/tffp6bp.

25. "Another Brick in the Wall, Part 2," track 5 on Pink Floyd, *The Wall*, Harvest/Columbia, 1979. "Another Brick in the Wall" is the title of three songs set to variations of the theme on Pink Floyd's 1979 rock opera *The Wall*. The album and "Part 2" of the song were

banned in South Africa in 1980 after the song became a protest anthem against racial inequalities in education. See also "Another Brick in the Wall," Pink-Floyd-Lyrics.com, accessed March 21, 2020, https://tinyurl.com/v8n2kbv.

26. Matthew 28:6 KJV.

27. Kenneth Stampp, *The Peculiar Institution: Slavery in the Ante-Bellum South.*

28. See Michael Hardt and Antonio Negri, *Empire* (Cambridge, MA: Harvard University Press, 2001), 124–25.

29. Hardt and Negri, *Empire*, 125.

30. See Edward W. Said, *Orientalism* (New York: Random House, 1978).

31. See Hélène Cixous, *The Hélène Cixous Reader*, ed. Susan Sellers (London: Routledge, 1994).

32. Hardt and Negri, *Empire*, 127.

33. Catherine Malabou, *What Should We Do with Our Brain?*, trans. Sebastian Rand (New York: Fordham University Press, 2008), 6.

34. Enrique Dussel, *Beyond Philosophy: Ethics, History, Marxism, and Liberation Theology*, ed. Eduardo Mendieta (Lanham: Rowman and Littlefield, 2003), 6.

35. See Jürgen Moltmann, *The Crucified God: The Cross of Christ as the Foundation and Criticism of Christian Theology* (New York: HarperCollins, 1991).

36. Luke 23:24.

37. Matt 27:46 and Mark 15:34.

38. John 19:30.

39. I use the word "sublation" not necessarily as Hegel does, but as a way to express neutralization and obviation of a particular phenomenon. Usually, the reference is to death and finality. I also use the term to express both the positive and negative in a dyadic.

40. See James Henry Harris, *Beyond the Tyranny of the Text: Preaching in Front of the Bible to Create a New World* (Nashville: Abingdon Press, 2019).

41. See Hegel, *Phenomenology of Spirit*, 117.

42. Hegel, *Phenomenology of Spirit*, 119.

43. Hegel, *Phenomenology of Spirit*, 119.

44. see Hegel, *Phenomenology of Spirit*.

45. See Friedrich Nietzsche, *Human, All Too Human,* trans. by R. J. Hollingdale (United Kingdom: Cambridge University Press, 1996).

46. Hegel, *Phenomenology of Spirit*, 111.

47. Hegel, *Phenomenology of Spirit*, 111.
48. This language is from the graduate seminar at the University of Virginia, "Hegel, Materialism and Theology" taught by Paul D. Jones, Spring 2013. I was a graduate student who later earned a degree in philosophical theology, ethics, and culture.
49. Hegel, *Phenomenology of Spirit*, 115.
50. Hegel, *Phenomenology of Spirit*, 115.

CHAPTER 7

1. See Mark Twain, *Adventures of Huckleberry Finn.*

CHAPTER 8

1. Malidoma Patrice Somé, *The Healing Wisdom of Africa: Finding Life Purpose through Nature, Ritual, and Community* (New York: Jeremy P Tarcher/Putnam, 1998), 54.
2. Toni Morrison, *Beloved* (New York: New American Library, 1987), 5.
3. Morrison, *Beloved*, 7.
4. Morrison, *Beloved*, 15.
5. Morrison, *Beloved*, 73.
6. Morrison, *Beloved*, 200.
7. Morrison, *Beloved*, 275.
8. Morrison, *Beloved*, 274.
9. Morrison, *Beloved*, 324.
10. Morrison, *Beloved*, 275.
11. Primo Levi, *Survival in Auschwitz* (New York: Orion Press, 1959), 8.
12. "Freedom in the Air," in *The Norton Anthology of African American Literature,* eds. Henry Louis Gates Jr. and Nellie Y. McKay (New York: W. W. Norton, 1997), 20.
13. See Hegel's *Phenomenology of Spirit*, 104–138.
14. Roland Hayes, born enslaved in Curryville, Georgia, in 1887, was an American singer who's wife and daughter sat in a white people-only section in a Georgia shoe store and the family was thrown out for it. This incident inspired Langston Hughes's poem. See Joanne M. Owens, "Roland Hayes (1887–1977)," New Georgia Encyclopedia, last edited July 16, 2018, https://tinyurl.com/s85jef5.
15. Sharon M. Draper, *Stella by Starlight* (New York: Atheneum/Caitlyn Dlouhy Books, 2015), 1.

16. This reasoning results from a discussion with my colleague, Dr. Robert Wafawanaka, Associate Professor of Old Testament and Hebrew at the School of Theology, Virginia Union University, Richmond, VA, July 2015.

CHAPTER 9

1. Job 1:10.
2. Job 23:2–7.
3. Tremper Longman III, *Job: Baker Commentary on the Old Testament Wisdom and Psalms* (Grand Rapids, MI: Baker Academic, 2012) 425.
4. Job 38:1–5.
5. Job 38:34.
6. Job 40:15.
7. Job 41:1.
8. 1 Cor 15:51–58.
9. Job 8:1-3, 6.
10. Job 3:1–10.
11. Job 2:9.
12. Job 3:11–23.
13. Job 2:9.

CHAPTER 11

1. See Rom 10:14.
2. Joel 2:28–29.
3. Bettye Collier-Thomas, *Daughters of Thunder: Black Women Preachers and Their Sermons, 1850–1979*, (San Francisco, Jossey-Bass, 1997).
4. Collier-Thomas, *Daughters of Thunder*, 17.
5. Collier-Thomas, *Daughters of Thunder*, 11.
6. Collier-Thomas, *Daughters of Thunder*, 11.
7. Jarena Lee in Milton C. Sernett, *African American Religious History: A Documentary Witness* (Durham, NC: Duke University Press, 1999), 172.
8. Sernett, *Religious History*, 172.
9. Acts 4:18–20.
10. Mark 14:66–71.
11. Ludwig Wittgenstein, *Tractatus Logico-Philosophicus*, trans. C. K. Ogden (Mineola, NY: Dover Publications, 1999). This is the last line in his book.

12. When Martin Luther (1483–1586) was brought before the imperial council, or Diet of Worms, in 1521 on charges that no one should provide him shelter. The edict stated Luther should be captured and punished as a heretic because of his disagreement with the Catholic Church. This quote is his response to the charges.
13. Martin Luther King Jr., " Letter from a Birmingham Jail," African Studies Center at the University of Pennsylvania, accessed March 21, 2020, https://tinyurl.com/r6kwhl3.
14. Jer 18:1–6 CEV.
15. Jer 1:17–19 GNT.
16. Jer 18:4 GNT.
17. Jer 18:5–8 NRSV.
18. Jer 18:8 NRSV.
19. Isa 45:18 NRSV.
20. See Luke 23:46 NRSV.
21. See Chanta M. Haywood, *Prophesying Daughters: Black Women Preachers and the Word, 1823–1913* (Columbia, MO: Missouri University Press, 2003), 21.
22. See Derrick Bell, *Faces at the Bottom of the Well: The Permanence of Racism* (New York: Basic Books, 1992).
23. Charles H. Long, *Signification: Signs, Symbols, and Images in the Interpretation of Religion* (Minneapolis: Fortress Press, 1986), 60.
24. Conversation with Vanderbilt Professor Victor Anderson in Memphis during the 2018 Society for the Study of Black Religion meeting, March 16, 2018.
25. See Rom 5:20 GNT.
26. Rom 8:18 GNT.
27. Mark 3:20–27 GNT.
28. Haywood, *Prophesying Daughters*, 3.
29. Martin Buber. *Good and Evil* (New York: Scriber and Sons, 1953).
30. Buber, *Good and Evil.*
31. See Mark 2:8 RSV.
32. Langston Hughes, "Mother to Son," from *The Collected Works of Langston Hughes*, 2002.
33. "Said I Wasn't Gonna Tell Nobody," track 2 on Sam & Dave, *Double Dynamite*, Stax Records, 1966.
34. See Jer 20:9 NRSV.

CHAPTER 12

1. Rom 8:22.
2. Amos 5:23 RSV.
3. Charles H. Long, *The Collective Writings of Charles H. Long: Ellipsis* (London: Bloomsbury Academic, 2018).
4. Long, *Significations*, 59.
5. Long, *Significations*, 59.
6. Jas 3:9–10.
7. Esth 1:1–12.
8. "Esther," in *New Bible Commentary*, eds. Gordon J. Wenham, J. A. Motyer, D.A. Carson, and R.T. France (Downers Grove, IL: Inter-Varsity Press, 1994), 442.
9. "Esther," 443.
10. See Collier-Thomas, *Daughters of Thunder*, 41–53.
11. Cor 9:16.
12. Phil 1:18.
13. The language here is borrowed from the reference made in the poem "Mending Wall" by American poet Robert Frost.
14. Robert Frost, "The Mending Wall," PoetryFoundation.org, accessed March 21, 2020, https://tinyurl.com/w4nx3ze.
15. Rev 22:17.
16. Catherine A. Brekus, *Strangers and Pilgrims: Female Preaching in America, 1740–1845* (Chapel Hill: The University of North Carolina Press, 1998), 7.
17. Ernest J. Gaines, *A Lesson Before Dying* (New York: Alfred A. Knopf, 1993).
18. Amos 5:21–24.
19. Phil 1:15–18.
20. 1 Cor 8:1–3.
21. William M. Sonnett, "World Should Heed Pope's Call for Love," *Richmond Times-Dispatch*, September 27, 2006, A10.
22. 1 Cor 8:1b.
23. 1 Cor 13:1–2.
24. Jer 31:34.
25. Alex Varughese and Mitchel Modine, *Jeremiah 26–52: A Commentary in the Wesleyan Tradition* (Kansas City, MO: Beacon Hill Press, 2010), 159.
26. See Jer 31:34 and Heb 8:12.

27. Paul Tillich, *The Eternal Now* (New York: Charles Scribner's Sons, 1963), 129.

CHAPTER 13

1. This entire chapter is inspired and sustained by the writings of James H. Cone, especially *The Cross and the Lynching Tree* and *God of the Oppressed.*
2. See James H. Harris, "Practicing Liberation in the Black Church," Religion Online, accessed March 23, 2020, https://tinyurl.com /rda9qtc.
3. James H. Cone *God of the Oppressed* (New York: The Seabury Press, 1975), 163.
4. Disgruntled congregant, excerpts of an email message to author after hearing a sermon preached on suffering, May 10, 2015.
5. Cone, *The Cross and the Lynching Tree*, 177.
6. Cone, *The Cross and the Lynching Tree*, 2.
7. Cone, *The Cross and the Lynching Tree*, 4.
8. Cone, *The Cross and the Lynching Tree*, 11.
9. See for example, Equal Justice Initiative, *Lynching in America: Confronting the Legacy of Racial Terror* (Montgomery, Alabama: Equal Justice Initiative), https://tinyurl.com/vcs3elh. The reference is to the lynching of Black people in America where historians and sociologists estimate over four thousand persons have been lynched since 1865. See also Steven Budiansky, *The Bloody Shirt: Terror After the Civil War* (New York: Plume, 2008).
10. Cone, *The Cross and the Lynching Tree*, 3.
11. Cone, *The Cross and the Lynching Tree*, 31.
12. Cone, *The Cross and the Lynching Tree*, 96.
13. Cone, *The Cross and the Lynching Tree*, 114; from Hughes's poem "Christ in Alabama."
14. Cone, *The Cross and the Lynching Tree*, 112.
15. Cone, *The Cross and the Lynching Tree*, 22.
16. Cone, *The Cross and the Lynching Tree*, 22.
17. Cone, *The Cross and the Lynching Tree*, 70.
18. Cone, *The Cross and the Lynching Tree*, 72.
19. Cone, *The Cross and the Lynching Tree*, 101.
20. Cone, *The Cross and the Lynching Tree*, 106.
21. Cone, *The Cross and the Lynching Tree*, 103.

22. Cone, *The Cross and the Lynching Tree*, 104.
23. Cone, *The Cross and the Lynching Tree*, 105.
24. Richard Pérez-Peña, "Woman Linked to 1955 Emmett Till Murder Tells Historian Her Claims Were False," *New York Times*, January 27, 2017, https://tinyurl.com/wngpkph.
25. Cone, *The Cross and the Lynching Tree*, 66.
26. Cone, *The Cross and the Lynching Tree*, 67.
27. 2 Cor. 4:8–9; Cone, *The Cross and the Lynching Tree*, 68.
28. Cone, *The Cross and the Lynching Tree*, 120.
29. Cone, *The Cross and the Lynching Tree*, 120.
30. Cone, *The Cross and the Lynching Tree*, 121.
31. Cone, *The Cross and the Lynching Tree*, 121.
32. Cone, *The Cross and the Lynching Tree*, 121.
33. As we see in the novel *To Kill A Mockingbird* and in the real-life trial and execution of the Martinsville Seven, where seven Black men from Martinsville, Virginia, were convicted and executed in 1951 for raping a white woman.
34. Cone, *The Cross and the Lynching Tree*, 6–7.
35. Cone, *The Cross and the Lynching Tree*, 123, as cited in Albert J. Raboteau, " 'The Blood of the Martyrs Is the Seed of Faith': Suffering in the Christianity of American Slaves," in *The Courage to Hope: From Black Suffering to Human Redemption*, eds. Quinton H. Dixie and Cornel West (Boston: Beacon Press, 1999), 31.
36. Cone, *The Cross and the Lynching Tree*, 127.
37. Cone, *The Cross and the Lynching Tree*, 127.
38. Cone, *The Cross and the Lynching Tree*, 128.
39. Cone, *The Cross and the Lynching Tree*, 127.
40. Cone, *The Cross and the Lynching Tree*, 130.
41. Cone, *The Cross and the Lynching Tree*, 135.
42. Cone, *The Cross and the Lynching Tree*, 137.
43. Cone, *The Cross and the Lynching Tree*, 144.
44. Cone, *The Cross and the Lynching Tree*, 145.
45. Cone, *The Cross and the Lynching Tree*, 144.
46. Cone, *The Cross and the Lynching Tree*, 146.
47. Cone, *The Cross and the Lynching Tree*, 150.
48. Ps 23:4.
49. Cone, *The Cross and the Lynching Tree*, 127.

INDEX